WORLD TRADE ORGANIZATION

A Handbook on the WTO Dispute Settlement System

A WTO Secretariat Publication

The Secretariat has prepared this training guide to assist public understanding of the WTO dispute settlement system. It is not intended to provide a legal interpretation of the Dispute Settlement Understanding.

Prepared for publication by the Legal Affairs Division and the Appellate Body

CAMBRIDGE
UNIVERSITY PRESS

PUBLISHED BY THE PRESS SYNDICATE OF THE UNIVERSITY OF CAMBRIDGE
The Pitt Building, Trumpington Street, Cambridge, United Kingdom

CAMBRIDGE UNIVERSITY PRESS
The Edinburgh Building, Cambridge CB2 2RU, UK
40 West 20th Street, New York, NY 10011–4211, USA
477 Williamstown Road, Port Melbourne, VIC 3207, Australia
Ruiz de Alarcón 13, 28014 Madrid, Spain
Dock House, The Waterfront, Cape Town 8001, South Africa

http://www.cambridge.org

First published 2004

Printed in the United Kingdom at the University Press, Cambridge

Typefaces Times 10/12pt.   *System* LATEX 2_ε [TB]

A catalogue record for this book is available from the British Library

ISBN 0 521 84192 5 hardback
ISBN 0 521 60292 0 paperback

CONTENTS

PREFACE

There have been over 300 disputes brought to the World Trade Organization (WTO) since its creation in January 1995 and these disputes cover a wide range of economic activities.

The WTO dispute settlement system is the backbone of today's multilateral trading regime. It was created by Member governments during the Uruguay Round in the conviction that a stronger, more binding system to settle disputes would help to ensure that the WTO's carefully negotiated trading rules are respected and enforced. The system, sometimes referred to as the "WTO's unique contribution to the stability of the global economy", is based on, but constitutes a major improvement over, the previous GATT dispute settlement system. As such, it has greatly enhanced the stability and predictability of the rules of international trade to the benefit of businesses, farmers, workers and consumers around the world.

The primary purpose of this training guide is to explain the WTO dispute settlement system to an interested person with little or no knowledge of how this system functions. However, with its detailed content, it could also serve as a very useful "handbook" to experienced practitioners of WTO Law. It explains the historic evolution of the current system and explores the practices that have arisen in its operation since its entry into force on 1 January 1995.

Special thanks should be addressed to those from the Legal Affairs Division, the Appellate Body Secretariat and the Information and Media Relations Division who have assisted in researching, drafting, editing, proof-reading and designing this publication.

BRUCE WILSON
Director
Legal Affairs Division
World Trade Organization
November 2003

INTRODUCTION TO THIS HANDBOOK

The WTO dispute settlement system plays an important role in clarifying and enforcing the legal obligations contained in the WTO Agreement. It has gained a strong practical relevance as more than 300 disputes have been brought from 1 January 1995 through October 2003. While dispute settlement is certainly not the only activity taking place within the WTO, it has become an important part of the practical reality of the Organization. WTO dispute settlement has also become an important tool in the management by WTO Members of their international economic relations at large.

The objective of this handbook is to give the general reader a good understanding of the practical operation of this system. Working through this guide, the reader will be introduced to all elements of the dispute settlement process, from the initiation of a case through to the implementation of the decision. The reader will find it useful to have the "Legal Texts" (i.e. a text of the WTO Agreement, especially Annex 2 containing the Dispute Settlement Understanding) at hand whenever working with the present material and to look up each of the cited provisions in order to understand the primary sources. The Legal Texts are available as a book or electronically on the WTO website at http://www.wto.org/english/docs_e/legal_e/legal_e.htm. However, for the convenience of the reader, the main provisions of the DSU and other WTO legal texts have been reproduced in this document, either in the body or in the Annexes.

ABBREVIATIONS

DSB	Dispute Settlement Body
DSU	Understanding on Rules and Procedures Governing the Settlement of Disputes (also referred to as the Dispute Settlement Understanding)
GATS	General Agreement on Trade in Services
GATT	General Agreement on Tariffs and Trade
SCM	Subsidies and Countervailing Measures
SPS	Sanitary and Phytosanitary Measures
TBT	Technical Barriers to Trade
TRIPS	Trade-Related Aspects of Intellectual Property Rights
WTO	World Trade Organization
WTO Agreement	Marrakesh Agreement Establishing the World Trade Organization

TABLE OF CASES CITED IN THIS PUBLICATION

Short Title	Full Case Title and Citation
Argentina – Footwear (EC)	Appellate Body Report, *Argentina – Safeguard Measures on Imports of Footwear*, WT/DS121/AB/R, adopted 12 January 2000, DSR 2000:I, 515
Argentina – Hides and Leather	Panel Report, *Argentina – Measures Affecting the Export of Bovine Hides and Import of Finished Leather*, WT/DS155/R and Corr.1, adopted 16 February 2001
Argentina – Hides and Leather	Award of the Arbitrator, *Argentina – Measures Affecting the Export of Bovine Hides and Import of Finished Leather – Arbitration under Article 21.3(c) of the DSU*, WT/DS155/10, 31 August 2001
Australia – Ammonium Sulphate	Working Party Report, *The Australian Subsidy on Ammonium Sulphate*, adopted 3 April 1950, BISD II/188
Australia – Salmon	Appellate Body Report, *Australia – Measures Affecting Importation of Salmon*, WT/DS18/AB/R, adopted 6 November 1998, DSR 1998:VIII, 3327
Brazil – Aircraft	Appellate Body Report, *Brazil – Export Financing Programme for Aircraft*, WT/DS46/AB/R, adopted 20 August 1999, DSR 1999:III, 1161
Canada – Aircraft	Appellate Body Report, *Canada – Measures Affecting the Export of Civilian Aircraft*, WT/DS70/AB/R, adopted 20 August 1999, DSR 1999:III, 1377
Canada – Autos	Appellate Body Report, *Canada – Certain Measures Affecting the Automotive Industry*, WT/DS139/AB/R, WT/DS142/AB/R, adopted 19 June 2000, DSR 2000:VI, 2995
Canada – Autos	Award of the Arbitrator, *Canada – Certain Measures Affecting the Automotive Industry – Arbitration under Article 21.3(c) of the DSU*, WT/DS139/12, WT/DS142/12, 4 October 2000, DSR 2000:X, 5079

INTRODUCTION TO THE WTO DISPUTE SETTLEMENT SYSTEM

IMPORTANCE OF THE WTO DISPUTE SETTLEMENT SYSTEM

The best international agreement is not worth very much if its obligations cannot be enforced when one of the signatories fails to comply with such obligations. An effective mechanism to settle disputes thus increases the practical value of the commitments the signatories undertake in an international agreement. The fact that the Members of the WTO established the current dispute settlement system during the Uruguay Round of Multilateral Trade Negotiations underscores the high importance they attach to compliance by all Members with their obligations under the WTO Agreement.

Settling disputes in a timely and structured manner is important. It helps to prevent the detrimental effects of unresolved international trade conflicts and to mitigate the imbalances between stronger and weaker players by having their disputes settled on the basis of rules rather than having power determine the outcome. Most people consider the WTO dispute settlement system to be one of the major results of the Uruguay Round. After the entry into force of the WTO Agreement in 1995, the dispute settlement system soon gained practical importance as Members frequently resorted to using this system.

THE DISPUTE SETTLEMENT UNDERSTANDING

The current dispute settlement system was created as part of the WTO Agreement during the Uruguay Round. It is embodied in the Understanding on Rules and Procedures Governing the Settlement of Disputes, commonly referred to as the Dispute Settlement Understanding and abbreviated "DSU" (referred to as such in this guide). The DSU, which constitutes Annex 2 of the WTO Agreement, sets out the procedures and rules that define today's dispute settlement system. It should however be noted that, to a large degree, the current dispute settlement system is the result of the evolution of rules, procedures and practices developed over almost half a century under the GATT 1947.

Explanatory note: The annexes of the WTO Agreement contain all the specific multilateral agreements. In other words, the WTO Agreement incorporates all agreements that have been concluded in the Uruguay Round. References in this guide to the "WTO Agreement" in general, therefore, include the totality of these rules. However, the WTO Agreement itself, if taken in isolation from its annexes, is a short Agreement containing 16 Articles that set out the institutional framework of the WTO as an international organization. Specific references to the WTO Agreement (e.g. "Article XVI of the WTO Agreement") relate to these rules.

FUNCTIONS, OBJECTIVES AND KEY FEATURES OF THE DISPUTE SETTLEMENT SYSTEM

PROVIDING SECURITY AND PREDICTABILITY TO THE MULTILATERAL TRADING SYSTEM

A central objective of the WTO dispute settlement system is to provide security and predictability to the multilateral trading system (Article 3.2 of the DSU). Although international trade is understood in the WTO as the flow of goods and services between Members, such trade is typically not conducted by States, but rather by private economic operators. These market participants need stability and predictability in the governing laws, rules and regulations applying to their commercial activity, especially when they conduct trade on the basis of long-term transactions. In light of this, the DSU aims to provide a fast, efficient, dependable and rule-oriented system to resolve disputes about the application of the provisions of the WTO Agreement. By reinforcing the rule of law, the dispute settlement system makes the trading system more secure and predictable. Where non-compliance with the WTO Agreement has been alleged by a WTO Member, the dispute settlement system provides for a relatively rapid resolution of the matter through an independent ruling that must be implemented promptly, or the non-implementing Member will face possible trade sanctions.

PRESERVING THE RIGHTS AND OBLIGATIONS OF WTO MEMBERS

Typically, a dispute arises when one WTO Member adopts a trade policy measure that one or more other Members consider to be inconsistent with the obligations set out in the WTO Agreement. In such a case, any Member that feels aggrieved is entitled to invoke the procedures and provisions of the dispute settlement system in order to challenge that measure.

If the parties to the dispute do not manage to reach a mutually agreed solution, the complainant is guaranteed a rules-based procedure in which the merits of its claims will be examined by an independent body (panels and the Appellate Body). If the complainant prevails, the desired outcome is to secure the withdrawal of the measure found to be inconsistent with the WTO Agreement. Compensation and countermeasures (the suspension of obligations) are available only as secondary and temporary responses to a contravention of the WTO Agreement (Article 3.7 of the DSU).

Thus, the dispute settlement system provides a mechanism through which WTO Members can ensure that their rights under the WTO Agreement can be enforced. This system is equally important from the perspective of the respondent whose measure is under challenge, since it provides a forum for the respondent to defend itself if it disagrees with the claims raised by the complainant. In this way, the dispute settlement system serves to preserve the Members' rights and obligations under the WTO Agreement (Article 3.2 of the DSU). The rulings of the bodies involved (the DSB, the Appellate Body, panels and arbitrations[1]) are intended to reflect and correctly apply the rights and obligations as they are set out in the WTO Agreement. They must not change the WTO law that is applicable between the parties or, in the words of the DSU, add to or diminish the rights and obligations provided in the WTO agreements (Articles 3.2 and 19.2 of the DSU).

CLARIFICATION OF RIGHTS AND OBLIGATIONS THROUGH INTERPRETATION

The precise scope of the rights and obligations contained in the WTO Agreement is not always evident from a mere reading of the legal texts. Legal provisions are often drafted in general terms so as to be of general applicability and to cover a multitude of individual cases, not all of which can be specifically regulated. Whether the existence of a certain set of facts gives rise to a violation of a legal requirement contained in a particular provision is, therefore, a question that is not always easy to answer. In most cases, the answer can be found only after interpreting the legal terms contained in the provision at issue.

In addition, legal provisions in international agreements often lack clarity because they are compromise formulations resulting from multilateral negotiations. The various participants in a negotiating process often reconcile their diverging positions by agreeing to a text that can be understood in more than one way so as to satisfy the demands of different domestic constituents. The negotiators may thus understand a particular provision in different and opposing ways.

For those reasons, as in any legal setting, individual cases often require an interpretation of the pertinent provisions. One might think that such an interpretation cannot occur in WTO dispute settlement proceedings because Article IX:2 of the WTO Agreement provides that the Ministerial Conference and the General Council of the WTO have the "exclusive authority to adopt interpretations" of the WTO Agreement. However, the DSU expressly states that the dispute settlement system is intended to clarify the provisions of the WTO Agreement "in accordance with customary rules of interpretation of public international law" (Article 3.2 of the DSU).

The DSU, therefore, recognizes the need to clarify WTO rules and mandates that this clarification take place pursuant to customary rules of interpretation. In

---

[1] The composition and tasks of these bodies will be explained below in the sections on The Dispute Settlement Body (DSB) on page 17, Panels on page 21 and the Appellate Body on page 22.

addition, Article 17.6 of the DSU implicitly recognizes that panels may develop legal interpretations. The "exclusive authority" of Article IX:2 of the WTO Agreement must therefore be understood as the possibility to adopt "authoritative" interpretations that are of general validity for all WTO Members – unlike interpretations by panels and the Appellate Body, which are applicable only to the parties and to the subject matter of a specific dispute. Accordingly, the DSU mandate to clarify WTO rules is without prejudice to the rights of Members to seek authoritative interpretations under Article IX:2 of the WTO Agreement (Article 3.9 of the DSU).

As regards the methods of interpretation, the DSU refers to the "customary rules of interpretation of public international law" (Article 3.2 of the DSU). While customary international law is normally unwritten, there is an international convention that has codified some of these customary rules of treaty interpretation. Notably, Articles 31, 32 and 33 of the Vienna Convention on the Law of Treaties embody many of the customary rules of interpretation of public international law. While the reference in Article 3.2 of the DSU does not refer directly to these Articles, the Appellate Body has ruled that they can serve as a point of reference for discerning the applicable customary rules.[2] The three Articles read as follows:

Article 31

General rule of interpretation

1. A treaty shall be interpreted in good faith in accordance with the ordinary meaning to be given to the terms of the treaty in their context and in the light of its object and purpose.

2. The context for the purpose of the interpretation of a treaty shall comprise, in addition to the text, including its preamble and annexes:

(a) any agreement relating to the treaty which was made between all the parties in connection with the conclusion of the treaty;

(b) any instrument which was made by one or more parties in connection with the conclusion of the treaty and accepted by the other parties as an instrument related to the treaty.

3. There shall be taken into account, together with the context:

(a) any subsequent agreement between the parties regarding the interpretation of the treaty or the application of its provisions;

(b) any subsequent practice in the application of the treaty which establishes the agreement of the parties regarding its interpretation;

(c) any relevant rules of international law applicable in the relations between the parties.

4. A special meaning shall be given to a term if it is established that the parties so intended.

---

[2] Appellate Body Report, *US – Gasoline*, DSR 1996: I, 3 at 15; Appellate Body Report, *Japan – Alcoholic Beverages II*, DSR 1996: I, 97 at 104.

Article 32

Supplementary means of interpretation

Recourse may be had to supplementary means of interpretation, including the preparatory work of the treaty and the circumstances of its conclusion, in order to confirm the meaning resulting from the application of Article 31, or to determine the meaning when the interpretation according to Article 31:

(a) leaves the meaning ambiguous or obscure; or

(b) leads to a result which is manifestly absurd or unreasonable.

Article 33

Interpretation of treaties authenticated in two or more languages

1. When a treaty has been authenticated in two or more languages, the text is equally authoritative in each language, unless the treaty provides or the parties agree that, in case of divergence, a particular text shall prevail.

2. A version of the treaty in a language other than one of those in which the text was authenticated shall be considered an authentic text only if the treaty so provides or the parties so agree.

3. The terms of the treaty are presumed to have the same meaning in each authentic text.

4. Except where a particular text prevails in accordance with paragraph 1, when a comparison of the authentic texts discloses a difference of meaning which the application of Articles 31 and 32 does not remove, the meaning which best reconciles the texts, having regard to the object and purpose of the treaty, shall be adopted.

As can be seen from these articles on treaty interpretation, the WTO Agreement is to be interpreted according to the ordinary meaning of the words in the relevant provision, viewed in their context and in the light of the object and purpose of the agreement. The ordinary meaning of a term in a provision is to be discerned on the basis of the plain text. The definitions given to this term in a dictionary can be of assistance in that purpose. "Context" refers to the kinds of conclusions that can be drawn on the basis of, for example, the structure, content or terminology in other provisions belonging to the same agreement, particularly the ones preceding and following the rule subject to interpretation. The "object and purpose" refers to the explicit or implicit objective of the rule in question or the agreement as a whole.

In practice, panels and the Appellate Body seem to rely more on the ordinary meaning and on the context than on the object and purpose of the provisions to be interpreted. The negotiating history of the agreement is merely a subsidiary tool of interpretation (Article 32 of the Vienna Convention). This tool is to be used only as confirmation of the interpretation according to the ordinary meaning, context and object and purpose or if that interpretative result is ambiguous, obscure, manifestly absurd or unreasonable. One of the corollaries of the rules on interpretation is that meaning and effect must be given to all terms of an agreement, rather than reducing whole parts of an agreement to redundancy or inutility.[3] Conversely, the process of interpretation does not permit reading words into an agreement that are not there.[4] With respect to Article 33 of the Vienna Convention, the WTO Agreement is authentic in English, French and Spanish.

"MUTUALLY AGREED SOLUTIONS" AS "PREFERRED SOLUTION"

Although the dispute settlement system is intended to uphold the rights of aggrieved Members and to clarify the scope of the rights and obligations, which gradually achieves higher levels of security and predictability, the primary objective of the system is not to make rulings or to develop jurisprudence. Rather, like other judicial systems, the priority is to settle disputes, preferably through a mutually agreed solution that is consistent with the WTO Agreement (Article 3.7 of the DSU). Adjudication is to be used only when the parties cannot work out a mutually agreed solution. By requiring formal consultations as the first stage of any dispute,[5] the DSU provides a framework in which the parties to a dispute must always at least attempt to negotiate a settlement. Even when the case has progressed to the stage of adjudication, a bilateral settlement always remains possible, and the parties are always encouraged to make efforts in that direction (Articles 3.7 and 11 of the DSU).

PROMPT SETTLEMENT OF DISPUTES

The DSU emphasizes that prompt settlement of disputes is essential if the WTO is to function effectively and the balance of rights and obligations between the Members is to be maintained (Article 3.3 of the DSU). It is well known that, to be achieved, justice must not only provide an equitable outcome but also be swift. Accordingly, the DSU sets out in considerable detail the procedures and corresponding deadlines to be followed in resolving disputes. The detailed procedures are designed to achieve efficiency, including the right of a complainant to move forward with a complaint even in the absence of agreement by the respondent (Articles 4.3 and 6.1 of the DSU). If a case is adjudicated, it should normally take no more than one year for a panel ruling and no more than 16 months if the case is appealed (Article 20 of the DSU). If the complainant deems the case urgent, consideration of the case should take even less time (Articles 4.9 and 12.8 of the DSU).

---

[3] Appellate Body Report, *US – Gasoline*, DSR 1996: I, 3 at 23.

[4] Appellate Body Report, *EC – Computer Equipment*, para. 83.

[5] *See* below the section on Consultations on page 43.

These time-frames might still appear long, considering that time for implementation will have to be added after the ruling.[6] Also, for the entire duration of the dispute, the complainant may still suffer economic harm from the challenged measure; and even after prevailing in dispute settlement, the complainant will receive no compensation for the harm suffered before the time by which the respondent must implement the ruling.

However, one must take into account that disputes in the WTO are usually very complex in both factual and legal terms. Parties generally submit a considerable amount of data and documentation relating to the challenged measure, and they also put forward very detailed legal arguments. The parties need time to prepare these factual and legal arguments and to respond to the arguments put forward by the opponent. The panel (and the Appellate Body) assigned to deal with the matter needs to consider all the evidence and arguments, possibly hear experts, and provide detailed reasoning in support of its conclusions. Considering all these aspects, the dispute settlement system of the WTO functions relatively fast and, in any event, much faster than many domestic judicial systems or other international systems of adjudication.

PROHIBITION AGAINST UNILATERAL DETERMINATIONS

WTO Members have agreed to use the multilateral system for settling their WTO trade disputes rather than resorting to unilateral action (Article 23 of the DSU). That means abiding by the agreed procedures and respecting the rulings once they are issued – and not taking the law into their own hands.

If Members were to act unilaterally, this would have obvious disadvantages that are well known from the history of the multilateral trading system. Imagine that one Member accuses another Member of breaking WTO rules. As a unilateral response, the accusing Member could decide to take a countermeasure, i.e. to infringe WTO obligations with regard to the other Member (by erecting trade barriers). Under traditional international law, that Member could argue that it has acted lawfully because its own violation is justified as a countermeasure in response to the other Member's violation that had occurred first. If, however, the accused Member disagrees on whether its measure truly infringes WTO obligations, it will not accept the argument of a justified countermeasure. On the contrary, it may assert that the countermeasure is illegal and, on that basis, it may feel justified in taking a countermeasure against the first countermeasure. The original complainant, based on its legal view on the matter, is likely to disagree and to consider that second countermeasure illegal. In response, it may adopt a further countermeasure. This shows that, if the views differ, unilateral actions are not able to settle disputes harmoniously. Things may spiral out of control and, unless one of the parties backs down, there is a risk of escalation of mutual trade restrictions, which may result in a "trade war".

---

[6] *See* below in the section on the Time-period for implementation on page 76.

To prevent such downward spirals, the DSU mandates the use of a multilateral system of dispute settlement to which WTO Members must have recourse when they seek redress against another Member under the WTO Agreement (Article 23.1 of the DSU). This applies to situations in which a Member believes that another Member violates the WTO Agreement or otherwise nullifies or impairs benefits under the WTO agreements or impedes the attainment of an objective of one of the agreements.[7]

In such cases, a Member cannot take action based on unilateral determinations that any of these situations exist, but may only act after recourse to dispute settlement under the rules and procedures of the DSU. Whatever actions the complaining Member takes, it may only take them based on the findings of an adopted panel or Appellate Body report or arbitration award (Article 23.2(a) of the DSU). The Member concerned must also respect the procedures foreseen in the DSU for the determination of the time-period for implementation[8] and impose countermeasures only on the basis of an authorization by the DSB (Article 23.2(b) and (c) of the DSU). This excludes unilateral actions such as those described above.

EXCLUSIVE JURISDICTION

By mandating recourse to the multilateral system of the WTO for the settlement of disputes, Article 23 of the DSU not only excludes unilateral action, it also precludes the use of other fora for the resolution of a WTO-related dispute.

COMPULSORY NATURE

The dispute settlement system is compulsory. All WTO Members are subject to it, as they have all signed and ratified the WTO Agreement as a single undertaking,[9] of which the DSU is a part. The DSU subjects all WTO Members to the dispute settlement system for all disputes arising under the WTO Agreement. Therefore, unlike other systems of international dispute resolution, there is no need for the parties to a dispute to accept the jurisdiction of the WTO dispute settlement system in a separate declaration or agreement. This consent to accept the jurisdiction of the WTO dispute settlement system is already contained in a Member's accession to the WTO. As a result, every Member enjoys assured access to the dispute settlement system and no responding Member may escape that jurisdiction.

---

[7] On these causes of action, see below the section on the Types of complaints and required allegations in GATT 1994 on page 29.

[8] *See* below the section on the Time-period for implementation on page 76.

[9] Single undertaking means that the WTO Agreement had to be signed in its totality (except for Agreements signed in Annex 4 known as plurilateral agreements). Signatories were not allowed to sign only individual parts of the entire package.

PARTICIPANTS IN THE DISPUTE SETTLEMENT SYSTEM

PARTIES AND THIRD PARTIES

The only participants in the dispute settlement system are the Member governments of the WTO, which can take part either as parties or as third parties. The WTO Secretariat, WTO observer countries, other international organizations, and regional or local governments are not entitled to initiate dispute settlement proceedings in the WTO.

The DSU sometimes refers to the Member bringing the dispute as the "complaining party" or the "complainant" (this guide mostly uses the term "complainant"). No equivalent short term is used for the "party to whom the request for consultations is addressed". The DSU sometimes also speaks of "Member concerned". In practice, the terms "respondent" or "defendant" are commonly used; this guide mostly uses the term "respondent".

NO NON-GOVERNMENTAL ACTORS

Since only WTO Member governments can bring disputes, it follows that private individuals or companies do not have direct access to the dispute settlement system, even if they may often be the ones (as exporters or importers) most directly and adversely affected by the measures allegedly violating the WTO Agreement. The same is true of other non-governmental organizations with a general interest in a matter before the dispute settlement system (which are often referred to as NGOs). They, too, cannot initiate WTO dispute settlement proceedings.

Of course, these organizations can, and often do, exert influence or even pressure on the government of a WTO Member with respect to the triggering of a dispute. Indeed, several WTO Members have formally adopted internal legislation under which private parties can petition their governments to bring a WTO dispute.[10]

There are divergent views among Members on whether non-governmental organizations may play a role in WTO dispute settlement proceedings, for example, by filing *amicus curiae* submissions with WTO dispute settlement bodies. According to WTO jurisprudence, panels and the Appellate Body have the discretion to accept or reject these submissions, but are not obliged to consider them.[11]

---

[10] For example, sections 301 *et seq.* of the United States Trade Act of 1974 or the Trade Barriers Regulation of the European Communities.

[11] *Amicus curiae* means "friend of the court" and the term "*amicus curiae* brief" stands for a submission from sources other than a party or third party in a panel proceeding or other than a participant or third participant in an appeal. This rather controversial issue will be addressed separately in the section on Amicus Curiae, at page 98.

SUBSTANTIVE SCOPE OF THE DISPUTE SETTLEMENT SYSTEM

THE "COVERED AGREEMENTS"

The WTO dispute settlement system applies to all disputes brought under the WTO agreements listed in Appendix 1 of the DSU (Article 1.1 of the DSU). In the DSU, these agreements are referred to as the "covered agreements". The DSU itself and the WTO Agreement (in the sense of Articles I to XVI) are also listed as covered agreements. In many cases brought to the dispute settlement system, the complainant invokes provisions belonging to more than one covered agreement.

The covered agreements also include the so-called Plurilateral Trade Agreements contained in Annex 4 to the WTO Agreement (Appendix 1 of the DSU), which are called "plurilateral" as opposed to "multilateral" because not all WTO Members have signed them. However, the applicability of the DSU to those Plurilateral Trade Agreements is subject to the adoption of a decision by the parties to each of these agreements setting out the terms for the application of the DSU to the individual agreement, including any special and additional rules or procedures (Appendix 1 of the DSU). The Committee on Government Procurement has taken such a decision[12], but not the Committee on Trade in Civil Aircraft for the Agreement on Trade in Civil Aircraft. Two other plurilateral agreements, the International Dairy Agreement and the International Bovine Meat Agreement, are no longer in force.

A SINGLE SET OF RULES AND PROCEDURES

By applying to all these covered agreements, the DSU provides for a coherent and integrated dispute settlement system. It puts an end to the former "GATT *à la carte*", where each agreement not only had a different set of signatories but also separate dispute settlement rules.[13] Subject to certain exceptions, the DSU is applicable in a uniform manner to disputes under all the WTO agreements. In some instances, there are so-called "special and additional rules and procedures" on dispute settlement contained in the covered agreements (Article 1.2 and Appendix 2 of the DSU). These are specific rules and procedures "designed to deal with the particularities of disputes under a specific covered agreement". They take precedence over the rules in the DSU to the extent that there is a difference between the rules and procedures of the DSU and the special and additional rules and procedures (Article 1.2 of the DSU). Such a "difference" or conflict between the DSU and the special rules exists only "where the provisions of the DSU and the special or additional rules and procedures of a covered agreement cannot be read as complementing each other" because they are mutually inconsistent such that adherence to the one

---

[12] Notification Under Appendix 1 of the DSU, Communication from the chairman of the Committee on Government Procurement, WT/DSB/7, 12 July 1996.

[13] *See* below the section on Dispute settlement under the Tokyo Round "codes" on page 14.

provision would lead to a violation of the other provision.[14] Only in that case and to that extent, do the special additional provisions prevail and do the DSU rules not apply.

DEVELOPING COUNTRY MEMBERS AND THE DISPUTE SETTLEMENT SYSTEM

The DSU also addresses the particular status of developing country Members of the WTO, although the approach taken differs from that of the other covered agreements. Unlike those agreements, which set out the Members' substantive trade obligations, the DSU chiefly specifies the procedures under which such substantive obligations can be enforced. Accordingly, in the dispute settlement system, special and differential treatment[15] does not take the form of reducing obligations, providing enhanced substantive rights or granting transition periods. Rather, it takes a procedural form, for instance, by making available to developing country Members additional or privileged procedures, or longer or accelerated deadlines. These rules of special and differential treatment will be mentioned in subsequent chapters in the relevant procedural context in which they apply. The rules of special and differential treatment and other aspects of the developing country's role in the dispute settlement system are also the subject of a separate chapter.[16]

---

[14] Appellate Body Report, *Guatemala – Cement I*, paras. 65 and 66.

[15] "Special and differential treatment" is a technical term used throughout the WTO Agreement to designate those provisions that are applicable only to developing country Members.

[16] *See* below the sections on Developing country Members in dispute settlement – theory and practice on page 109; Special and differential treatment on page 111; and Legal assistance on page 114.

HISTORIC DEVELOPMENT OF THE WTO DISPUTE SETTLEMENT SYSTEM

The WTO dispute settlement system is often praised as one of the most important innovations of the Uruguay Round. This should not, however, be misunderstood to mean that the WTO dispute settlement system was a total innovation and that the previous multilateral trading system based on GATT 1947 did not have a dispute settlement system.

On the contrary, there was a dispute settlement system under GATT 1947 that evolved quite remarkably over nearly 50 years on the basis of Articles XXII and XXIII of GATT 1947. Several of the principles and practices that evolved in the GATT dispute settlement system were, over the years, codified in decisions and understandings of the contracting parties to GATT 1947. The current WTO system builds on, and adheres to, the principles for the management of disputes applied under Articles XXII and XXIII of GATT 1947 (Article 3.1 of the DSU). Of course, the Uruguay Round brought important modifications and elaborations to the previous system, which will be mentioned later.[1] This chapter provides a brief overview of the historic roots of the current dispute settlement system.

THE SYSTEM UNDER GATT 1947 AND ITS EVOLUTION OVER THE YEARS

ARTICLES XXII AND XXIII AND EMERGING PRACTICES

The rudimentary rules in Article XXIII:2 of GATT 1947 provided that the contracting parties themselves, acting jointly, had to deal with any dispute between individual contracting parties. Accordingly, disputes in the very early years of GATT 1947 were decided by rulings of the Chairman of the GATT Council. Later, they were referred to working parties composed of representatives from all interested contracting parties, including the parties to the dispute. These working parties adopted their reports by consensus decisions. They were soon replaced by panels made up of three or five independent experts who were unrelated to the parties of the dispute. These panels wrote independent reports with recommendations and rulings for resolving the dispute, and referred them to the GATT Council. Only upon approval by the GATT Council did these reports become legally binding on

---

[1] *See* below the section on Major changes in the Uruguay Round on page 15.

the parties to the dispute. The GATT panels thus built up a body of jurisprudence, which remains important today, and followed an increasingly rules-based approach and juridical style of reasoning in their reports.

The contracting parties to GATT 1947 progressively codified and sometimes also modified the emerging procedural dispute settlement practices. The most important pre-Uruguay Round decisions and understandings were:

- The Decision of 5 April 1966 on Procedures under Article XXIII;[2]
- The Understanding on Notification, Consultation, Dispute Settlement and Surveillance, adopted on 28 November 1979;[3]
- The Decision on Dispute Settlement, contained in the Ministerial Declaration of 29 November 1982;[4]
- The Decision on Dispute Settlement of 30 November 1984.[5]

WEAKNESSES OF THE GATT DISPUTE SETTLEMENT SYSTEM

Some key principles, however, remained unchanged up to the Uruguay Round, the most important being the rule of positive consensus that existed under GATT 1947. For example, there needed to be a positive consensus in the GATT Council in order to refer a dispute to a panel. Positive consensus meant that there had to be no objection from any contracting party to the decision. Importantly, the parties to the dispute were not excluded from participation in this decision-making process. In other words, the respondent could block the establishment of a panel. Moreover, the adoption of the panel report also required a positive consensus, and so did the authorization of countermeasures against a non-implementing respondent. Such actions could also be blocked by the respondent.

One might think that such a system could not possibly have worked. Why would a respondent not use its right to block the establishment of a panel if it thought that it might lose the case? Why would the losing party not block the adoption of the panel report? How could a party refrain from using its veto against the authorization of countermeasures, from which it would suffer economically? If domestic judicial systems were to operate on the basis of such a consensus rule, they would probably fail in most instances.

Quite surprisingly, this was generally not the experience of the dispute settlement system of GATT 1947. Individual respondent contracting parties mostly refrained from blocking consensus decisions and allowed disputes in which they were involved to proceed, even if this was to their short-term detriment. They did so because they had a long-term systemic interest and knew that excessive use of the veto right would result in a response in kind by the others. Accordingly, panels were

---

[2] BISD 14S/18.   [3] BISD 26S/210.   [4] BISD 29S/13.   [5] BISD 31S/9.

established and their reports frequently adopted, albeit often with delays (even though the authorization of countermeasures was only granted once).

On the basis of empirical research, it has been concluded that the GATT 1947 dispute settlement system brought about solutions satisfying the parties in a large majority of the cases. However, it must be noted that, by their nature, such statistics can only cover complaints that were actually brought. Certainly, there were a significant number of disputes that were never brought before the GATT because the complainant suspected that the respondent would exercise its veto. Thus, the *risk* of a veto also weakened the GATT dispute settlement system. In addition, such vetoes actually occurred, especially in economically important or politically sensitive areas such as anti-dumping. Finally, there was a deterioration of the system in the 1980s as contracting parties increasingly blocked the establishment of panels and the adoption of panel reports.

Even when panel reports were adopted, the risk of one party blocking adoption must often have influenced the panels' rulings. The three panelists knew that their report had also to be accepted by the losing party in order to be adopted. Accordingly, there was an incentive to rule not solely on the basis of the legal merits of a complaint, but to aim for a somewhat "diplomatic" solution by crafting a compromise that would be acceptable to both sides.

Hence, the structural weaknesses of the old GATT dispute settlement system were significant even though many disputes were ultimately resolved. As noted in the late 1980s, when the Uruguay Round negotiations were ongoing, the situation deteriorated, especially in politically sensitive areas or because some contracting parties attempted to achieve trade-offs between ongoing disputes and matters being negotiated. This resulted in a decreasing confidence by the contracting parties in the ability of the GATT dispute settlement system to resolve the difficult cases. In turn, this also led to more unilateral action by individual contracting parties, who, instead of invoking the GATT dispute settlement system, would take direct action against other parties in order to enforce their rights.[6]

DISPUTE SETTLEMENT UNDER THE TOKYO ROUND "CODES"

Several of the plurilateral agreements emerging from the Tokyo Round of Multilateral Trade Negotiations, the so-called Tokyo Round "Codes", for example the one on Anti-Dumping, contained code-specific dispute settlement procedures. Like the codes as a whole, these specific dispute settlement procedures were applicable only to the signatories of the codes, and only with regard to the specific subject matter. If the multilateral trading system before the establishment of the WTO was often referred to as a "GATT *à la carte*", this also applied to dispute settlement. In some instances, where rules pertaining to a specific subject matter existed both in GATT

---

[6] This is now excluded by Article 23.1 DSU. *See* above the section on the Prohibition against unilateral determinations on page 7.

1947 and in one of the Tokyo Round Codes, a complainant also had some leeway for "forum-shopping" and "forum-duplication", i.e. choosing the agreement and the dispute settlement mechanism that promised to be the most beneficial to its interests, or launching two separate disputes under different agreements on the same matter.

In terms of how satisfactorily the dispute settlement system under these codes functioned, the record was less favourable than it was for GATT 1947, i.e. consensus was blocked quite frequently.

THE URUGUAY ROUND AND THE DECISION OF 1989

As the inherent problems in the GATT dispute settlement system led to increasing problems in the 1980s, many contracting parties to GATT 1947, both developing and developed countries, felt that the system needed improving and strengthening. Negotiations on dispute settlement were accordingly included and given high priority on the agenda of the Uruguay Round negotiations.

By 1989, midway through the Uruguay Round negotiations, the contracting parties were ready to implement some preliminary results of the negotiations ("early harvest") on certain issues and accordingly adopted the Decision of 12 April 1989 on Improvements to the GATT Dispute Settlement Rules and Procedures.[7] The decision was to apply on a trial basis until the end of the Uruguay Round and already contained many of the rules later embodied in the DSU, such as a right to a panel and strict time-frames for panel proceedings. However, there was no agreement yet on the important issue of the procedure to be used for the adoption of panel reports. Nor was appellate review foreseen at that stage.

MAJOR CHANGES IN THE URUGUAY ROUND

As part of the results of the Uruguay Round, the DSU introduced a significantly strengthened dispute settlement system. It provided more detailed procedures for the various stages of a dispute, including specific time-frames. As a result, the DSU contains many deadlines, so as to ensure prompt settlement of disputes. The new dispute settlement system is also an integrated framework that applies to all covered agreements with only minor variations.[8]

Arguably, its most important innovation is that the DSU eliminated the right of individual parties, typically the one whose measure is being challenged, to block the establishment of panels or the adoption of a report. Now, the DSB automatically establishes panels and adopts panel and Appellate Body reports unless there is a consensus not to do so. This "negative" consensus rule contrasts sharply with the

---

[7] BISD 36S/61.   [8] *See* above the section on A single set of rules and procedures on page 10.

practice under the GATT 1947 and also applies, in addition to the establishment of panels and the adoption of panel and Appellate Body reports, to the authorization of countermeasures against a party which fails to implement a ruling.[9]

Other important new features of the WTO dispute settlement system are the appellate review of panel reports and a formal surveillance of implementation following the adoption of panel (and Appellate Body) reports.

---

[9] *See* further below in the section on Decision-making in the DSB on page 18.

WTO BODIES INVOLVED IN THE DISPUTE SETTLEMENT PROCESS

The operation of the WTO dispute settlement process involves the parties and third parties to a case, the DSB, panels, the Appellate Body, the WTO Secretariat, arbitrators, independent experts and several specialized institutions. This chapter gives an introduction to the WTO bodies involved in the dispute settlement system. The involvement of the parties and third parties, the primary participants in a dispute settlement proceeding, has already been outlined above.[1] The precise tasks and roles of each of the actors involved in the dispute settlement process will become clear in the later chapter on the stages of the dispute settlement process.

Among the WTO bodies involved in dispute settlement, one can distinguish between a political institution, the DSB, and independent, quasi-judicial institutions such as panels, the Appellate Body and arbitrators.

THE DISPUTE SETTLEMENT BODY (DSB)

FUNCTIONS AND COMPOSITION

The General Council discharges its responsibilities under the DSU through the DSB (Article IV:3 of the WTO Agreement). Like the General Council, the DSB is composed of representatives of all WTO Members. These are governmental representatives, in most cases diplomatic delegates who reside in Geneva (where the WTO is based) and who belong to either the trade or the foreign affairs ministry of the WTO Member they represent. As civil servants, they receive instructions from their capitals on the positions to take and the statements to make in the DSB. As such, the DSB is a political body.

The DSB is responsible for administering the DSU, i.e. for overseeing the entire dispute settlement process.

The DSB has the authority to establish panels, adopt panel and Appellate Body reports, maintain surveillance of implementation of rulings and recommendations and authorize the suspension of obligations under the covered agreements (Article 2.1 of the DSU). A later chapter on the stages of the dispute settlement procedure will explain exactly what all these actions mean. In less technical terms, the DSB is responsible for the referral of a dispute to adjudication (establishing a panel); for making the adjudicative decision binding (adopting the reports); generally, for

---

[1] *See* above the section on Parties and third parties on page 9.

supervising the implementation of the ruling; and for authorizing "retaliation" when a Member does not comply with the ruling.

The DSB meets as often as is necessary to adhere to the time-frames provided for in the DSU (Article 2.3 of the DSU). In practice, the DSB usually has one regular meeting per month. When a Member so requests, the Director-General convenes additional special meetings. The staff of the WTO Secretariat provides administrative support for the DSB (Article 27.1 of the DSU).

DECISION-MAKING IN THE DSB

The general rule is for the DSB to take decisions by consensus (Article 2.4 of the DSU). Footnote 1 to Article 2.4 of the DSU defines consensus as being achieved if *no* WTO Member, present at the meeting when the decision is taken, formally objects to the proposed decision. This means that the chairperson does not actively ask every delegation whether it supports the proposed decision, nor is there a vote. On the contrary, the chairperson merely asks, for example, whether the decision can be adopted and if no one raises their voice in opposition, the chairperson will announce that the decision has been taken or adopted. In other words, a delegation wishing to block a decision is obliged to be present and alert at the meeting, and when the moment comes, it must raise its flag and voice opposition. Any Member that does so, even alone, is able to prevent the decision.

However, when the DSB establishes panels, when it adopts panel and Appellate Body reports and when it authorizes retaliation, the DSB must approve the decision *unless* there is a consensus *against* it (Articles 6.1, 16.4, 17.14 and 22.6 of the DSU). This special decision-making procedure is commonly referred to as "negative" or "reverse" consensus. At the three mentioned important stages of the dispute settlement process (establishment, adoption and retaliation), the DSB must automatically decide to take the action ahead, unless there is a consensus not to do so. This means that one sole Member can always *prevent* this reverse consensus, i.e. it can avoid the blocking of the decision (being taken). To do so that Member merely needs to insist on the decision being approved.

No Member (including the affected or interested parties) is excluded from participation in the decision-making process. This means that the Member requesting the establishment of a panel, the adoption of the report or the authorization of the suspension of concessions can ensure that its request is approved by merely placing it on the agenda of the DSB. In the case of the adoption of panel and Appellate Body reports, there is at least one party which, having prevailed in the dispute, has a strong interest in the adoption of the report(s). In other words, any Member intending to block the decision to adopt the report(s) has to persuade all other WTO Members (including the adversarial party in the case) to join its opposition or at least to stay passive. Therefore, a negative consensus is largely a theoretical possibility and, to date, has never occurred. For this reason, one speaks of the quasi-automaticity of these decisions in the DSB. This contrasts sharply with the situation that prevailed under GATT 1947 when panels could be established, their reports adopted and retaliation authorized only on the basis of a positive consensus. Unlike under GATT 1947, the DSU thus provides no opportunity for blockage by individual Members in decision-making on these important matters. Negative consensus applies nowhere else in the WTO decision-making framework other than in the dispute settlement system.

When the DSB administers the dispute settlement provisions of a plurilateral trade agreement (of Annex 4 of the WTO Agreement), only Members that are parties to that agreement may participate in decisions or actions taken by the DSB with respect to disputes under these agreements (Articles 2.1 of the DSU).

With respect to the more operational aspects of the DSB's work, the Rules of Procedure for Meetings of the DSB[2] provide that the Rules of Procedure for Sessions of the Ministerial Conference and Meetings of the General Council[3] apply, subject to a few special rules on the chairperson and except as otherwise provided in the DSU. An important organizational aspect of these general rules is the requirement for Members to file items to be included on the agenda of an upcoming meeting no later than on the working day before the day on which the notice of the meeting is to be issued, which is at least ten calendar days before the meeting (Rule 3 of the Rules of Procedure). In practice, this means that items for the agenda must be made on the 11th day before the DSB meeting, and on the 12th or 13th day if the 11th day were to fall on a Saturday or Sunday.

ROLE OF THE CHAIRPERSON

The DSB has its own chairperson, who is usually one of the Geneva-based ambassadors, i.e. a chief of mission of a Member's permanent representation to the WTO (Article IV:3 of the WTO Agreement). The chairperson is appointed by a consensus decision of the WTO Members. The chairperson of the DSB has mainly procedural functions, that is, passing information to the Members, chairing the meeting, calling up and introducing the items on the agenda, giving the floor to delegations wishing to speak, proposing and, if taken, announcing the requested decision. The chairperson of the DSB is also the addressee of the Members' communications to the DSB.

In addition, the chairperson has several responsibilities in specific situations. For instance, the chairperson determines, upon request by a party and in consultation with the parties to the dispute, the rules and procedures in disputes involving several covered agreements with conflicting "special or additional rules and procedures"[4] if the parties cannot agree on the procedure within 20 days (Article 1.2 of the DSU). The chairperson can also be authorized by the DSB to draw up special

---

[2] WT/DSB/9, 16 January 1997.   [3] WT/L/161, 25 July 1996.
[4] *See* above the section on A single set of rules and procedures on page 10.

terms of reference pursuant to Article 7.3 of the DSU. The DSB chairperson is further entitled to extend, after consultation with the parties, the time-period for consultations involving a measure taken by a developing country Member, if the parties cannot agree that the consultations have concluded (Article 12.10 of the DSU). In dispute settlement cases involving a least-developed country Member, the least-developed country can request the DSB chairperson to offer his/her good offices, conciliation and mediation before the case goes to a panel (Article 24.2 of the DSU). Lastly, the DSB chairperson is to be consulted before the Director-General determines the composition of the panel under Article 8.7 of the DSU,[5] and before the Appellate Body adopts or amends its Working Procedures (Article 17.9 of the DSU).

THE DIRECTOR-GENERAL AND THE WTO SECRETARIAT

The Director-General of the WTO may, acting in an ex officio capacity, offer his/her good offices, conciliation or mediation with a view to assisting Members to settle a dispute (Article 5.6 of the DSU).[6] In a dispute settlement procedure involving a least-developed country Member, when a satisfactory solution has not been found during consultations, the Director-General will, upon request by the least-developed country Member, offer his or her good offices, conciliation or mediation in order to help the parties resolve the dispute, before a request for a panel is made (Article 24.2 of the DSU). The Director-General convenes the meetings of the DSB and appoints panel members upon the request of either party, and in consultation with the Chairman of the DSB and the Chairman of the relevant Council or Committee, where the parties cannot agree on the composition within 20 days (Article 8.7 of the DSU).[7] The Director-General also appoints the arbitrator(s) for the determination of the reasonable period of time for implementation, if the parties cannot agree on the period of time and on the arbitrator (footnote 12 to Articles 21.3(c) of the DSU),[8] or for the review of the proposed suspension of obligations in the event of non-implementation (Article 22.6 of the DSU). The appointment of an arbitrator under Article 22 by the Director-General is an alternative to the original panelists undertaking the task, if they are unavailable.[9]

The staff of the WTO Secretariat, which reports to the Director-General, assists Members in respect of dispute settlement at their request (Article 27.2 of the DSU), conducts special training courses (Article 27.3 of the DSU) and provides additional legal advice and assistance to developing country Members in matters relating to

---

[5] *See* further below in the section on the Composition of the panel on page 50.
[6] *See* further below in the section on Mediation, conciliation and good offices on page 93.
[7] *See* further below in the section on the Composition of the panel on page 50.
[8] *See* further below in the section on the Time-period for implementation on page 76.
[9] *See* further below in the section on Authorization and arbitration on page 83.

dispute settlement within the parameters of impartiality called for by Article 27.2 of the DSU.[10] The Secretariat also assists parties in composing panels by proposing nominations for potential panelists to hear the dispute (Article 8.6 of the DSU), assists panels once they are composed (Article 27.1 of the DSU),[11] and provides administrative support for the DSB.

PANELS

FUNCTIONS AND COMPOSITION OF PANELS

Panels are the quasi-judicial bodies, in a way tribunals, in charge of adjudicating disputes between Members in the first instance. They are normally composed of three, and exceptionally five, experts selected on an ad hoc basis.[12] This means that there is no permanent panel at the WTO; rather, a different panel is composed for each dispute. Anyone who is well qualified and independent (Articles 8.1 and 8.2 of the DSU) can serve as panelist. Article 8.1 of the DSU mentions as examples persons who have served on or presented a case to a panel, served as a representative of a Member or of a contracting party to GATT 1947 or as a representative to the Council or Committee of any covered agreement or its predecessor agreement, or who have worked in the Secretariat, taught or published on international trade law or policy, or served as a senior trade policy official of a Member. The WTO Secretariat maintains an indicative list of names of governmental and non-governmental persons, from which panelists may be drawn (Article 8.4 of the DSU). WTO Members regularly propose names for inclusion in that list, and, in practice, the DSB always approves their inclusion without debate. It is not necessary to be on the list in order to be proposed as a potential panel member in a specific dispute. Although some individuals have served on more than one panel, most serve only on one panel. There is thus no institutional continuity of personnel between the different ad hoc panels. Whoever is appointed as a panelist serves independently and in an individual capacity, and not as a government representative or as a representative of any organization (Article 8.9 of the DSU).

The panel composed for a specific dispute must review the factual and legal aspects of the case and submit a report to the DSB in which it expresses its conclusions as to whether the claims of the complainant are well founded and the measures or actions being challenged are WTO-inconsistent. If the panel finds that the claims are indeed well founded and that there have been breaches by a Member of WTO obligations, it makes a recommendation for implementation by the respondent (Articles 11 and 19 of the DSU).

---

[10]   *See* further below in the section on Legal assistance on page 114.

[11]   *See* further below in the section on Administrative and legal support on page 22.

[12]   According to the procedure explained below in the section on the Composition of the panel on page 50.

The WTO Secretariat is responsible for the administrative aspects of the dispute settlement procedures, as well as for assisting panels on the legal and procedural aspects of the dispute at issue (Article 27.1 of the DSU). This means, on the one hand, dealing with the panel's logistical arrangements, i.e. organizing the panelists' travel to Geneva where panel meetings take place, preparing the letters inviting the parties to the meetings with the panels, receiving the submissions and forwarding them to the panelists etc. On the other hand, assisting panels also means providing them with legal support by advising on the legal issues arising in a dispute, including the jurisprudence of past panels and the Appellate Body. Because panels are not permanent bodies, the Secretariat serves as the institutional memory to provide some continuity and consistency between panels, which is necessary to achieve the DSU's objective of providing security and predictability to the multilateral trading system (Article 3.2 of the DSU). The Secretariat staff assisting a panel usually consists of at least one secretary and one legal officer. Often, one of the two belongs to the division of the Secretariat responsible for the covered agreement invoked,[13] and the other to the Legal Affairs Division. The staff of the Rules Division assists panels dealing with disputes on trade remedies (anti-dumping and subsidies).

APPELLATE BODY

TASKS AND BACKGROUND

Unlike panels, the Appellate Body is a permanent body of seven members entrusted with the task of reviewing the legal aspects of the reports issued by panels. The Appellate Body is thus the second and final stage in the adjudicatory part of the dispute settlement system. As it did not exist in the old dispute settlement system under GATT 1947, the addition of this second adjudicatory stage was one of the major innovations of the Uruguay Round of Multilateral Trade Negotiations.

One important reason for the creation of the Appellate Body is the more automatic nature of the adoption of panel reports since the inception of the DSU.[14] In the current dispute settlement system, individual Members of the WTO are no longer able to prevent the adoption of panel reports, unless they have at least the tacit approval of all the other Members represented in the DSB. The resulting virtual automatic nature of the adoption of panel reports not only took away the previous possibility that the "losing" party could block the adoption of the report, it also

---

[13] For example, the Services Division for GATS disputes, the Intellectual Property Division for TRIPS disputes, the Agriculture and Commodities Division for disputes on the Agreement on Agriculture and the SPS Agreement.

[14] *See* above the section on Decision-making on page 18.

took away the possibility for parties or other Members to reject panel reports due to a substantive disagreement with the panel's legal analysis. Wherever one single Member, typically the party "winning" the dispute, is primarily guided by its intention to win the dispute, such rejection is impossible even if the panel report is legally flawed. Under the old dispute settlement system of GATT 1947, by contrast, some panel reports were not adopted because the legal interpretation of a particular GATT provision was unacceptable to the contracting parties from a substantive legal perspective. While this is no longer possible, the appellate review carried out by the Appellate Body now has the function of correcting possible legal errors committed by panels. In doing so, the Appellate Body also provides consistency of decisions, which is in line with the central goal of the dispute settlement system to provide security and predictability to the multilateral trading system (Article 3.2 of the DSU).

If a party files an appeal against a panel report, the Appellate Body reviews the challenged legal issues and may uphold, reverse or modify the panel's findings (Article 17.13 of the DSU).

COMPOSITION AND STRUCTURE OF THE APPELLATE BODY

The DSB established the Appellate Body in 1995,[15] after which the seven first Appellate Body members were appointed. The DSB appoints the members by consensus (Article 2.4 of the DSU), for a four-year term and can reappoint a person once (Article 17.2 of the DSU). An Appellate Body member can, therefore, serve a maximum of eight years. On average, every two years a part of the Appellate Body membership changes.

Appellate Body members must be persons of recognized authority, with demonstrated expertise in law, international trade and the subject matter of the covered agreements generally, and they must not be affiliated with any government (Article 17.3 of the DSU). Most Appellate Body members have so far been university professors, practising lawyers, past government officials or senior judges. Being an Appellate Body member is theoretically only a part-time occupation. However, the workload and, conversely, the ability to pursue substantial other professional activities, depends on the number of appeals being filed, given that Appellate Body members must be available at all times and on short notice (Article 17.3 of the DSU).

The seven Appellate Body members must be broadly representative of the membership of the WTO (Article 17.3 DSU), although they do not act as representatives of their own countries but rather they represent the WTO membership as a whole. The first seven members were citizens of Egypt, Japan, Germany, New Zealand,

---

[15] Decision Establishing the Appellate Body, Recommendations by the Preparatory Committee for the WTO approved by the Dispute Settlement Body on 10 February 1995, WT/DSB/1, dated 19 June 1995.

the Philippines, the United States and Uruguay. The current seven members are:

- Professor Georges Abi-Saab, Egypt, appointed in 2000;
- Mr James Bacchus, United States, appointed in 1995;[16]
- Professor Luiz Olavo Baptista, Brazil, appointed in 2001;
- Mr A. V. Ganesan, India, appointed in 2000;
- Mr John Lockhart, Australia, appointed in 2001;
- Professor Giorgio Sacerdoti, Italy, appointed in 2001;
- Professor Yasuhei Taniguchi, Japan, appointed in 2000.

Either three or four Appellate Body members have always been citizens of a developing country Member. According to the Working Procedures for Appellate Review,[17] the seven Appellate Body members elect one of their number as Chairman who serves a term of one or maximum two years (paragraph 5 of the Working Procedures). The current Chairman is James Bacchus who has held this position since 2001. The Chairman is responsible for the overall direction of the Appellate Body business, especially with regard to its internal functioning (paragraph 3 of the Working Procedures).

APPELLATE BODY SECRETARIAT

The Appellate Body Secretariat provides legal assistance and administrative support to the Appellate Body (Article 17.7 of the DSU). To ensure the independence of the Appellate Body, this Secretariat is only linked to the WTO Secretariat administratively, but is otherwise separate. The Appellate Body Secretariat is housed together with the WTO Secretariat at the WTO headquarters in Geneva, where both the panels and the Appellate Body hold their meetings.

ARBITRATORS

In addition to panels and the Appellate Body, arbitrators, either as individuals or as groups, can be called to adjudicate certain questions at several stages of the dispute settlement process. Arbitration is available as an alternative to dispute resolution by panels and the Appellate Body (Article 25 of the DSU), although it is a possibility that has so far very rarely been used.[18] Arbitration results are not appealable but can be enforced through the DSU (Articles 21 and 22 of the DSU).

---

[16] At the time of publication, Mr James Bacchus' mandate was due to expire on 10 December 2003. On 7 November 2003, the DSB selected Ms Merit Janow, United States, to replace Mr Bacchus for a four-year term beginning on 11 December 2003.

[17] *See* further below in the section on the Rules on the appellate review on page 63.

[18] *See* further below in the section on Arbitration pursuant to Article 25 of the DSU on page 95.

Much more frequent are two other forms of arbitration foreseen in the DSU for specific situations and questions in the process of implementation, i.e. after the DSB has adopted a panel (and, if applicable, an Appellate Body) report, and the "losing" party is bound to implement the DSB rulings and recommendations. The first such situation, which an arbitrator may be called to decide on, is the establishment of the "reasonable period of time" granted to the respondent for implementation (Article 21.3(c) of the DSU).[19] The second is where a party subject to retaliation may also request arbitration if it objects to the level or the nature of the suspension of obligations proposed (Article 22.6 of the DSU).[20] These two forms of arbitration are thus limited to clarifying very specific questions in the process of implementation and they result in decisions that are binding for the parties.

EXPERTS

Disputes often involve complex factual questions of a technical or scientific nature, for instance when the existence or degree of a health risk related to a certain product is the subject of contention between the parties. Because panelists are experts in international trade but not necessarily in those scientific fields, the DSU gives panels the right to seek information and technical advice from experts. They may seek information from any relevant source, but before seeking information from any individual or body within the jurisdiction of a Member, the panel must inform that Member (Article 13.1 of the DSU). In addition to the general rule of Article 13 of the DSU, the following provisions in the covered agreements explicitly authorize or require panels to seek the opinions of experts when they deal with questions falling under these agreements:

– Article 11.2 of the Agreement on Sanitary and Phytosanitary Measures;
– Articles 14.2, 14.3 and Annex 2 of the Agreement on Technical Barriers to Trade;
– Articles 19.3, 19.4 and Annex 2 of the Agreement on Implementation of Article VII of GATT 1994;
– Articles 4.5 and 24.3 of the Agreement on Subsidies and Countervailing Measures (SCM Agreement).

Where a panel considers it necessary to consult experts in order to discharge its duty to make an objective assessment of the facts, it may consult either individual experts or appoint an expert review group to prepare an advisory report (Article 13.2 of the DSU).

Rules for the establishment of expert review groups and their procedures are contained in Appendix 4 to the DSU. Expert review groups perform their duties

---

[19] *See* further below the section on the Time-period for implementation on page 76.
[20] *See* further below the section on Authorization and arbitration on page 83.

under the panel's authority and report to the panel. The panel determines their terms of reference and detailed working procedures. The final reports of expert review groups are issued to the parties to the dispute when submitted to the panel. Expert review groups only have an advisory role. The ultimate decision on the legal questions and the establishment of the facts on the basis of the expert opinions remains the domain of the panel. Participation in expert review groups is restricted to persons of professional standing and experience in the field in question. Citizens of parties to the dispute cannot serve on an expert review group without the joint agreement of the parties to the dispute, except in exceptional circumstances when the panel considers that the need for specialized scientific expertise cannot otherwise be fulfilled. Government officials of parties to the dispute may not serve on an expert review group. Members of expert review groups serve in their individual capacity and not as government representatives, nor as representatives of any organization. Governments or organizations must not give them instructions with regard to matters before an expert review group.

Where panels have so far resorted to experts, they did not establish expert review groups, but consulted experts on an individual basis. They have selected them in consultation with the parties, given them a list of questions to which each expert individually responded in writing, and convened a special meeting with the experts at which these and other questions were discussed with the panelists and the parties. The panel report usually reflected both the written responses of the experts to the panel's questions as well as a transcript of the discussions at the meeting with the panel.

RULES OF CONDUCT

Under the DSU, the "players" in a dispute settlement process are subject to certain rules designed to ensure due process and unbiased decisions. Persons called to participate in the dispute settlement process as panelists, Appellate Body members or arbitrators must carry out their tasks in an impartial and independent manner. There must not be any *ex parte* communications (the panel is not entitled to communicate with individual parties except in the presence of the other party or parties) between the parties and the panel or Appellate Body members concerning matters under their consideration (Article 18.1 of the DSU).

More specifically, the DSB has adopted Rules of Conduct for the DSU,[21] which aim at guaranteeing the integrity, impartiality and confidentiality of the dispute settlement system. These Rules of Conduct are applicable to all "covered persons" which include panel members, Appellate Body members, experts assisting panels, arbitrators, members of the Textile Monitoring Body, and WTO Secretariat and Appellate Body Secretariat staff.

---

[21] WT/DSB/RC/1, 11 December 1996.

Under the Rules of Conduct, "covered persons" are required to be independent and impartial, to avoid direct or indirect conflicts of interest, and to respect the confidentiality of dispute settlement proceedings. In particular, any covered person is required to disclose the existence or development of any interest, relationship or matter that he or she could reasonably be expected to know and that is likely to affect, or give rise to justifiable doubts as to that person's independence or impartiality. Such disclosure has to include information on financial, professional and other active interests as well as considered statements of public opinion and employment or family interests.

A violation of any of these requirements by a covered person gives the parties to the dispute a right to challenge the participation of that person in the dispute settlement proceeding and to request the exclusion of that person from any further participation in the process. In the case of Secretariat staff, the challenge is addressed to the Director-General.

LEGAL BASIS FOR A DISPUTE

This chapter will explain the conditions under which Members of the WTO can invoke the provisions of the dispute settlement system; that is, what constitutes a valid basis for a complaint by one Member against another Member.

LEGAL PROVISIONS IN THE MULTILATERAL TRADE AGREEMENTS AND THE DSU

DSU – Reference to the "covered agreements"

Article 1.1 of the DSU stipulates that its rules and procedures apply to "disputes brought pursuant to the consultation and dispute settlement provisions of the . . . 'covered agreements'". The basis or cause of action for a WTO dispute must, therefore, be found in the "covered agreements" listed in Appendix 1 to the DSU, namely, in the provisions on "consultation and dispute settlement" contained in those WTO agreements. In other words, it is not the DSU, but rather the WTO agreements that contain the substantive rights and obligations of WTO Members, which determine the possible grounds for a dispute.

Dispute settlement provisions in the covered agreements

These provisions on "consultation and dispute settlement" are:

- Articles XXII and XXIII of GATT 1994;
- Article 19 of the Agreement on Agriculture;
- Article 11 of the Agreement on the Application of Sanitary and Phytosanitary Measures;
- Article 8.10 of the Agreement on Textiles and Clothing;
- Article 14 of the Agreement on Technical Barriers to Trade;
- Article 8 of the Agreement on Trade-Related Investment Measures;
- Article 17 of the Agreement on Implementation of Article VI of GATT 1994;[1]

---

[1] Commonly called the Anti-Dumping Agreement.

- Article 19 of the Agreement on Implementation of Article VII of GATT 1994;[2]
- Articles 7 and 8 of the Agreement on Preshipment Inspection;
- Articles 7 and 8 of the Agreement on Rules of Origin;
- Article 6 of the Agreement on Import Licensing Procedures;
- Articles 4 and 30 of the Agreement on Subsidies and Countervailing Measures;
- Article 14 of the Agreement on Safeguards;
- Articles XXII and XXIII of the General Agreement on Trade in Services;
- Article 64 of the Agreement on Trade-Related Aspects of Intellectual Property Rights.

Many of these provisions simply refer to Articles XXII and XXIII of GATT 1994,[3] or have been drafted using Articles XXII and XXIII as a model. Article XXIII deserves being considered first and given special attention. Obviously, a dispute can be, and often is, brought under more than one covered agreement. In such a case, the question of the proper legal basis has to be assessed separately for the claims made under different agreements.

TYPES OF COMPLAINTS AND REQUIRED ALLEGATIONS IN GATT 1994

The GATT 1994 contains "consultation and dispute settlement provisions" in both Articles XXII and XXIII. However, it is Article XXIII:1(a) to (c) which sets out the specific circumstances in which a WTO Member is entitled to a remedy. Article XXIII:2 originally specified the form that this remedy could take, but the consequences of a successful recourse to the dispute settlement system nowadays are set out in more detail in the DSU. Article XXIII of GATT 1994 therefore retains its significance chiefly for specifying in paragraph 1 the conditions under which a Member can invoke the dispute settlement system. Article XXIII:1 of GATT 1994 states:

> Nullification or Impairment
> 1. If any contracting party should consider that any benefit accruing to it directly or indirectly under this Agreement is being nullified or impaired or that the attainment of any objective of the Agreement is being impeded as the result of

---

[2] Commonly called the Customs Valuation Agreement.

[3] This is the case for all the provisions listed above, except: Article 8.10 of the Agreement on Textiles and Clothing; Article 17 of the Agreement on Implementation of Article VI of GATT 1994; Article 19 of the Agreement on Implementation of Article VII of GATT 1994; Article 4 of the Agreement on Subsidies and Countervailing Measures and Articles XXII and XXIII of the General Agreement on Trade in Services.

(a) the failure of another contracting party to carry out its obligations under this Agreement, or

(b) the application by another contracting party of any measure, whether or not it conflicts with the provisions of this Agreement, or

(c) the existence of any other situation,

the contracting party may, with a view to the satisfactory adjustment of the matter, make written representations or proposals to the other contracting party or parties which it considers to be concerned. Any contracting party thus approached shall give sympathetic consideration to the representations or proposals made to it.

THE DIFFERENT TYPES OF COMPLAINTS UNDER ARTICLE XXIII:1 OF GATT 1994

In subparagraphs (a), (b) and (c), Article XXIII:1 provides for three alternative options (i.e. (a) "or" (b) "or" (c)) on which a complainant may rely. However, Article XXIII:1 starts with an introductory clause containing the condition that a Member "consider that any benefit accruing to it directly or indirectly under this Agreement is being nullified or impaired or that the attainment of any objective of the Agreement is being impeded". This must be the result of one of the scenarios specified in subparagraphs (a), (b) and (c).

The first, and by far, the most common complaint is the so-called "violation complaint" pursuant to Article XXIII:1(a) of GATT 1994. This complaint requires "nullification or impairment of a benefit" as a result of "the failure of another [Member] to carry out its obligations" under GATT 1994. This "failure to carry out obligations" is just a different way of referring to a legal inconsistency with, or violation of, the GATT 1994. There also needs to be "nullification or impairment" as a result of the alleged legal inconsistency.

The second type of complaint is the so-called "non-violation complaint" pursuant to Article XXIII:1(b) of GATT 1994. A non-violation complaint may be used to challenge any measure applied by another Member, even if it does not conflict with GATT 1994, provided that it results in "nullification or impairment of a benefit". There have been a few such complaints both under GATT 1947 and in the WTO.

The third type of complaint is the so-called "situation complaint" pursuant to Article XXIII:1(c) of GATT 1994. Literally understood, it could cover any situation whatsoever, as long as it results in "nullification or impairment". However, although a few such situation complaints have been raised under the old GATT, none of them has ever resulted in a panel report. In the WTO, Article XXIII:1(c) of GATT 1994 has not so far been invoked by any complainant.

Given the admissibility of "non-violation" and "situation complaints", the scope of the WTO dispute settlement system is broader than that of other international dispute settlement systems which are confined to adjudicating only violations of agreements. Simultaneously, the WTO dispute settlement system is narrower than those other systems, in the sense that a violation must also result in nullification or impairment (or possibly the impeded attainment of an objective). This particularity of the system for settlement of international trade disputes reflects the intention to maintain the negotiated balance of concessions and benefits between the WTO Members. It was GATT practice and it is now WTO law that a violation of a WTO provision triggers a rebuttable presumption of nullification or impairment of trade benefits (Article 3.8 of the DSU).

In summary, the WTO dispute settlement system provides for three kinds of complaints: (a) "violation complaints", (b) "non-violation complaints" and (c) "situation complaints". Violation complaints are by far the most frequent. Only a few cases have been brought on the basis of an allegation of non-violation nullification or impairment of trade benefits. No "situation complaint" has ever resulted in a panel or Appellate Body report based on Article XXIII:1(c) of GATT 1994.

Violation complaint

As outlined above, a violation complaint will succeed when the respondent fails to carry out its obligations under GATT 1994 or the other covered agreements, and this results directly or indirectly in nullification or impairment of a benefit accruing to the complainant under these agreements. If it can be established before a Panel and the Appellate Body that these two conditions are satisfied, the complainant will "win" the dispute.

In practice, the first of these two conditions, the violation, plays a much more important role than the second condition, nullification or impairment of a benefit. This is due to the fact that nullification or impairment is "presumed" to exist whenever a violation has been established. This presumption evolved in GATT jurisprudence[4] and is today codified in Article 3.8 of the DSU. Article 3.8 is concerned only with violation complaints ("where there is an infringement"). The presumption set out in this article relates to nullification or impairment once it has been *established* that there is a breach of an obligation. The presumption does not address the question *whether there is* such a violation, and it should not be confused with this question.[5]

The effect of the legal presumption is that of a reversal of the burden of proof. The concept of a legal presumption and the language in the last sentence of Article 3.8 of the DSU imply that the presumption set out by Article 3.8 of the DSU can be rebutted. However, there has been no single case of a successful rebuttal in the history of GATT and the WTO to date. GATT panels rejected all attempts to demonstrate that there was no actual trade impact.[6] For instance, the fact that an import quota had not been fully utilized was insufficient for proving the absence

---

[4] Panel Report, *Uruguay – Recourse to Article XXIII*, para. 15.

[5] The Appellate Body has confirmed this separation in Appellate Body Report, *US – Wool Shirts and Blouses*, DSR 1997: I, 323 at 334 and 335.

[6] Eg. Panel Report, *Italy – Agricultural Machinery*, paras. 21–22; Panel Report, *Canada – FIRA*, para. 6.7.

of nullification or impairment of benefits because quotas give rise to increased transaction costs and uncertainties that could affect investment plans.[7] In another case, a panel rejected the claim that the GATT-inconsistent measure caused no or insignificant trade effects arguing that the national treatment requirement in GATT 1947 did not protect expectations on export volumes, but expectations on the competitive relationship between imported and domestic products.[8] The Appellate Body has endorsed this reasoning.[9] One GATT panel went as far as to observe that the presumption had, in *practice*, operated as an irrefutable presumption.[10]

In the practice of the WTO dispute settlement system, panels typically cite Article 3.8 of the DSU (other than disputes brought under the GATS) once they have concluded that the defendant has violated a rule of a covered agreement. Unless the defendant (exceptionally) makes an attempt to rebut the presumption, panels dedicate no more than a brief paragraph at the end of their reports to the issue of nullification or impairment. It should be noted that the types of complaints brought under the GATS are slightly different.[11]

NON-VIOLATION COMPLAINT

One might wonder about the legitimacy of the non-violation complaint, given that the WTO Agreement contains all the rights and obligations on which the Members agreed in their negotiations. Why should there be a remedy against actions that are not inconsistent with these rights and obligations, in other words, measures that the WTO Agreement does not preclude?

The reason is that an international trade agreement such as the WTO Agreement can never be a complete set of rules without gaps. As a result, it is possible for WTO Members to take measures that comply with the letter of the agreement, but nevertheless frustrate one of its objectives or undermine trade commitments contained in the agreement. More technically speaking, the benefit a Member legitimately expects from another Member's commitment under the WTO Agreement can be frustrated both by measures proscribed in the WTO Agreement and by measures consistent with it. If one Member frustrates another Member's benefit by taking a measure otherwise consistent with the WTO Agreement, this impairs the balance between the mutual trade commitments of the two Members. The non-violation complaint provides for a means to redress this imbalance.

A GATT panel has described the purpose of the unusual remedy of the non-violation complaint as encouraging contracting parties to make tariff concessions. When the value of a tariff concession has been impaired by a contracting party

---

[7]   Panel Report, *Japan – Leather II* (US), paras. 54–56.
[8]   Panel Report, *US – Superfund*, para. 5.1.9.
[9]   Appellate Body Report, *EC – Bananas III*, paras. 252 and 253.
[10] Panel Report, *US – Superfund*, para. 5.1.7.
[11] See below the section on Types of dispute in the GATS on page 35.

giving that concession as a result of the application of a GATT-consistent measure, the contracting party receiving such concession – whose expectation of improved competitive opportunities is frustrated by that measure – must be given a right of redress.[12]

It would be wrong to believe that the non-violation complaint has a wide scope of application and is suitable to address all sorts of measures otherwise consistent with GATT 1994 and the other covered agreements. Panels and the Appellate Body have stated that the remedy in Article XXIII:1(b) "should be approached with caution and should remain an exceptional remedy".[13] One panel has added: "The reason for this caution is straightforward. Members negotiate the rules that they agree to follow and only exceptionally would expect to be challenged for actions not in contravention of those rules."[14]

Article 26.1 of the DSU specifically addresses non-violation complaints in the sense of Article XXIII:1(b) of GATT 1994 and requires the complainant to "present a detailed justification in support of any complaint relating to a measure which does not conflict with the relevant covered agreement". No presumption applies in non-violation cases as regards nullification or impairment. The text of Article XXIII:1(b), combined with the concept of nullification or impairment of a benefit,[15] gives rise to three conditions whose existence a complainant must establish, in order to be successful with a non-violation complaint. These three conditions are: (1) the application of a measure by a Member of the WTO; (2) the existence of a benefit accruing under the applicable agreement; and (3) the nullification or impairment of a benefit as a result of the application of the measure.[16]

The first condition means that the measure applied is attributable to the government of the respondent Member. Purely private conduct, taken by itself, would not satisfy this condition. If a government simply tolerates private restrictive conduct, this also could not be challenged with the non-violation complaint. A different situation is that where the government actively supports or encourages such private actions.[17] With respect to the second condition, complainants have in the past been able to rely on the legitimate expectation of improved market access opportunities resulting from the relevant tariff concessions. As to the third condition, this benefit is nullified or impaired when the measure in question has the effect of upsetting the competitive relationship between imported and domestic goods and the complainant was not able to reasonably anticipate the application of the measure when it was negotiating the concession.

---

[12] Panel Report, *EEC – Oilseeds I*, para. 144.
[13] Panel Report, *Japan – Film*, para. 10.37.   [14] Panel Report, *Japan – Film*, para. 10.36.
[15] Note that Article 26.1 of the DSU also covers the other kind of non-violation complaint, which combines the "measure applied by a Member" with the impeded "attainment of any objective" of GATT 1994, instead of combining the non-violating measure with "nullification or impairment of a benefit", as typically happens in non-violation complaints.
[16] Panel Report, *EC – Asbestos*, para. 8.283.   [17] *See* also Article 11.3 of the Agreement on Safeguards.

There have been 14 cases in which a non-violation claim under Article XXIII:1(b) of GATT 1947 has been considered by working parties and panels. In six of these cases, the claim under Article XXIII:1(b) was successful[18] and, on three of these occasions, the report was adopted by the GATT Council.

SITUATION COMPLAINT

The negotiating history indicates that Article XXIII:1(c) of GATT 1947, the so-called "situation complaint", was intended to play a role in situations of macro-economic emergency (e.g. general depressions, high unemployment, collapse of the price of a commodity, balance-of-payment difficulties). Under GATT 1947 practice, contracting parties relied on Article XXIII:1(c) in a few cases in order to complain about withdrawn concessions, failed re-negotiations of tariff concessions and non-realized expectations on trade flows. However, none of these complaints ever resulted in a panel ruling based on Article XXIII:1(c).[19] Therefore neither GATT nor WTO jurisprudence provides guidance as to the criteria for a legitimate situation complaint.

From the plain text of Article XXIII:1(c), one can deduce that there needs to be a situation other than those mentioned in subparagraphs (a) and (b) of Article XXIII:1 and nullification or impairment of a benefit (or the impeded attainment of an objective of GATT 1994). Article 26.2(a) of the DSU provides that the complaining party must "present a detailed justification in support of any argument" with respect to the situation complaint.

Article 26.2 of the DSU also provides that the rules and procedures of the DSU apply only to situation complaints up to the circulation of the panel report. Regarding the adoption of a panel report and the surveillance and implementation of recommendations and rulings in these cases, the old dispute settlement rules and procedures contained in the Decision of 12 April 1989[20] continue to apply. This means that there is no reverse consensus rule applying to the adoption of the panel report and the authorization of the suspension of obligations in the event of non-implementation of rulings with respect to situation complaints. In other words, any Member could block these decisions in the DSB by preventing a positive consensus.[21] So far, this provision has never been invoked by any Member.

---

[18] Working Party Report, *Australia – Ammonium Sulphate*; Panel Report, *Germany – Sardines*; Panel Report, *EC – Citrus*, 7 February 1985, unadopted, L/5776; Panel Report, *EEC – Canned Fruit*; Panel Report, *EEC – Oilseeds I*; Panel Report, *EEC – Oilseeds II*.

[19] *See* GATT, Analytical Index, pp. 668–671 (6th updated edition 1995).   [20] BISD 36S/61–67.

[21] Article 26.2 of the DSU also implicitly excludes the possibility of an appeal against a panel report based on a situation complaint. This appears to preclude the Appellate Body from reviewing the legal criteria found by a panel to be the requirements of a valid situation complaint on the basis of Article XXIII:1(c) of GATT 1994 and Article 26.2 of the DSU.

SYNTHESIS FOR PRACTICAL PURPOSES

In summary, it can be said that there are two types of complaints which play a practical role in the WTO dispute settlement process. These are the violation complaint and, far less frequently, the non-violation complaint, as described above. It is possible for one case to simultaneously involve both these types of complaints, for instance when raised in the alternative ("if the Panel finds that there is no violation, the complainant submits that it would have to find that there is non-violation nullification or impairment").[22]

TYPES OF DISPUTE IN THE OTHER MULTILATERAL AGREEMENTS ON TRADE IN GOODS

As stated above, most of the multilateral agreements on trade in goods (which are contained in Annex 1A of the WTO Agreement) other than GATT 1994 include an express reference to Articles XXII and XXIII of GATT or paraphrase the criteria contained therein. In those cases, the requirements and options for a complaint are the same as discussed above. Minor adaptations are of course necessary because, for instance, the failure to carry out an obligation under the agreement then refers to the respective agreement, not to GATT 1994. Similarly, the benefit must be one accruing under that agreement. Accordingly, the following section will only highlight the instances in which there are departures from what was explained in the context of GATT 1994.

The SCM Agreement also refers to Articles XXII and XXIII of GATT 1994 (Article 30). However, in Article 4, it specifically provides otherwise in relation to the prohibited subsidies as defined in Article 3 (export subsidies and import substitution subsidies) by not requiring any claim of nullification or impairment of a benefit. As a consequence, Article 3.8 of the DSU is not applicable.[23]

TYPES OF DISPUTE IN THE GATS

The dispute settlement provisions of the GATS (which is contained in Annex 1B of the WTO Agreement) are contained in Articles XXII and XXIII of that Agreement. The GATS only provides for two types of complaints, the violation complaint and the non-violation complaint.[24] There is no situation complaint and the

---

[22] Eg. in *Japan – Film*, and *EC – Asbestos*.

[23] Not in the sense that there is no presumption of nullification or impairment, but in the sense that there is no nullification or impairment that needs to be presumed.

[24] These are the two types of complaint that play a practical role in GATT 1994.

GATT 1994 clause referring to the scenario that "the attainment of any objective of the Agreement is being impeded" also does not exist.

As regards the violation complaint, Article XXIII:1 of the GATS provides that a WTO Member that considers that another Member has failed to carry out its obligations under the GATS may have recourse to the DSU. The GATS thus abandoned the notion of nullification or impairment as a requirement in addition to the failure to carry out obligations. Consequently, Article 3.8 of the DSU is of no relevance to complaints brought under the GATS.

The non-violation complaint of GATS resembles that of GATT 1994 because a Member can allege nullification or impairment of a benefit it could reasonably expect to accrue to it under a specific commitment of another Member in the absence of a conflict with the provisions of GATS (Article XXIII:3).

TYPES OF DISPUTE IN THE TRIPS AGREEMENT

In Article 64.1, the TRIPS Agreement (which is contained in Annex 1C of the WTO Agreement) contains a reference to Articles XXII and XXIII of GATT 1994. On that basis, one would say that all the above as explained in the context of GATT 1994 also applies to disputes under the TRIPS Agreement. In other words, there are three different types of complaints that could be brought under the TRIPS Agreement. However, Article 64.2 of the TRIPS Agreement excluded non-violation and situation complaints for the first five years from the entry into force of the WTO Agreement. Article 64.3 mandated the Council for TRIPS to examine the scope and modalities for non-violation and situation complaints during the five-year moratorium and to submit recommendations to the Ministerial Conference for approval by consensus.

The five-year deadline of Article 64.2 expired on 31 December 1999, but the TRIPS Council has not so far submitted recommendations to the Ministerial Conference, nor has the Ministerial Conference approved any recommendations in that regard. This has resulted in a controversy among Members over whether, in the absence of an approved recommendation on scope and modalities, complaints of the type set out in Article XXIII:1(b) and 1(c) of GATT 1994 are possible since the expiry of the Article 64.2 moratorium. Despite this controversy, no non-violation and situation complaints were brought by Members under the TRIPS Agreement.

At their fourth ministerial session in 2001, ministers of the WTO Members renewed the moratorium contained in Article 64.2 and directed the TRIPS Council to continue its examination of the scope and modalities for non-violation and situation complaints and to make recommendations to the fifth session of the Ministerial Conference that took place in September 2003.[25] However, the fifth session was concluded without any action on this matter.

---

[25] Para. 11.1 of the Doha Decision on Implementation.

DISPUTES ON ARTICLES I TO XVI OF THE WTO AGREEMENT AND THE DSU

Articles I to XVI of the WTO Agreement and the DSU do not contain specific provisions concerning consultations and dispute settlement to deal with matters arising under the WTO Agreement itself (in the sense of Articles I to XVI) or the DSU itself. However, these two Agreements do fall within the category of "covered agreements", as they are listed in Appendix 1 to the DSU. The second sentence of Article 1.1 of the DSU also provides specifically that the dispute settlement system applies to disputes under the WTO Agreement (in the sense of Articles I to XVI) and the DSU.

To date, there have been two cases in which a complainant has claimed a breach by a Member of a provision of the DSU, namely Article 23.1.[26] Moreover, one provision of the WTO Agreement (in the sense of Articles I to XVI), namely Article XVI:4, is a frequent basis for violation complaints.

---

[26] Panel Report, *US – Section 301 Trade Act*; Panel Report and Appellate Body Report, *US – Certain EC Products*.

POSSIBLE OBJECT OF A COMPLAINT – JURISDICTION OF PANELS AND THE APPELLATE BODY

The previous chapter explored what constitutes a valid basis for a complaint in the WTO dispute settlement system and explained the different types of complaints available under the covered agreements. The present chapter addresses the jurisdiction of WTO panels and the Appellate Body by exploring the question of the *object* of the complaint. To put it more simply: *against what* can the complaint be directed? For example, in a violation complaint, what types of action by a Member are covered by a commitment in a covered agreement? Can only acts of administrative authorities be challenged or also legislative acts? Can the complainant invoke the dispute settlement system only against legally binding acts of Members or also against non-binding acts taken by the Members' authorities? Can the challenge only be directed against governmental conduct or also against behaviour of private individuals? Can it be directed only against positive action or also against omissions, i.e. the failure to act?

Answers to these questions are important because they serve to delineate the jurisdiction of WTO panels and the Appellate Body.

ARTICLE 1.1 OF THE DSU

One could give a simple and formalistic answer to the question of jurisdiction: the WTO dispute settlement system has jurisdiction over any dispute between WTO Members arising under any of the covered agreements (Article 1.1 of the DSU). How the object of a dispute is viewed in legal terms depends on the content of the agreements (i.e. on the type of complaint possible under the agreement in question, combined with the substantive provision in question). For example, a violation complaint under Article X, Y or Z of GATT 1994 can be directed against anything that might violate those provisions. In such a case, a panel would probably not spend any time deciding whether the complainant is challenging a proper measure, but rather would simply assess whether what is alleged to violate the invoked article actually does so. There is no doubt that the panel would have jurisdiction to answer that question.

At the same time, it is possible conceptually to categorize the possible objects of a complaint on the basis of the common structure of the provisions of the covered agreements. Such categorization follows below.

ACTION AND INACTION; BINDING AND NON-BINDING ACTS OF MEMBERS

If a complaint is based on a provision that prohibits certain actions (e.g. Article XI of GATT 1994 which prohibits, among other things, export restrictions), only positive action (e.g. a law, regulation or decision impeding the exportation of goods to other WTO Members or other forms of measures imposing restrictions) can violate such a provision. Inaction as such (the failure to adopt such a law, regulation or decision) could not breach this obligation.[1] The positive action in question could be a formal regulation, but also an informal instruction issued by the government, if, as in the Article XI example above, it effectively restricts exports.[2]

The situation is different under WTO agreement provisions that do not prohibit certain behaviour, but rather require positive action. The TRIPS Agreement, for example, obliges Members in Article 25.1 to provide for the protection of new or original independently created industrial designs. In Article 26, it defines what this protection has to include. This is a typical obligation to take *positive action* by passing and applying a law granting this protection. Accordingly, inaction or an omission will be at the heart of a violation complaint which can be brought in a situation where a Member has either done nothing, i.e. not passed any laws, or where the laws passed and applied for some reason do not meet the required standards.

Obligations to take positive action are prominent within the TRIPS Agreement, but also exist in other covered agreements. Notification and transparency requirements (e.g. Article 12.2 of the Agreement on Safeguards or Article X:1 of GATT 1994) or consultation requirements (Article 12.3 of the Agreement on Safeguards) are other examples. What can become the object of a violation complaint, therefore, essentially depends on the obligations underlying the claim. Whatever activity can violate these obligations of the Members can also be challenged by a complainant.

Article 6.2 of the DSU, which obliges the complainant to identify in its request for the establishment of a panel the specific "measures" at issue, should not be understood to impose the requirement that a complaint can only be brought against a "measure" in the sense of a positive act, which would exclude *inaction*. The Appellate Body has dealt with the term "measure" in Article 6.2 of the DSU and stated, with reference to previous GATT and WTO jurisprudence, that a "measure" may be *any* act of a Member, whether or not legally binding, including a government's non-binding administrative guidance and also an omission or a failure to act on the part of a Member.[3] This must be so because Article 6.2 of the DSU applies to all complaints and, as pointed out above with the example of Article 25 of the

---

[1] The failure to abrogate a law that impedes exports should not be qualified as omission in the technical sense, as the violation is found in the law in question, which is a positive act.
[2] Panel Report, *Japan – Semi-Conductors*, para. 117.
[3] Appellate Body Report, *Guatemala – Cement I*, footnote 47.

TRIPS Agreement, complaints are also possible against the failure of a Member to take action where the WTO provision in question requires positive action.

ONLY GOVERNMENTAL MEASURES OF MEMBERS?

As a general rule, only government measures can be the object of WTO complaints.

Concerning violation complaints, it is recalled that the WTO Agreement is an international agreement binding the WTO Members under public international law. The obligations contained in the WTO Agreement, as such, therefore bind only the signatory States and separate customs territories. It follows that non-governmental, private actors cannot infringe these obligations. However, there can be instances in which certain private behaviour has strong ties to some governmental action. Whether this permits the attribution of the private behaviour to the Member in question, and therefore is actionable under the WTO, will obviously depend on the particularities of each case.[4]

As regards the non-violation complaint, Article XXIII:1(b) of GATT 1994 requires the application of a measure by another Member. A purely private activity without government involvement would therefore not satisfy that requirement.[5] However, in practice, things are not always so clear-cut, and there have been several trade disputes involving private actions having some governmental connection or endorsement. On the basis of the panel reports in such disputes, the panel in *Japan – Film* defined "sufficient government involvement" as the decisive criterion as to whether a private action may be deemed to be a governmental "measure".[6]

Finally, a situation complaint could arguably apply to situations in which private parties have taken some action against which the Member did not act but this has never been tested in either the GATT or WTO dispute settlement systems.

MEASURES TAKEN BY REGIONAL OR LOCAL SUBDIVISIONS OF A MEMBER

Under traditional public international law, subjects of international law, typically States, are responsible for the activities of all branches of government within their system of governance, and also for all regional levels or other subdivisions of government. This principle also applies in WTO law, except where the covered agreements expressly deal with this question and exclude acts taken by regional or local governments from the coverage of certain obligations. Article 22 of the DSU specifically confirms that the dispute settlement system can be invoked in

---

[4] Panel Report, *Japan – Semi-Conductors*, para. 117; Panel Report, *EEC – Dessert Apples*, para. 126; Panel Report, *Argentina – Hides and Leather*, paras. 11.17, 11.22 and 11.51.
[5] Panel Report, *Japan – Film*, para. 10.52.   [6] Panel Report, *Japan – Film*, para. 10.56.

respect of measures taken by regional or local governments or authorities within the territory of a Member. There are particular rules, however, applying in the implementation phase. Where a measure taken by a regional or local authority is inconsistent with a provision of a covered agreement, the Member must take such reasonable measures as may be available to it to ensure observance (Article 22.9 of the DSU, Article XXIV:12 of GATT 1994 and Article I:3(a) of the GATS).[7] Article 14 of the TBT Agreement attributes to Members acts of non-governmental organizations regulated by the Agreement.[8]

THE POSSIBILITY OF CHALLENGING LAWS "AS SUCH"

WTO complaints are often directed against specific administrative measures taken by authorities of a Member pursuant to domestic laws, for example, anti-dumping duties imposed by an anti-dumping authority following an investigation of certain imports. However, the underlying law itself may also violate a WTO legal obligation or otherwise nullify or impair benefits under the covered agreements. Article XVI:4 of the WTO Agreement makes clear that Members must ensure the conformity of their laws, regulations and administrative procedures with their obligations under the WTO Agreement, including its Annexes. Accordingly, Members frequently invoke the dispute settlement system against a law as such, independently of, or without waiting for, the application of that law. For example, claims about taxes which discriminate against imports and contravene Article III:2 of GATT 1994 are typically directed at the tax legislation and not at the tax imposed on a specific shipment of goods at a specific time in the recent past. Successfully challenging the law as such gives the advantage that the respondent's implementation, ideally the withdrawal or modification of the inconsistent measure (Article 3.7 of the DSU), would equally address the law as such and not be limited to an isolated case of application of such law.

DISCRETIONARY AND MANDATORY LEGISLATION

There is an important distinction in WTO law between challenging a law as such and challenging the application of that law. Under GATT 1947, panels had already developed the concept that, when legislation as such is the object of a complaint, mandatory and discretionary legislation must be distinguished from each other. The Appellate Body has endorsed this distinction.[9] Only legislation that *mandates* a violation of WTO obligations can be found as such to be inconsistent with those obligations. By contrast, legislation that merely gives discretion to the executive

---

[7] *See* further below the section on Obligations in the event of a "regional or local violation" on page 90.

[8] *See* further below the section on Obligations in the event of a "regional or local violation" on page 90.

[9] Appellate Body Report, *US – 1916 Act*, para. 88, with references to GATT panel reports.

authority of a Member to act inconsistently with the WTO Agreement cannot be challenged as such. In such a case, only the actual application of such legislation in a manner that is inconsistent with the WTO Agreement is subject to challenge. Thus, where discretionary authority is vested in the executive branch of a WTO Member, it cannot be assumed that the WTO Member will fail to implement its obligations under the WTO Agreement in good faith.[10] According to this approach, the test is whether or not the legislation in question allows the administrative authorities to abide by that Member's WTO obligations.

Nonetheless, one panel took issue with this distinction as a principle applying to all WTO obligations. This panel insisted that it depends on the precise WTO provision in question and whether the provision precludes only mandatory laws or also discretionary ones.[11] The Appellate Body recently stated that it is "not . . . precluding the possibility that a Member could violate its WTO obligations by enacting legislation granting discretion to its authorities to act in violation of its WTO obligation."[12]

LEGISLATION NOT YET IN FORCE

There are times when a piece of domestic legislation has already been adopted, but has not yet entered into force. In other words, the law has been adopted in its final form, but with the stipulation that it will be effective only from a future date. Can such laws be challenged in the WTO dispute settlement system before they enter into force, given that the legislative authorities have completed their work of crafting the law and the entry into effect is only a matter of time and thus automatic? Or is it premature to challenge such a law, given that it has no legal effect until the date of entry into force, which would exclude any violation of WTO law and might also prevent nullification or impairment of any benefit for the time being?

Several dispute settlement panels have dealt with this type of question and have found that the challenge was not premature in these specific instances because the entry into force was automatic at a future date and did not depend on further legislative action. Even though the legal effect of such a measure will only occur in the future, the measure already had an impact on the market participants engaging in international trade prior to its coming into force because these market participants typically plan their transactions ahead of time.[13]

---

[10] Appellate Body Report, *US – Section 211 Appropriations Act*, para. 259.

[11] Panel Report, *US – Section 301 Trade Act*, paras. 7.53–7.54.

[12] Appellate Body Report, *US – Countervailing Measures on Certain EC Products*, footnote 334 to para. 159.

[13] For instance, the panel in *US – Superfund* insisted that Articles III and XI of GATT 1947 also purport to create the predictability needed to plan future trade. It noted that the coming into force of the tax at issue at the beginning of the second year following that of the dispute was a time-frame within which the trade and investment decisions that could be influenced by the tax would be taken. *See* Panel Report, *US – Superfund*, para. 5.2.2.

THE PROCESS – STAGES IN A TYPICAL WTO DISPUTE SETTLEMENT CASE

This chapter explains all the various stages through which a dispute can pass in the WTO dispute settlement system. There are two main ways to settle a dispute once a complaint has been filed in the WTO: (i) the parties find a mutually agreed solution, particularly during the phase of bilateral consultations; and (ii) through adjudication, including the subsequent implementation of the panel and Appellate Body reports, which are binding upon the parties once adopted by the DSB. There are three main stages to the WTO dispute settlement process: (i) consultations between the parties; (ii) adjudication by panels and, if applicable, by the Appellate Body; and (iii) the implementation of the ruling, which includes the possibility of countermeasures in the event of failure by the losing party to implement the ruling.

CONSULTATIONS

OBJECTIVE OF CONSULTATIONS

The preferred objective of the DSU is for the Members concerned to settle the dispute between themselves in a manner that is consistent with the WTO agreements (Article 3.7 of the DSU). Accordingly, bilateral consultations between the parties are the first stage of formal dispute settlement (Article 4 of the DSU). They give the parties an opportunity to discuss the matter and to find a satisfactory solution without resorting to litigation (Article 4.5 of the DSU). Only after such mandatory consultations have failed to produce a satisfactory solution within 60 days may the complainant request adjudication by a panel (Article 4.7 of the DSU).[1] Even when consultations have failed to resolve the dispute, it always remains possible for the parties to find a mutually agreed solution at any later stage of the proceedings.[2]

A majority of disputes so far in the WTO have not proceeded beyond consultations, either because a satisfactory settlement was found, or because the complainant

---

[1]   The parties to a dispute can depart from the requirement of consultations through mutual agreement under Article 25.2 of the DSU if they resort to arbitration as an alternative means of dispute settlement.

[2]   It is not this possibility of, and preference for, mutually agreeable solutions, which distinguishes the dispute settlement system of the WTO from typical domestic judicial systems, but the formal prerequisite of prior consultations. However, many of these domestic systems are moving towards the inclusion of alternative means of dispute resolution as a formal prerequisite for judicial action such as, for instance, a prior attempt to find an amicable solution with a mediator.

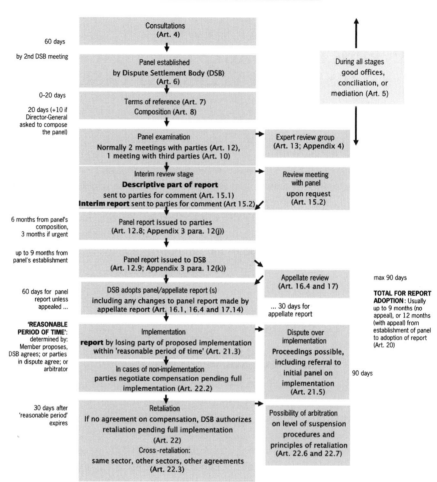

Flow Chart of the Dispute Settlement Process

decided for other reasons not to pursue the matter further. This shows that consultations are often an effective means of dispute resolution in the WTO and that the instruments of adjudication and enforcement in the dispute settlement system are by no means always necessary.

Together with good offices, conciliation and mediation,[3] consultations are the key non-judicial/diplomatic feature of the dispute settlement system of the WTO. Consultations also allow the parties to clarify the facts of the matter and the claims of the complainant, possibly dispelling misunderstandings as to the actual nature of

---

[3] These forms of "alternative" dispute settlement are voluntary and provided for under Article 5 DSU. *See* further below the section on Mediation, conciliation and good offices on page 93.

the measure at issue. In this sense, consultations serve either to lay the foundation for a settlement or for further proceedings under the DSU.

LEGAL BASIS AND REQUIREMENTS FOR A REQUEST FOR CONSULTATIONS

The request for consultations formally initiates a dispute in the WTO and triggers the application of the DSU. Very often, informal discussions on the matter between capital-based officials or between the Geneva delegations of the Members involved precede the formal WTO consultations. However, even where prior consultations occurred, it remains necessary for the complainant to go through the consultation procedure set forth in the DSU as a prerequisite for further proceedings in the WTO.

The complaining Member addresses the request for consultations to the responding Member, but must also notify the request to the DSB and to relevant Councils and Committees overseeing the agreement(s) in question (Article 4.4 of the DSU). Members only have to send one single text of their notification to the Secretariat, specifying the other relevant Councils or Committees. The Secretariat then distributes it to the specified relevant bodies.[4] The request for consultations informs the entire Membership of the WTO and the public at large of the initiation of a WTO dispute. The complainant has to make the request pursuant to one or more of the covered agreements (Articles 4.3 and 1.1 of the DSU), specifically under the respective provision on consultations of the covered agreement(s) in question.[5] Consultations are thus subject to the provisions of Article 4 of the DSU *and* the respective individual WTO agreement.

Under GATT 1994 and those covered agreements that refer to the consultations and dispute settlement provisions of GATT 1994, two legal bases are available for launching a dispute with a request for consultations, that is, either Articles XXII:1 or XXIII:1 of GATT 1994. Similarly, under GATS, consultations can be initiated under either Articles XXII:1 or XXIII:1.

For practical purposes, the main difference between these two legal bases relates to the ability of other WTO Members to join as third parties, which is possible only when consultations are held pursuant to Article XXII of GATT 1994, Article XXII:1 of GATS, or the corresponding provisions in other covered agreements (Article 4.11 of the DSU).[6] Hence, the choice between Articles XXII:1 and XXIII:1 of GATT 1994 is a strategic one, depending on whether the complainant wants to make it possible for other Members to participate. If the complainant invokes Article XXII:1, the admission of interested third parties depends on the respondent, who may or

---

[4] *See* DSB, Working Practices Concerning Dispute Settlement Procedures, As agreed by the DSB, WT/DSB/6, 6 June 1996, page 2; and DSB, Minutes of the Meeting of 19 July 1995, WT/DSB/M/6, page 12.

[5] For the provisions on consultation and dispute settlement in the covered agreement, *see* above the section on Dispute settlement provisions in the covered agreements on page 28.

[6] The corresponding consultation provisions in the covered agreements are listed in footnote 4 to the DSU.

may not accept them.[7] By choosing Article XXIII:1, the complainant is able to prevent the involvement in the consultations of third parties. This option may be attractive for a complainant who intends to work towards a mutually agreed solution with the respondent without interference from other Members.

A request for consultations must be submitted in writing and must give the reasons for the request. This includes identifying the measures at issue and indicating the legal basis for the complaint (Article 4.4 of the DSU). In practice, such requests for consultations are very brief; often they are no more than one or two pages long, yet they must be sufficiently precise. Because requests for consultations are always the first official WTO document emerging in a specific dispute and each dispute has its own WT/DS number, requests for consultations carry the document symbol WT/DS###/1 (except in the case of issues falling under the Agreement on Textiles and Clothing where different procedures apply).

FRUITFULNESS OF ACTION UNDER THE DISPUTE SETTLEMENT SYSTEM

Before initiating consultations, a Member is obliged to exercise its judgement as to whether action under the dispute settlement system would be fruitful, the aim of the dispute settlement mechanism being to secure a positive solution to the dispute (Article 3.7 of the DSU). By its express terms, Article 3.7 of the DSU entrusts the Members of the WTO with the self-regulating responsibility of exercising their own judgement in deciding whether they consider it would be fruitful to bring a case.

PROCEDURE FOR CONSULTATIONS

The respondent (i.e. the Member to whom the request for consultations is addressed), is obliged to accord sympathetic consideration to, and afford adequate opportunity for, consultations (Article 4.2 of the DSU). Consultations typically take place in Geneva and are confidential (Article 4.6 of the DSU), which also means that the WTO Secretariat is not involved. The fact that they take place behind closed doors also means that their content remains undisclosed to any panel subsequently assigned the matter.

Unless otherwise agreed, the respondent must reply to the request within ten days and must enter into consultations in good faith within a period of no more than 30 days after the date of receipt of the request for consultations. If the respondent fails to meet any of these deadlines, the complainant may immediately proceed to the adjudicative stage of dispute settlement and request the establishment of a panel (Article 4.3 of the DSU). If the respondent engages in consultations, the complainant can proceed to the request for establishment of a panel at the earliest

---

[7] *See* below in the section on Third parties in consultations, at page 47.

60 days after the date of receipt of the request for consultations, provided that no satisfactory solution has emerged from the consultations. However, the consultation stage can also be concluded earlier if the parties jointly consider that consultations have failed to settle the dispute (Article 4.7 of the DSU). In practice, parties to a dispute often allow themselves significantly more time than the minimum of 60 days.

In cases of urgency, including those that concern perishable goods, Members must enter into consultations within a period of no more than ten days after the date of receipt of the request. If the consultations fail to settle the dispute within a period of 20 days after the date of receipt of the request, the complaining party may request the establishment of a panel (Article 4.8 of the DSU).

THIRD PARTIES IN CONSULTATIONS

A WTO Member that is neither the complainant nor the respondent may be interested in the matters the parties to a dispute are discussing in their consultations. There are various reasons for such an interest: for example, that other Member may have a trade interest and so feels similarly aggrieved by the challenged measure; it may, on the contrary, benefit from that measure; or it may be concerned about the challenge because it maintains a measure similar to that of the respondent. The Member in question may also have an interest in being present at discussions on any mutually agreeable solution because such a solution may affect its interests.

Such other Member may request to join consultations if it has a substantial trade interest in the matter being discussed and if consultations were requested pursuant to Article XXII:1 of GATT 1994, Article XXII:1 of GATS or the corresponding provisions of the other covered agreements. The request must be addressed to the consulting Members and the DSB within ten days after the date of the circulation of the original request for consultations.[8] The responding Member must also agree that the claim of substantial trade interest is well founded. If the respondent disagrees, there is no recourse through which the interested Member can impose its presence at the consultations, no matter how legitimate the invoked substantial trade interest may be. However, the interested Member can always request consultations directly with the respondent (Article 4.11 of the DSU), which would open a new, separate dispute settlement proceeding.

THE PANEL STAGE

If the consultations have failed to settle the dispute, the complaining party may request the establishment of a panel to adjudicate the dispute. As mentioned earlier, the complainant may do so any time 60 days after the date of receipt by the

---

[8] Requests to be joined in consultations are in almost all cases submitted to the DSB.

respondent of the request for consultations, but also earlier if the respondent either did not respect the deadlines for responding to the request for consultations or if the consulting parties jointly consider that consultations have failed to settle the dispute (Article 4.7 of the DSU). Where consultations do not yield a satisfactory result for the complainant, the procedure starting with the panel stage offers the complainant the possibility to uphold its rights or protect its benefits under the WTO Agreement. This procedure is equally important for the respondent as an opportunity to defend itself because it may disagree with the complainant on either the facts or the correct interpretation of obligations or benefits under the WTO Agreement. The adjudicative stage of dispute settlement is intended to resolve a legal dispute, and both parties must accept any rulings as binding (although they are always able to try to settle the dispute amicably at any time).

ESTABLISHMENT OF A PANEL

The request for establishment of a panel initiates the phase of adjudication. A request for the establishment of a panel must be made in writing and is addressed to the Chairman of the DSB. This request becomes an official document in the dispute in question and is circulated to the entire WTO membership.[9] In order to be included in the agenda of a DSB meeting, the request for establishment of a panel must be filed at least 11 days in advance (Rule 3 of the Rules of Procedure). It must indicate whether consultations were held, identify the specific measures at issue, and provide a brief, but sufficiently clear, summary of the legal basis of the complaint (Article 6.2 of the DSU).

The content of the request for establishment of the panel is crucial. Under Article 7.1 of the DSU, such request determines the standard terms of reference for the panel's examination of the matter. In other words, the request for the establishment of a panel defines and limits the scope of the dispute and thereby the extent of the panel's jurisdiction. Only the measure or measures identified in the request become the object of the panel's review and the panel will review the dispute only in the light of the provisions cited in the complainant's request. In addition to determining the panel's terms of reference, the request for establishment of the panel also has the function of informing the respondent and third parties of the basis for the complaint.[10]

It is thus important to draft the request for the establishment of a panel with sufficient precision so as to avoid having the respondent raise preliminary objections against individual claims or having the panel decline to rule on certain aspects of the complaint. Providing "a brief summary of the legal basis of the complaint sufficient

---

[9]   The request for the establishment of a panel is also a public document, but there is no standard number for the request for establishment of a panel because the number of documents emerging from a dispute after the request for consultations (WT/DS###/1) and before the request for the establishment of a panel varies (third parties requesting to be joined to consultations, acceptance of third parties by the respondent).

[10]   Appellate Body Report, *EC – Bananas III*, para. 142.

to present the problem clearly" means that the legal claims, but not the arguments,[11] must all be specified sufficiently in the request for the establishment of a panel. If the initial request does not specify a certain *claim*, the request cannot subsequently be "cured" by a complaining party's argumentation in the written submissions or in oral statements to the panel.[12] The mere listing of the articles of the agreements allegedly breached may, in the particular circumstances of the case, be sufficient to satisfy the minimum requirements of Article 6.2 of the DSU,[13] but this must be examined on a case-by-case basis.[14] In several cases of (preliminary) objections by the respondent, panels and the Appellate Body have asked whether the respondent's ability to defend itself was prejudiced by the alleged lack of clarity in the panel request.[15]

Panels have standard terms of reference, unless the parties to the dispute agree otherwise within 20 days from the establishment of the panel (Article 7.1 of the DSU). If other than standard terms of reference are agreed upon, any Member may raise any point in that respect in the DSB (Article 7.3 of the DSU).

Establishing panels is one of the functions of the DSB and is one of the three situations in which the decision of the DSB does not require a consensus. In the first DSB meeting in which such a request is made, the responding Member can still block the panel's establishment, as was the case in the dispute settlement system under GATT 1947. At the second DSB meeting where the request is made, however, the panel will be established, unless the DSB decides by consensus not to establish the panel (i.e. the "negative" consensus rule applies (Article 6.1 of the DSU)). This second meeting usually takes place around one month later, but the complainant can also request a special meeting of the DSB within 15 days of the request, provided that at least ten days' advance notice of the meeting is given (footnote 5 to Article 6.1 of the DSU).

The rule of negative (or reverse) consensus means that the complainant ultimately has a guarantee that the requested panel will be established if it so wishes. The only possibility to prevent the establishment is a consensus in the DSB against establishment, but this will not happen as long as the complainant is unwilling to join in that consensus. In other words, as long as the complainant, even alone and against the opposition of all other WTO Members, insists on the establishment of the panel, it is impossible for the DSB to reach a consensus against establishment. Therefore,[16] one speaks of a virtually automatic DSB decision to establish a panel.

---

[11] On the distinction between claims and arguments, see below the section on the Claims versus arguments on page 101.

[12] Appellate Body Report, *EC – Bananas III*, para. 143.

[13] Appellate Body Report, *EC – Bananas III*, para. 141.

[14] Appellate Body Report, *Korea – Dairy*, para. 127.

[15] Appellate Body Report, *Korea – Dairy*, para. 127; Appellate Body Report, *Thailand – H-Beams*, para. 95.

[16] It would be contradictory, unusual circumstances aside, to request a panel and simultaneously to refrain from objecting to an attempted consensus in the DSB not to establish the panel.

THIRD PARTIES BEFORE THE PANEL

The complaining and the responding Members are the parties to the disputes. Other Members have an opportunity to be heard by panels and to make written submissions as third parties, even if they have not participated in the consultations. In order to participate in the panel procedure, these Members must have a substantial interest in the matter before the panel and they must notify their interest to the DSB (Article 10.2 of the DSU).

In practice, the DSB applies a ten-day deadline from the establishment of the panel for Members to reserve their rights as third parties. At the meeting at which the panel is established, it is sufficient to do so orally. During the following ten days, the substantial interest and the desire of Members to participate as third parties must be notified to the DSB in writing through the WTO Secretariat.

There is a difference between "substantial trade interest" which is required for third parties in consultations and "substantial interest" before the panel. Most significant is the fact that it is possible to join consultations only with the respondent's acceptance (and in the case of non-acceptance, there is no recourse to enforce participation). On the other hand, any Member who invokes a systemic interest, in practice, is admitted to a panel procedure as a third party without any scrutiny whether the interest truly is "substantial".

Third parties receive the parties' first written submissions to the panel and present their views orally to the panel during the first substantive meeting (Article 10.3 of the DSU).[17] Third parties have no rights beyond these although a panel can, and often does, extend the rights of participation of third parties in individual cases.

COMPOSITION OF THE PANEL

Even after a panel has been established by the DSB, it still must be composed because there are no permanent panels nor permanent panelists in the WTO. Instead, panels must be composed ad hoc for each individual dispute, with the selection of three or five members, pursuant to procedures laid down in the DSU (Article 8 of the DSU).

Panels are composed of three persons unless the parties to the dispute agree, within ten days from the establishment of the panel, to a panel composed of five panelists (Article 8.5 of the DSU). The Secretariat proposes nominations for the panel to the parties to the dispute (Article 8.6 of the DSU). Potential candidates must meet certain requirements in terms of expertise and independence (Articles 8.1 and 8.2 of the DSU). The WTO Secretariat maintains an indicative list of names of governmental and non-governmental persons, from which panelists may be drawn (Article 8.4 of the DSU) although other names can be considered as well. WTO Members regularly propose names for inclusion in that list, and, in practice, the DSB almost always approves their inclusion without debate. As noted, it is not

---

[17] *See* below in the section on Submissions and oral hearings on page 54.

necessary to be on the indicative list in order to be proposed as a potential panel member in a specific dispute. Citizens of a party or a third party to a dispute may not serve as panelists without the agreement of the parties (Article 8.3 of the DSU). When a dispute is between a developing country Member and a developed country Member the panel must, upon request by the developing country Member, include at least one panelist from a developing country Member (Article 8.10 of the DSU). Traditionally, many panelists are trade delegates of WTO Members or capital-based trade officials, but former Secretariat officials, retired government officials and academics also regularly serve on panels. These individuals perform the task of a panelist on a part-time basis, in addition to their usual professional activity.

When the Secretariat proposes qualified individual nominations as panelists, the parties must not oppose these nominations except for compelling reasons (Article 8.6 of the DSU). In practice, many Members make quite extensive use of this clause and oppose nominations very frequently. In such cases, there is no review regarding whether the reasons given are truly compelling. Rather, the Secretariat proposes other names. If, according to this method, there is no agreement between the parties on the composition of the panel within 20 days after the date of its establishment by the DSB, either party may request the Director-General of the WTO to determine the composition of the panel. Within ten days after sending this request to the chairperson of the DSB, the Director-General appoints the panel members in consultation with the chairperson of the DSB and the chairperson of the relevant Council or Committee, after consulting with the parties (Article 8.7 of the DSU).[18] The availability of this procedure is important because it prevents a respondent from blocking the entire panel proceeding by delaying (forever) the composition of the panel, which is what sometimes happens in other systems of international dispute resolution. Of course, the parties are always free to devote more than 20 days attempting to agree on the composition of the panel as long as none of them requests the Director-General to intervene.

The selected panelists must fulfil their task in full independence and not as representatives of a government or other organization for which they might happen to work. Members are prohibited from giving panelists instructions or seeking to influence them with regard to matters before the panel (Article 8.9 of the DSU).

SPECIAL RULES ON COMPOSITION

The Ministerial *Decision on Certain Dispute Settlement Procedures for the General Agreement on Trade in Services*, adopted in Marrakesh on 15 April 1994, and paragraph 4 of the GATS Annex on Financial Services expressly provide for the selection of panelists to ensure that panels have the relevant specific expertise in the sector that is the subject of the dispute.

---

[18] This procedure is available, whether the disagreement relates to one, two or all three panel members.

MULTIPLE COMPLAINANTS

Given that governmental measures regulating trade often affect trade with many WTO Members, there is frequently more than one other Member taking issue with a measure allegedly breaching WTO law or impairing benefits under the WTO agreements. Past practice shows that Members have used various strategies available under the dispute settlement rules to protect their commercial interests:

- The most passive strategy has been to hold back completely and hope that another Member raises the issue, proceeds through the entire dispute settlement process and ultimately secures the withdrawal of a measure if it has been found WTO-inconsistent. If this happens, all WTO Members benefit from that withdrawal.[19] Whether the Member which invoked the dispute settlement system benefits from that withdrawal to a greater extent than the passive Member(s) will largely depend on the respective trade flows in the products or services concerned.
- A more active strategy has been to participate as a third party in a dispute between two other Members involving a measure of interest. Compared to the passive option, being a third party offers the advantage of receiving information on the dispute, namely, the initial submissions, and of being heard by the panel and the parties. But the panel report does not include conclusions and recommendations with respect of third parties. A third party can always, however, switch to a more active role at a later stage and initiate a dispute settlement proceeding in its own right (Article 10.4 of the DSU).
- The most active strategy available would be that of being a complainant in one's own right by requesting consultations and a panel either in parallel to other complainants or jointly with other (co-)complainants. Both these variations exist in practice.

ESTABLISHMENT AND COMPOSITION IN THE CASE OF MULTIPLE COMPLAINANTS

In the case of multiple complainants, i.e. more than one Member requesting the establishment of a panel related to the same matter, Article 9.1 of the DSU applies and calls for the DSB, whenever feasible, to establish a single panel to examine these complaints taking into account the rights of all Members concerned.[20] For

---

[19] In the case of non-violation nullification or impairment, this strategy may not work equally well because there is no obligation to withdraw the measure (Article 26.1(b) of the DSU). The mutually satisfactory adjustment found by the parties in the phase of implementation may well provide for a benefit granted by the respondent that is particularly beneficial to the complainant, or the complainant may withdraw a reciprocal benefit. The passive Member whose benefit has also been (and continues to be) nullified or impaired would not profit from these adjustments to a similar degree.

[20] Pursuant to Article 10.4 of the DSU, this rationale also applies if a third party initiates its own complaint regarding a measure that is already the subject of a panel proceeding.

example, in *US – Shrimp*, the DSB decided to establish one single panel, despite a separate request made by India after the establishment of a panel at the joint request of Malaysia and Thailand and a separate request of Pakistan.[21] The "feasibility" of establishing a single panel obviously depends on factors such as the timing of the various disputes being more or less similar. If there is a long period of time between the different requests for establishment of a panel, establishing a single panel may be unfeasible, for instance if the panel that has been established first has already held its substantive meetings. When the time lag between the two disputes is less, establishing a single panel can be feasible if the parties, for instance, agree on a shorter time-period for consultations.

If it is not feasible to establish a single panel and more than one panel is established, the same persons should, if possible, serve as panelists on each of the separate panels and the timetables should be harmonized (Article 9.3 of the DSU). In *EC – Hormones*, for instance, the complaint of Canada (WT/DS48) and that of the United States (WT/DS26) were reviewed by two separate panels composed of the same individuals.

These two solutions serve to ensure that there is a consistent legal approach on the different complaints. With various panels composed of different panelists, who would work separately and not know each others' reasoning and decision (panel procedures are confidential until the circulation of the report), there is a risk that the different panel reports could depart one from another and even be contradictory.[22]

THE PANEL PROCEDURE

Once established and composed, the panel now exists as a collegial body and can start its work. One of the first tasks for the panel is to draw up a calendar for the panel's work (Article 12.3 of the DSU). The procedure is primarily set out in Article 12 and Appendix 3 to the DSU, but offers a certain degree of flexibility. The panel can follow different procedures after consulting the parties (Article 12.1 of the DSU, paragraph 11 of Appendix 3). In practice, panels generally follow the working procedures of Appendix 3 to the DSU, but often adopt additional rules where the specific dispute so requires. This usually happens in consultations or in agreement with the parties during the panel's "organizational" meeting with the parties. If this is not possible, the panel takes a decision on the working schedule and notifies the parties. The calendar of work thus adopted on the basis of the suggested timetable in Appendix 3 to the DSU sets dates and deadlines for the key

---

[21] Note by the Secretariat, *US – Shrimp*, WT/DS58/9, 17 April 1997.
[22] Although the Appellate Body could rectify such inconsistencies, divergent rulings by different panels would not enhance the credibility of these panel decisions and not serve the purpose of providing security and predictability to the multilateral trading system, which is one of the goals of the dispute settlement system (Article 3.2 of the DSU). If there is no appeal rectifying the inconsistencies, the divergent panel conclusions and recommendations could even be mutually incompatible and lead to insurmountable problems in the process of implementation.

stages of the panel proceeding, (e.g. the dates by which submissions have to be filed, the oral hearings (called "first" or "second substantive meeting") take place, and when the interim and the final panel report are to be issued, etc.).

SUBMISSIONS AND ORAL HEARINGS

In accordance with the panel's calendar, the substantive panel process may start with an exchange of submissions between the parties on any preliminary issue raised by the respondent. For example, a respondent may challenge the sufficiency or clarity of the request for the establishment of the panel.[23] In such cases, the panel may issue a preliminary ruling, but it can also reserve its ruling for the final panel report.[24]

When there are no such preliminary issues, the parties start by exchanging a first set of written submissions. The complainant normally is the first to file its submission, to which the respondent replies in its first submission (Article 12.6 of the DSU). The third parties usually file their submissions after the parties have filed theirs. The third parties, who are entitled to receive the parties' first written submissions (Article 10.3 of the DSU), often side with the positions taken by one of the parties.

The DSU envisages that the Secretariat is to receive these submissions and transmit them to the other party or parties to the dispute (Article 12.6 of the DSU). In practice, however, these submissions are filed with the Secretariat DS Registry[25] only in the number requested for the panel, whereas the parties and third parties serve copies directly on the other parties and third parties, often through the letter boxes of their Geneva delegations in the WTO building.

The parties' written submissions are quite extensive documents sometimes of considerable length and often with elaborate annexes. They clarify the facts of the case and contain legal arguments, which often rely substantially on prior jurisprudence of panels and the Appellate Body. The complainant's submission usually attempts to establish that the claim of a violation or of non-violation nullification or impairment is substantiated. The respondent typically tries to refute the factual and legal allegations and arguments put forward by the complainant. In contrast to the parties' submissions, third party submissions are usually a lot shorter, often only a few pages long, and comment on the parties' factual and legal arguments.

All these submissions are kept confidential (Article 18.2 of the DSU and paragraph 3 of the Working Procedures in Appendix 3 to the DSU), but the panel report, which is ultimately circulated to all Members and made public, reflects and summarizes the factual and legal allegations and arguments of the parties before the

---

[23] *See* above in the section on the Establishment of a panel on page 48.

[24] In the latter case, the parties might have to present some of their arguments in the alternative, if they do not know whether a certain claim forms part of the panel's terms of reference.

[25] In 2002, the Secretariat established a dispute settlement registry which receives and files the submissions and maintains the official record for every dispute at the panel stage.

panel (in the so-called descriptive part of the panel report). In addition, the parties are free to disclose their own submissions to the public (Article 18.2 of the DSU and paragraph 3 of the Working Procedures in Appendix 3 to the DSU). Several Members publish their submissions on their own websites, as soon as they are filed, after an oral hearing, or once the procedure is concluded.[26]

In drawing up their working procedures for a specific dispute, panels sometimes request the parties and third parties to submit executive summaries of their submissions. To some extent, these summaries are used in drafting the descriptive part of the panel report.

After the exchange of the first written submissions, the panel convenes a first oral hearing, called the first substantive (as opposed to "organizational") meeting. Like all meetings, this meeting takes place at the WTO headquarters in Geneva, and is similar to an oral hearing before a court, but the setting is more informal. Contrary to practice in many domestic judiciaries, this oral hearing is not public. Only the parties and third parties to the dispute, the panelists, the Secretariat staff supporting the panel, and the interpreters are entitled to attend this meeting.

At this meeting, which is recorded on tape, the parties present their views orally, mostly on the basis of a prepared statement also distributed in writing to the panel and the other parties (paragraph 9 of the Working Procedures in Appendix 3). After hearing the complainant(s) and the respondent, the panel accords the third parties an opportunity to present their views orally during a special session dedicated to the third parties' presentations (Article 10.2 of the DSU, paragraph 6 of the Working Procedures in Appendix 3). This means that, under the normal procedures, third parties are not present prior to this special third party session, when the parties present their views orally, but only while all the third parties present their cases. Accordingly, they all leave the room after all third parties have spoken (unless the panel adopts a different procedure).

After the oral statements, the parties (and third parties) are invited to respond to questions from the panel and from the other parties in order to clarify all the legal and factual issues (paragraph 8 of the Working Procedures in Appendix 3). These questions are usually distributed in written form, but discussed in the oral hearing to the extent that parties (and third parties) are ready to respond to them orally. After the conclusion of the first substantive meeting, the parties are usually requested, within a deadline of several days, to submit written answers to the panel's and the other parties' questions, irrespective of whether they have already been discussed orally.

---

[26] These websites can be useful resources for an example of how these submissions are structured and written and of specific legal statements in various areas of WTO law. Examples of these websites of active players in the dispute settlement system are: http://www.acwl.ch/cases/SubmenuCase.htm for the (developing country) parties represented by the Advisory Centre on WTO Law; http://www.dfat.gov.au/trade/negotiations/wto˙disputes.html for Australia; http://www.dfait-maeci.gc.ca/tna-nac/dispute-e.asp for Canada; http://mkaccdb.eu.int/miti/dsu for the European Communities; http://www.dft.govt.nz/support/legal/default.html for New Zealand; http://ustr.gov/enforcement/briefs.shtml for the United States.

Approximately four weeks after the first panel meeting, the parties simultaneously exchange written rebuttals, also called the second written submissions. In
these submissions, which are not provided to the third parties, the parties respond
to each other's first written submissions and oral statements made at the first substantive meeting. Thereafter, the panel holds a second substantive meeting with the
parties (panels have the power to schedule a third (or more) meetings in a dispute).
The parties once again orally present factual and legal arguments at this second
oral hearing and respond to further questions from the panel and the other party,
first orally, then in writing. Sometimes a Panel holds a third meeting, in particular
when an expert hearing takes place.

In cases of multiple complaints on the same matter where a single panel is
established, the written submissions of each of the complainants must be made
available to the other complainants, and each complainant has the right to be present
when any one of the other complainants presents its views to the panel (Article 9.2
of the DSU).

DELIBERATION OF THE PANEL AND PREPARATION OF THE PANEL REPORT

After the oral hearings are concluded, the panel goes into internal deliberations to
review the matter and to reach conclusions as to the outcome of the dispute and the
reasoning in support of such outcome. The panel is mandated to make an objective
assessment of the relevant factual questions and legal issues in order to assess
the conformity of the challenged measure with the covered agreement(s) invoked
by the complainant (Article 11 of the DSU). Simply put, the panel examines the
correctness of the complainant's claim that the respondent has acted inconsistently
with its WTO obligations.[27] Thus, the panel's mandate is to apply existing WTO
law, not to make law. Article 19.2 of the DSU emphasizes that panels and the
Appellate Body must not add to or diminish the rights and obligations set forth in
the covered agreements.

The panel's deliberations are confidential and its report is drafted in the absence
of the parties (Article 14.1 and 14.2 of the DSU and paragraph 3 of the Working
Procedures in Appendix 3 to the DSU). Article 18.1 of the DSU also prohibits any
ex parte communications with the panel on the matter under consideration, which
means that the panel is not entitled to communicate with individual parties except
in the presence of the other party or parties.

The panel report is divided into two main parts: the so-called "descriptive part"
and the "findings". The descriptive part is usually the longer part, and is typically composed of an introduction, the factual aspects, the claims of the parties

---

[27] Or – in the rare case of a non-violation complaint – whether the challenged WTO-consistent measure
nullifies or impairs benefits accruing to the complainant under the covered agreement invoked.

(also sometimes called "Findings Requested"), and, most importantly, a summary of the factual and legal arguments of the parties and third parties.

The panel first issues a draft descriptive part to the parties for written comments (Article 15.1 of the DSU). In accordance with the proposed timetable in Appendix 3 to the DSU, parties are invited to make comments on the draft descriptive part within two weeks. This gives the parties an opportunity to ensure that all their key arguments are reflected in the descriptive part and to rectify errors and perceived imprecisions.

FINDINGS, CONCLUSIONS AND RECOMMENDATIONS AND SUGGESTIONS ON IMPLEMENTATION

The latter part of the panel report is generally referred to as the "Findings". This is the section setting out the panel's reasoning to support its final conclusions as to whether the complainant's claim should be upheld or rejected. This reasoning is a comprehensive discussion of the applicable law in light of the facts established by the panel on the basis of the evidence before it and in the light of the arguments submitted by the parties (Article 12.7 of the DSU).

In the typical case of a violation complaint, the panel decides whether there has been a violation of the invoked provision(s) of one or more covered agreement(s). (As discussed above,[28] the additional requirement of nullification or impairment, where applicable, takes up no more than a short paragraph at the end of the conclusions referring to the presumption of Article 3.8 of the DSU.) In the much less frequent case of a non-violation complaint, the panel decides whether a benefit accruing to the complainant under a covered agreement has been nullified or impaired as a result of a measure that nonetheless conforms with the covered agreement in question. Individual panelists have the right to express a separate opinion in the panel report, but they must do so anonymously (Article 14.3 of the DSU).

The panel's findings are usually very detailed and specific, often with long legal discussions of whether or not the respondent has acted inconsistently with the covered agreements invoked by the complainant. It is often said that the dispute settlement system has evolved over the years from a diplomatic forum to a more judicial or juridical system. In the early days of GATT 1947, panel conclusions were not always as specific and did not always express clear legal results as is the case today.[29]

Where the panel concludes that the challenged measure is inconsistent with a covered agreement, the panel report also contains a recommendation that the responding Member bring the challenged measure into conformity with WTO law (Article 19.1 of the DSU, first sentence). In practice, these recommendations are

---

[28] *See* the section on the Violation complaint on page 31.
[29] *See*, for example, Panel Report, *Belgian Family Allowances*, para. 8.

formulated as recommendations to the DSB that it request the Member concerned to bring its measure into conformity. The panel may also suggest ways in which the Member concerned could implement the recommendation (Article 19.1 of the DSU, second sentence). However, the panel is not obliged to make such a suggestion ("may"), even when requested by the complainant(s). If the panel makes use of its right to suggest possible ways of implementation, such "suggestions" on how the respondent "could" put itself into compliance are not binding on the responding party. The responding party enjoys the freedom to choose any of the various options that may exist to bring about compliance. All the respondent is obliged to do is to make its measure(s) fully compatible with WTO law.

When a non-violation complaint succeeds, there is no obligation for the responding party to withdraw the measure found to nullify or impair benefits under, or impede an objective of the relevant covered agreement. In such cases the panel recommends that the Member concerned make an adjustment that is mutually satisfactory to the parties (Article 26.1(b) of the DSU). A possible form of adjustment would be that the respondent compensate the complainant with alternative trade opportunities to make up for the nullified or impaired benefit.

A special rule on the panel's recommendation also exists in respect of prohibited subsidies under the SCM Agreement: if the panel concludes that the challenged subsidy is prohibited, it must "recommend that the subsidizing Member withdraw the subsidy without delay" and must specify the time-period for this withdrawal (Article 4.7 of the SCM Agreement).

INTERIM REVIEW

The panel issues its report to the parties in an "interim" form and as a confidential document containing all the above elements, ideally two to four weeks after the receipt of comments on the descriptive part. The interim report contains the revised descriptive part, the findings, the conclusions and the recommendations, and, as the case may be, suggestions for implementation. It is thus a complete report, although it is not yet final. Parties are again entitled to make comments and may also request a meeting of the panel to further argue specific points raised with respect to the interim report. This is the interim review stage (Article 15 of the DSU). A party may request that the panel review precise aspects of the interim decision. The period of review must not exceed two weeks. The panel may hold an additional meeting with the two sides, which, in practice, the parties rarely request.

The interim report is the first substantial indication the parties receive as to the likely outcome of the panel report. Although the interim report is confidential, one or more of the parties often leak its content to the press.

The interim review is designed for a reconsideration of precise aspects of the panel report; it is rare for the parties to ask the panel to completely overturn its interim decision. The likelihood of a panel overturning its own (interim) decision would probably not be very high; the panel already knows the arguments of the party in question and has made up its mind.

However, insofar as facts are concerned, the situation is different because the appellate review is limited to legal questions (Article 17.6 of the DSU). The establishment of facts falls exclusively in the domain of panels, and the Appellate Body does not review factual questions. Accordingly, the interim review is the last opportunity for the parties to rectify any factual mistake in the panel report and parties should make use of that opportunity.

Irrespective of whether or not the panel modifies its findings after the interim review, its final report must contain a reference to the arguments raised by the parties during the interim review stage (Article 15.3 of the DSU). This typically becomes a separate section, in which the panel discusses the merits of the parties' comments during the interim review stage.

ISSUANCE AND CIRCULATION OF THE FINAL REPORT

The panel should submit its final report to the parties to the dispute within two weeks following conclusion of the interim review. Once the report is translated into the other official WTO languages,[30] it is circulated to all WTO Members and becomes a public WT/DS document (the symbol ends on "R", thus WT/DS###/R).

In cases of multiple complaints on the same matter where a single panel is established, the panel must submit separate reports if one of the parties involved so requests in a timely fashion (Article 9.2 of the DSU).[31]

DEADLINES, TIMETABLE AND SUSPENSION

Dispute settlement panels operate under strict deadlines, which illustrates the importance the Members attribute to a "prompt settlement"[32] of WTO disputes. As a general rule, a panel is required to issue the final report to the parties within six months from the date when it was composed (and, as the case may be, the terms of reference agreed). In cases of urgency, the panel attempts to issue its report to the parties within three months from the date of its composition (Article 12.8 of the DSU). When the panel considers that it cannot issue its report within six months (or three months in case of urgency), it must inform the DSB in writing of the reasons for the delay and provide an estimate of the period within which it will issue its report. The period from the establishment of the panel to the circulation of the report to the Members "should" in no case exceed nine months (Article 12.9 of the DSU). In practice, however, panel proceedings take an average of 12 months.

Panels may suspend their work at any time at the request of the complaining party for a period not exceeding 12 months. Such suspensions normally serve to allow the parties to find a mutually agreeable solution, which is the preference of the

---

[30] The three official languages of the WTO are English, French and Spanish. *See* the concluding paragraph of the WTO Agreement.
[31] Appellate Body Report, *US – Offset Act (Byrd Amendment)*, paras. 311–316.
[32] Article 3.3 of the DSU.

DSU (Article 3.7 of the DSU). If the suspension exceeds 12 months, the authority for the establishment of the panel lapses (Article 12.12 of the DSU). If unresolved, the dispute settlement proceedings would have to be started all over again.

Appendix 3 to the DSU provides a proposed timetable for panel work. This timetable may be adjusted depending on the circumstances of the case. There may also be additional meetings, i.e. more than two substantive meetings with the parties (Articles 12.1 and 12.2 of the DSU). Appendix 3 provides for the following time-periods, counted from one step to the next:

1. Receipt of the first written submissions of the parties:
   (a) Complaining party: 3–6 weeks
   (b) Party complained against: 2–3 weeks
2. First substantive meeting with the parties; third party
   session: 1–2 weeks
3. Receipt of written rebuttals of the parties: 2–3 weeks
4. Second substantive meeting with the parties: 1–2 weeks
5. Issuance of descriptive part of the report to the parties: 2–4 weeks
6. Receipt of comments by the parties on the descriptive part
   of the report: 2 weeks
7. Issuance of the interim report, including the findings and
   conclusions, to the parties: 2–4 weeks
8. Deadline for party to request review of part(s) of report: 1 week
9. Period of review by panel, including possible additional
   meeting with parties: 2 weeks
10. Issuance of final report to parties to dispute: 2 weeks
11. Circulation of the final report to the Members: 3 weeks

In cases of multiple complaints on the same matter where more than one panel is established, the timetable for the process before each panel should be harmonized to the greatest extent possible (Article 9.3 of the DSU). This can result in one or the other time-period being shortened or extended. Where a single panel is established, it must organize its examination and present its findings to the DSB in such a manner so as not to impair the rights that the parties to the dispute would have enjoyed had separate panels examined the complaints (Article 9.2 of the DSU).

Accelerated procedures are available under the terms of the Decision of 5 April 1966[33] when a developing country Member brings a complaint against a developed country Member and the developing country Member makes use of its right to invoke those accelerated procedures (Article 3.12 of the DSU).[34]

The SCM Agreement provides for accelerated procedures with several shorter time-periods with respect to disputes on prohibited subsidies and actionable

---

[33] BISD 14S/18. The Decision of 1966 is also reproduced in the Annex on page 185.
[34] Since the establishment of the WTO, this has so far not happened.

subsidies. Regarding prohibited subsidies, the complainant may request the establishment of a panel if consultations have not led to a mutually agreed solution within 30 days, and the DSB must immediately establish the panel, unless there is a consensus not to do so (Article 4.4 of the SCM Agreement). In other words, in a departure from the normal rules, the negative consensus rule applies at the first, and not just the second DSB meeting at which the request for establishment of the panel appears on the DSB agenda. The panel must circulate its report to all WTO Members within 90 days of the date of its composition and the establishment of its terms of reference (Article 4.6 of the SCM Agreement).

Dispute settlement with respect to *actionable* subsidies is also subject to some specific deadlines, including at the panel stage. For instance, the composition and terms of reference of the panel must be established within 15 days from the establishment of the panel (Article 7.4 of the SCM Agreement), and the panel must circulate its report to all Members within 120 days of the date of its composition and the establishment of its terms of reference (Article 7.5 of the SCM Agreement).

ADOPTION OF PANEL REPORTS

Although the panel report contains the findings and conclusions ruling on the substance of the dispute, it only becomes binding when the DSB has adopted it. This is why the DSU describes the function of panels as assisting the DSB in discharging its responsibilities under the DSU and the covered agreements (and as making such findings as will assist the DSB in making the recommendations or in giving the rulings provided for in the covered agreements, Article 11 of the DSU). The DSU provides that the DSB must adopt the report no earlier than 20 days, but no later than 60 days after the date of its circulation to the Members,[35] unless a party to the dispute formally notifies the DSB of its decision to appeal or the DSB decides by consensus not to adopt the report (Article 16.4 of the DSU).

If a party has notified its decision to appeal, the panel report cannot yet be adopted, given that the Appellate Body could modify or reverse it. In that case, the panel report will be considered for adoption by the DSB only after completion of the appeal (Article 16.4 of the DSU).

If there is no appeal by either party, the DSB is obliged to adopt the report, unless there is a so-called negative (or reverse) consensus, i.e. a consensus in the DSB against the adoption. This is (after the establishment of the panel) the second key instance in which the decision-making rule of reverse consensus applies in the WTO dispute settlement system. By contrast, under GATT 1947, a rule of positive

---

[35] If a meeting of the DSB is not scheduled during this period, such a meeting of the DSB must be held to discuss and adopt the report (footnote 7 to Article 16.4 DSU).

consensus applied at the stage of adopting panel reports. This gave the losing party the ability to block or veto the adoption of a report.[36]

Although the parties to a dispute are entitled to participate fully in the DSB's consideration of the panel report (Article 16.3 of the DSU), the adoption of panel reports no longer requires consensus in the WTO dispute settlement system. A single Member, typically the party having lost at the panel stage, cannot alone do much to prevent the adoption. One Member opposing the adoption of the report is not sufficient, nor is a majority; instead, what is needed to reject (or not to adopt) the panel report is a consensus against adoption by *all* Members represented at the relevant DSB meeting. In other words, one single Member insisting on adoption is sufficient in order to secure the adoption of the report. Normally, at least one party has an interest in the adoption because, overall, it prevailed with the panel. Even if many panel decisions are mixed in that not all the claims of violation of WTO law succeed, there is usually a "winner" (the complainant, if at least one claim is upheld, and the respondent, if all are dismissed) and a "loser" in the formal sense. Because the prevailing party has a natural interest in having the panel's conclusions become binding upon the parties, the adoption of panel reports is "quasi-automatic". Thus, rejection by (negative) consensus is more theoretical than real, and has never occurred in the WTO practice to date.

In order to be adopted in a DSB meeting, a panel report (which has not been appealed) must, however, be placed on the agenda of a DSB meeting. It is the practice that only WTO Members can request items to be put on the agenda of an upcoming DSB meeting (not the Secretariat). Thus, if no Member places a panel report on the DSB agenda for adoption, the adoption does not take place, even though this is not in conformity with Article 16.4 of the DSU. In the history of the WTO, only once has a panel report not been adopted for this reason (and not because a settlement between the parties intervened).[37]

The adoption procedure is without prejudice to the right of Members to express their views on a panel report (Article 16.4 of the DSU). The Members present at the DSB meeting in which a panel report is adopted, particularly Members that have been involved in the dispute as parties, often make use of this right to comment on the conclusions or the reasoning contained in the panel report. In circumstances where the panel developed unexpected reasoning or made unexpected findings, the parties and possibly other Members might want to put their objections on record.

In the early days of the WTO dispute settlement system, the chairperson of the DSB used to ask whether there was a consensus against the adoption of the report in question. Nowadays, he or she simply gives the floor to the parties to the dispute and then to other Members to express their opinions. It sometimes happens that a Member urges the other Members to oppose the report, but this typically has no consequence because a rejection of the report would require consensus of all the

---

[36] In this regard, *see* further above in the section on The system under GATT 1947 and its evolution over the years on page 12.

[37] Panel Report, *EC – Bananas III (Article 21.5 – EC)*, DSR 1999: II, at 783.

Members present at the meeting. The DSB chairperson, therefore, merely states that the DSB takes note of all the statements and adopts the report.

If there is no appeal, the dispute proceeds immediately to the implementation phase after the DSB has adopted the panel report.

There are special and additional rules with respect to the adoption of panel reports in the SCM Agreement. In disputes regarding both prohibited and actionable subsidies, the DSB must adopt the report within 30 days of its circulation to all Members, unless it decides by consensus not to adopt it or unless one of the parties notifies the DSB of its decision to appeal (Articles 4.8 and 7.6 SCM Agreement).

For the purposes of the description below of the further procedure, it is assumed that there is an appeal.

APPELLATE REVIEW

RULES ON THE APPELLATE REVIEW

The DSU does not devote many articles to the appellate review process. Except for Article 16.4 of the DSU, which refers to the notification of a party's decision to file an appeal, Article 17 is the only article dealing specifically with the structure, function and procedures of the Appellate Body. However, several general rules in the DSU are applicable both to the panel and the appellate processes, for instance, Articles 1, 3, 18 and 19 of the DSU. In addition, the Appellate Body has adopted its own Working Procedures for Appellate Review on the basis of the mandate and pursuant to the procedure stipulated in Article 17.9 of the DSU (in this section on appellate review referred to as "Working Procedures"[38]). The Appellate Body drew up its Working Procedures for the first time in 1996, and they have been amended several times since, the last time with effect from 1 May 2003.[39] These Working Procedures contain the detailed procedural rules for appeals and they range from the duties and responsibilities of Appellate Body members to the specific deadlines by which submissions must be filed in an appeal. The "gap-filling" Rule 16(1) of the Working Procedures permits an Appellate Body division under certain circumstances to adopt additional procedures for a particular appeal in which the need to do so arises.

DEADLINE FOR FILING AN APPEAL

If the panel report is appealed, the dispute is referred to the Appellate Body and, for the time being, the panel report cannot be adopted by the DSB. Article 16.4 of the DSU implies that the panel report must be appealed before it is adopted by the DSB. The article does not specify a clear deadline for the filing of an appeal. Rather the

---

[38] These procedures should not be confused with the panel Working Procedures in Appendix 3 to the DSU.
[39] *Working Procedures for Appellate Review*, WT/AB/WP/7, consolidated and revised version http://docsonline.wto.org/DDFDocuments/t/WT/AB/WP7.doc.

appellant must notify the DSB of its decision to appeal before the adoption of the panel report. This adoption may take place, at the earliest, on the 20th day after the circulation of the panel report and it must (in the absence of an appeal and of a negative consensus against adoption) occur within 60 days after the circulation. For any day between those limits, the adoption of the panel report can, according to Article 16.4 of the DSU, be placed on the agenda of the DSB (with ten days' notice required for requesting items to be put on the agenda). Since the appeal must be filed before adoption actually occurs,[40] the effective deadline for filing an appeal is variable and could be as short as 20 days, but it can also be longer, e.g. 60 days. Thus, if the party which emerged from the panel proceeding as the "winner" wants to shorten the deadline for the other party to file an appeal, it can do so by placing the panel report on the agenda for a DSB meeting to occur on the 20th day after the panel report has been circulated.

RIGHT TO APPEAL

Article 16.4 of the DSU makes clear that only the parties to the dispute, not the third parties, can appeal the panel report. Both the "winning" and the "losing" party (i.e. more than one party) can appeal a panel report. The reason is that either party in the dispute may disagree with the panel's conclusions: the respondent, whose challenged measure has been found to be inconsistent with the WTO Agreement or to nullify or impair a benefit, or the complainant, whose claims of violation or nullification or impairment have been rejected. In addition, a complainant, even though it may have "won" at the panel stage, may nevertheless not have been successful with all its claims, for example, if the panel only upheld two out of six claims of violation.

In addition, parties have in the past also appealed isolated panel findings they disagreed with (i.e. a legal interpretation developed by the panel), even though these findings were part of a reasoning which ultimately upheld that party's position. For example, in the second appeal under the WTO, in *Japan – Alcoholic Beverages II*, the United States appealed the panel report, even though it had been successful with its claim of a Japanese violation of Article III:2 of GATT 1994, because it disagreed with the panel's interpretation of Article III. The United States was not aggrieved as such by the panel's conclusion on the claim, but it had a systemic interest, reaching beyond the individual dispute, as to how Article III should be interpreted. In such a case, there could be more than one appeal on the same issue, one coming from the party having lost at the panel stage, and one from the winning party which disagrees with the reasoning.

The Working Procedures refer to two options of how multiple appeals can be filed. One option is that of one party initiating the appeal pursuant to Article 16.4

---

[40] It is quite common for appeals to be notified on the very morning of a DSB meeting scheduled to adopt a panel report. If the panel report was the only item on the agenda, the DSB meeting is then cancelled.

of the DSU, and, once that appellant has filed its notice of appeal and its appellant's submission, another party, knowing the extent of, and the reasons for the challenge, joins in with its own appeal. Such an appeal would expand the overall scope of the appellate review to cover other alleged errors in the panel report (Rule 23(1) of the Working Procedures). In the Working Procedures and in Appellate Body reports, this form of appeal is called "other appeal" and informally sometimes "cross-appeal".

The second option is that of more than one party using its right of appeal under Article 16.4 of the DSU. In that case, the Appellate Body deals with the various appeals jointly (Rules 23(4) and (5) of the Working Procedures).

If both of the two parties to a dispute challenge the panel report on appeal, each of them is, at the same time, appellant and appellee, but usually with regard to different portions of the panel report, i.e. they address different issues of law or legal interpretations covered in the panel report. The generic term for parties participating in the appeal as appellant or appellee is "participants".

THIRD PARTICIPANTS AT THE APPELLATE STAGE

Third parties cannot appeal a panel report.[41] However, third parties that have been third parties at the panel stage may also participate in the appeal as a so-called "third participant". Article 17.4 of the DSU provides that third parties may make written submissions to, and be given an opportunity to be heard by, the Appellate Body.

A WTO Member that has not been a third party at the panel stage, in contrast, is excluded from participation in the appellate review. It cannot "jump on board", if it identifies its interest in the dispute, for instance, in the light of the content of the panel report. Under the current practice, however, such Members may seek to submit a so-called *amicus curiae* brief,[42] which the Appellate Body is entitled to accept, but not obliged to consider.[43]

In the first years of the WTO dispute settlement system, third parties who wanted to participate in the appellate process as third participants had to file a written submission, stating their intention to participate as a third participant in the appeal and explaining the grounds and legal arguments in support of their position, within 25 days after the notice of appeal. Third parties who had not done so had no right to participate in the oral hearing before the Appellate Body. Over the years, however, a practice had developed of admitting such third parties as "passive observers" to the oral hearing, with the (explicit or tacit) agreement of the participants. Against the background of this practice and in an effort to enhance third party participation in

---

[41] Third parties are not directly affected by the decision: it is not their measure which has been found to breach WTO law or to nullify or impair benefits, nor is it their challenge of the measure which has been rejected.

[42] *See* further below the section on Amicus Curiae on page 98.

[43] Appellate Body Report, *EC – Sardines*, paras. 161–167. In *EC – Sardines*, Morocco chose precisely this form of action in order to submit its views to the Appellate Body.

appeals, the Working Procedures have recently been changed. They now no longer require a third party to file a third participants' submission in order to be entitled to attend the oral hearing before the Appellate Body. A third party now has the following options if it wants to be a third participant in an appellate review, with varying degrees of involvement. The third party may:

- file a third participants submission within 25 days of the notice of appeal, appear at the oral hearing and make an oral statement, if desired (Rules 24(1) and 27(3)(a) of the Working Procedures); or
- not file any submission, but notify the Appellate Body Secretariat in writing and within 25 days of the intention to appear at the oral hearing, and make an oral statement, if desired (Rules 24(2) and 27(3)(a) of the Working Procedures);
- not file any submission, and not make any notification within 25 days, but notify the Appellate Body Secretariat, preferably in writing and at the earliest opportunity, of the intention to appear at the oral hearing and request to make an oral statement, and make an oral statement if the Appellate Body has acceded to the request (Rules 24(4) and 27(3)(b) and (c) of the Working Procedures);
- not file any submission, and not make any notification within 25 days, but notify the Appellate Body Secretariat, preferably in writing and at the earliest opportunity, of the intention to appear at the oral hearing and appear at the oral hearing as passive observer (Rules 24(4) and 27(3)(b) of the Working Procedures).

OBJECT OF AN APPEAL

Appeals are limited to legal questions. They may only address issues of law covered in the panel report and legal interpretations developed by the panel (Article 17.6 of the DSU). An appeal cannot address the facts on which the panel report is based, for example, by requesting the examination of new factual evidence or by re-examining existing evidence. Evaluating the evidence and establishing the facts is the task of panels in the dispute settlement system. The distinction between legal and factual questions is therefore important in defining the scope of appellate review. In the abstract, it seems easy to distinguish between law and facts: for example whether or not a national authority has charged a 30 per cent tariff rather than a 20 per cent tariff on the importation of a certain shipment of goods and whether or not vodka and shochu are being produced through the distillation of fermented starch-containing products are clearly facts. More generally speaking, a fact is the occurrence of a certain event in time and space.[44]

In contrast, how the expression of "like products" in Article III:2 of GATT 1994 is to be interpreted is clearly a question of law. However, many of the more complex

---

[44] Appellate Body Report, *EC – Hormones*, para. 132.

questions that regularly arise in disputes are mixed questions of law *and* facts, or, in other words, questions that can be answered only on the basis of both a factual and a legal assessment. For example, the question of whether shochu and vodka are "like products" in the sense of Article III:2 of GATT 1994 is such a mixed legal and factual question. In such cases, the identification of the legal issue that can be subject to appeal hinges upon a more detailed and differentiated analysis of the question involved. The Appellate Body jurisprudence to date gives some guidance in that regard.

For instance, the legal appreciation of facts, or, in other words, a panel's application of a legal rule to specific facts, is a legal question and subject to appellate review. As the Appellate Body has stated, "[t]he consistency or inconsistency of a given fact or set of facts with the requirements of a given treaty provision is, however, a legal characterisation issue. It is a legal question."[45]

In contrast, the panel's examination and weighing of the submitted evidence, and its establishment of the facts, fall within the panel's discretion as the trier of facts and are normally not subject to appeal.[46] However, there are limits to the panel's discretion, to the extent that the panel's factual examination is subject to *legal* requirements, the compliance with which is a legal question that can be raised on appeal. Such a legal rule is contained in Article 11 of the DSU which obliges panels to "make an objective assessment of the matter before it, including an objective assessment of the facts of the case". The question of "whether or not a panel has made an objective assessment of the facts before it, as required by Article 11 of the DSU, is a legal question which, if properly raised on appeal, would fall within the scope of appellate review".[47] Thus, the Appellate Body can review the panel's appreciation of the evidence where the panel has exceeded the bounds of its discretion.[48] Where exactly those bounds lie remains to be fully explored. The Appellate Body has already had the opportunity to give several examples, which do not exhaust the universe of possible legal errors in the establishment of facts.[49] The Appellate Body has ruled that for a panel to "disregard", "distort" or "misrepresent" evidence, or a panel's "egregious errors" that would call into question the good faith of a panel, are issues that can be appealed.[50]

Article 11 of the DSU is also relevant where the issue is whether the panel applied the correct standard of review. This, however, is clearly a legal question and not one of establishing facts, since it relates to determining what legal standard panels must apply. This in turn determines which facts pertaining to which period of time are relevant to the legal examination.

---

[45] Appellate Body Report, *EC – Hormones*, para. 132.
[46] Appellate Body Report, *Korea – Alcoholic Beverages*, para. 161.
[47] Appellate Body Report, *EC – Hormones*, para. 132.
[48] Appellate Body Report, *US – Wheat Gluten*, para. 151.
[49] See, for example, Appellate Body Report, *EC – Hormones*, para. 133.
[50] Appellate Body Report, *EC – Hormones*, para. 133.

NOTICE OF APPEAL

According to Article 16.4 of the DSU, the appeal process begins when "a party to the dispute formally notifies the DSB of its decision to appeal" within the time-frame discussed above (i.e. before the DSB adopts the panel report).[51] Rule 20(1) of the Working Procedures requires a simultaneous filing of a notice of appeal with the Appellate Body Secretariat. Rule 20(2)(d)[52] of the Working Procedures requires that a notice of appeal include a brief statement of the nature of the appeal, including the allegations of errors in the issues of law covered in the panel report and legal interpretations developed by the panel. The notice of appeal also becomes an official WT/DS document.

In accordance with the possible object of appellate review,[53] these allegations of errors must relate to what the appellant wishes the Appellate Body to overturn. This can be a panel's *conclusion*, including the supporting reasoning that there is or there is not a violation of the covered agreement in question. It can also be an isolated *legal finding* which forms part of the panel's reasoning supporting a conclusion.

For example, the appellant can challenge a panel's *conclusion* and assert that the panel erred by finding that the respondent acted inconsistently with Articles X, Y or Z. The appellant can also challenge an isolated *legal finding* in the panel report and assert that the panel "erred in its interpretation of Article III:2 . . . in finding that 'likeness' can be determined purely on the basis of physical characteristics, consumer uses and tariff classification without considering also the context and purpose of Article III . . . and without considering . . . whether regulatory distinctions are made . . . 'so as to afford protection to domestic production'".[54]

Another matter that has come up in several appeals is whether the notice of appeal was sufficiently precise to meet the requirements set out in Rule 20(2)(d) of the Working Procedures. The Appellate Body has so far rejected all requests by appellees to dismiss appeals for being vague, ruling that it is sufficient for the notice of appeal merely to identify those panel findings or legal interpretations that the appellant believes were erroneous. The notice of appeal is not designed to be a summary or outline of the arguments of the appellant, which are to be set forth in the appellant's submission rather than in its notice of appeal.[55]

However, as a matter of due process, the notice of appeal serves to give the appellee notice of the findings appealed so that it can prepare its defence.[56] It is thus not necessary (nor sufficient) for the notice of appeal to cite the numbered paragraphs of the panel report containing the findings appealed, but it must be clear from the notice which panel findings or interpretations the Appellate Body is

---

[51] *See* above in the section on the Deadline for filing an appeal on page 63.
[52] Rules 20(2)(a) to (c) of the Working Procedures require several formalities, such as specifying the name and address of the party as well as identifying the panel report appealed.
[53] *See* above in the section on the Object of an appeal on page 66.
[54] *See* Appellate Body Report, *Japan – Alcoholic Beverages II*, DSR 1996: I, 97 at 99–100.
[55] Appellate Body Report, *US – Shrimp*, para. 95.
[56] Appellate Body Report, *EC – Bananas III*, para. 152.

asked to review.[57] Conversely, the Appellate Body would generally exclude from the scope of appellate review a finding that is not "covered" in the notice of appeal[58] or a claim of error (e.g. "the panel violated Article 11 DSU") that is not included[59] in the allegations of error set out in the notice of appeal.

After the filing of the notice of appeal, the WTO Secretariat transmits the complete panel record to the Appellate Body Secretariat pursuant to Rule 25 of the Working Procedures. The panel record includes the written submissions of the parties to the panel, their oral statements, their written responses to questions, exhibits introduced as evidence, the interim report, the interim review comments and the tapes of the substantive meetings.

COMPOSITION OF APPELLATE BODY DIVISIONS

Article 17.1 of the DSU provides that three of the seven Appellate Body members are to serve on each appeal and that the seven Members are to serve in rotation as further specified in the Working Procedures. Rule 6 of the Working Procedures calls this body of three Appellate Body members a "division". It provides for a selection of the three Members constituting a division on the basis of rotation, taking into account the principles of random selection but regardless of national origin. This is different from panels, where persons holding the citizenship of a party or third party cannot serve, except with the agreement of the parties. Thus, Appellate Body members who are citizens of Members involved in many disputes as either parties or third parties, like the United States or the European Union, are not excluded from serving on Appellate Body divisions hearing cases involving their countries of citizenship.

The three Appellate Body members who have been selected to serve on a particular appeal elect one of them to be presiding member of that division. The presiding member coordinates the overall conduct of the appellate proceeding, chairs the oral hearing and meetings related to that appeal and coordinates the drafting of the Appellate Body report (Rule 7(2) of the Working Procedures).

APPELLATE REVIEW PROCEDURE

No later than ten days after the date when the notice of appeal was filed, the appellant must file its written submission, setting out in detail its legal arguments as to why the panel committed a legal error and, as appropriate, the ruling the appellant requests the Appellate Body to make with regard to the contested panel findings (Rule 21(2) of the Working Procedures). Ten days may seem a short time, but an appellant is able to begin preparing its submission well before filing the notice of appeal, indeed

---

[57] *Ibid.*, para. 96.   [58] *See* Appellate Body Report, *EC – Bananas III*, para. 152.
[59] Appellate Body Report, *US – Countervailing Measures Concerning Certain EC Products*, paras. 72–75.

as soon as the interim panel report is issued or in any event when the final panel report is circulated.[60]

Like all documents that are filed in an appeal, the appellant must serve its submission on all the other parties or third parties (Rule 18(2) of the Working Procedures).

Within 15 days from the notice of appeal, a party to the dispute other than the original appellant may join in that appeal or appeal on the basis of other alleged errors in the panel report ("other appeal" or (informally) "cross appeal", Rule 23(1) of the Working Procedures).[61] Within 25 days from the notice of appeal, the appellee(s) have to file their submissions in which they respond to the allegations of error made by the appellant(s). The appellees' submissions must set out in detail whether or not and for what legal reasons the appellee(s) opposes(s) the appellant's challenge; and, in doing so, it will have to argue to what extent it agrees or disagrees with the Panel's conclusions (Rule 22(2) of the Working Procedures).

Also with 25 days from the notice of appeal, the third participant(s) must file their written submission(s), setting forth their position and legal arguments.[62]

Approximately 30 to 45 days after the notice of appeal, the Appellate Body division assigned to the case holds an oral hearing (Rule 27(1) of the Working Procedures), which is not open to the public (Article 17.10 of the DSU). At this oral hearing, the participants and the third participants make a brief opening statement, after which the Appellate Body division poses questions to the participants and third participants. The oral hearing is thus similar to the substantive meetings at the panel stage. The main differences between an oral hearing and a substantive meeting of the panel are: (i) there is only one oral hearing on appeal; (ii) oral statements are kept short; (iii) an oral hearing rarely lasts longer than one full day; and (iv) the participants in an oral hearing may not ask questions directly of each other.

DELIBERATION OF THE APPELLATE BODY AND PREPARATION OF THE APPELLATE BODY REPORT

After the oral hearing, the division exchanges views on the issues raised in the appeal with the four other Appellate Body members not on the division. This exchange of views is intended to give effect to the principle of collegiality in the Appellate Body and serves to ensure consistency and coherence in the jurisprudence of the Appellate Body (Rule 4(1) of the Working Procedures). Divergent or inconsistent lines of jurisprudence that might otherwise arise would detract from the security and predictability of the multilateral trading system, which is one of the main objectives of the dispute settlement system (Article 3.2 of the DSU). Nevertheless,

---

[60] *See* above the sections on the Interim review on page 58 and on the Issuance and circulation of the final report on page 59.

[61] *See* above in the section on the Right to appeal on page 64.

[62] *See* above in the section on Third participants at the appellate stage on page 65.

as prescribed by Article 17.1 of the DSU, only the assigned division may ultimately decide on the appeal (Rules 4(4) and 3(1) of the Working Procedures).

The Working Procedures also envisage that members of the Appellate Body and its divisions must make every effort to take their decisions by consensus. Where this is not possible, a majority vote takes place (Rule 3(2) of the Working Procedures). If an individual Appellate Body member includes a separate opinion in the Appellate Body report, it must be done anonymously (Article 17.11 of the DSU).

Following the exchange of views with the other Appellate Body members, the division concludes its deliberations and drafts the Appellate Body report. After the report is finalized and signed by the Appellate Body members of the division, it is translated into the two other official languages of the WTO. All deliberations of the Appellate Body are confidential, and the drafting of the report takes place without the presence of the participants and third participants (Article 17.10 of the DSU).

In contrast to the panel procedure, there is no interim review[63] at the Appellate Body stage.

Mandate of the Appellate Body and completing the legal analysis

With regard to the content of an Appellate Body report, the DSU prescribes that the Appellate Body must address each of the legal issues and panel interpretations that have been appealed (Articles 17.6 and 17.12 of the DSU). The Appellate Body may uphold, modify or reverse the legal findings and conclusions of the panel (Article 17.13 of the DSU). However, where certain legal findings of the panel are no longer relevant because they are related to or based on a legal interpretation reversed or modified by the division, the Appellate Body sometimes declares such panel findings as "moot and having no legal effect".

In many cases, the Appellate Body will partly modify the panel's legal findings and conclusions because it agrees with the panel's final conclusion but not necessarily with the panel's reasoning. If the Appellate Body agrees with both, it upholds the panel's findings and conclusions. Where the Appellate Body disagrees with the panel's conclusion, it reverses it.

Especially in this latter case, the function of the appellate proceeding must not only be seen in the review of panel reports. There is also a dispute to resolve (Articles 3.3 and 3.2 of the DSU). Where, for instance, the Appellate Body has reversed the panel's conclusion of a violation of a certain provision, the respondent's measure might instead be inconsistent with another WTO provision. Often, the complainant has also claimed an inconsistency with this other provision, either in the alternative, or cumulatively. However, often the panel, given its finding of a violation of the former provision, did not address this other alternative claim or it chose not to

---

[63] See above, section Interim review on page 58.

address the other cumulative claim for reasons of judicial economy.[64] In such a case, if the Appellate Body has limited itself to reversing the panel's erroneous findings and conclusion, the dispute would not be fully resolved. The complainant would then have to start all over again by initiating a new dispute settlement proceeding.

Two approaches are common in the procedures of many appellate tribunals whose mandate is limited to questions of law. One is to decide the outstanding issue at the appellate level. Indeed, many appellate tribunals have this authority (often without obligation) where the case is "ripe" for such a decision (i.e. no further facts must be explored). The other approach (the only one where a factual question remains open) is to send the case back to the trier of facts. In this situation, the panel is the trier of facts. The authority to send a case back to the lower level is called remand authority but does not exist in the WTO system.

Given this absence of remand authority in the WTO, the first approach, that is, having the Appellate Body decide the outstanding issue, becomes more compelling. Indeed, the Appellate Body has on a number of occasions "completed the legal analysis" in order to resolve a dispute. This has been possible only where there were sufficient factual findings in the panel report or undisputed facts in the panel record to enable the Appellate Body to address and decide on the outstanding issue. Where this has not been the case, the Appellate Body has been unable to complete the legal analysis because it is not entitled to make new factual findings. Moreover, an insufficiency of the facts is not the only reason the Appellate Body has declined to complete the legal analysis. In one instance, in *EC – Asbestos*, the Appellate Body declined to address a "novel" issue because it had not been argued in sufficient detail at the panel level, either in the case in question or in previous disputes.[65]

CONCLUSIONS AND RECOMMENDATIONS OF THE APPELLATE BODY

An Appellate Body report has two sections: the descriptive part and the findings section. The descriptive part contains the factual and procedural background of the dispute and summarizes the arguments of the participants and third participants. In the findings section, the Appellate Body addresses in detail the issues raised on appeal, elaborates its conclusions and reasoning in support of such conclusions, and states whether the appealed panel findings and conclusions are upheld, modified or reversed. It also contains additional relevant conclusions, for instance if the respondent has been found in violation of another WTO provision than the one the panel addressed.

As for recommendations and suggestions, Articles 19 and 26 of the DSU apply to Appellate Body reports as well as to panel reports.[66] Where the conclusion is that the

---

[64] *See* below the section on Judicial economy on page 102.

[65] *See* Appellate Body Report, *US – Section 211 Omnibus Appropriations Act*, para. 343 with references to the relevant cases.

[66] *See* above in the section on Findings, conclusions and recommendations and suggestions on implementation on page 57.

challenged measure is inconsistent with a covered agreement, the Appellate Body recommends that the responding Member brings the inconsistent measure into conformity with its obligations under the covered agreement in question (Article 19.1 of the DSU, first sentence). In practice, these recommendations are addressed to the DSB, which is then to request the Member concerned to bring its measure into conformity with the relevant provisions of WTO law. Like the panel, the Appellate Body may also suggest ways in which the Member concerned could implement the recommendation (Article 19.1 of the DSU, second sentence), but the Appellate Body has not so far made use of this right. When a non-violation complaint succeeds, the Appellate Body would normally recommend that the parties find a mutually satisfactory adjustment (Article 26.1(b) of the DSU).

Finally, the Appellate Body report is circulated to all WTO Members and becomes a public WT/DS document (the symbol ends on "AB/R", thus WT/DS###/AB/R). The participants frequently receive a confidential copy of the report up to one day in advance.

WITHDRAWAL OF AN APPEAL

Rule 30(1) of the Working Procedures permits an appellant to withdraw its appeal at any time. It falls within the discretion of WTO Members not only to initiate disputes, but also to terminate them. The possibility of withdrawing an appeal reflects the preference of the DSU for the parties to find a mutually agreeable solution to their dispute (Article 3.7 of the DSU).

A withdrawal normally terminates an initiated appellate procedure, as happened in *India – Autos*.[67] In that case, the Appellate Body issued a brief Appellate Body report setting out the procedural history of the appeal, and concluded that it had therefore completed its work in view of India's withdrawal.[68]

On three occasions, appellants have withdrawn their appeals in order to re-file an appeal shortly thereafter. Twice, this was done for scheduling reasons (i.e. to postpone the entire appeal process by a few weeks).[69] More recently, in *EC – Sardines*, the European Communities withdrew its appeal in response to Peru's challenge of the notice of appeal. Peru challenged the notice of appeal as insufficiently clear, to which the European Communities reacted by withdrawing and immediately filing a new, more detailed, notice of appeal. As in two other cases of withdrawn appeals, the withdrawal was explicitly conditioned upon the right to file a new notice of appeal. Peru then challenged the European Communities' right to withdraw a notice of appeal conditionally and to file another, second appeal. The Appellate Body rejected Peru's request to reject the appeal as inadmissible. It saw "no reason to interpret Rule 30 as granting a right to withdraw an appeal only if that withdrawal

---

[67] Appellate Body Report, *India – Autos*, paras. 14–18. [68] *Ibid.*, para. 18.
[69] Appellate Body Report, *US – FSC*, para. 4; Appellate Body Report, *US – Line Pipe*, para. 13.

is unconditional",[70] unless the condition undermines the fair, prompt and effective resolution of the dispute, and as long as the Member in question engages in dispute settlement procedures in good faith.[71]

DEADLINE FOR THE COMPLETION OF THE APPELLATE REVIEW

Appellate review proceedings must generally be completed within 60 days, and in no case take longer than 90 days from the date when the notice of appeal was filed. When an appellate procedure takes more than 60 days, the Appellate Body must inform the DSB of the reasons for the delay and give an estimate of the time until circulation of the report (Article 17.5 of the DSU). In most appeals thus far, the Appellate Body has circulated its report 90 days after the notification of appeal.[72] In a few cases of exceptional circumstances, and with the agreement of the participants, the Appellate Body has circulated its report later than within 90 days.[73]

The SCM Agreement provides for a shorter appellate deadline in disputes on prohibited subsidies: 30 days as a general time-frame and 60 days as maximum (Article 4.9 of the SCM Agreement). This 60-day maximum has also been exceeded in two appeals.[74]

ADOPTION OF THE REPORTS BY THE DISPUTE SETTLEMENT BODY

The DSB must adopt, and the parties must unconditionally accept, the Appellate Body report unless the DSB decides by consensus not to adopt the Appellate Body report within 30 days following its circulation to Members.[75] This adoption procedure is without prejudice to the right of Members to express their views on an Appellate Body report (Article 17.14 of the DSU).

Regarding the automaticity of adoption (except where there is a "reverse" consensus), the expression of Members' opinions and the practical requirement that the Appellate Body report be placed on the DSB agenda, the process is the same as

---

[70] One can conceive of the withdrawal as undoing the first notice of appeal. Therefore, within the deadline for filing (*see* above in the section on the Deadline for filing an appeal on page 63) the right of appeal continues to exist. The condition attached to the withdrawal in the present case was not a factual condition and did not reach outside the appellate procedure. It therefore created no procedural obstacles.

[71] Appellate Body Report, *EC – Sardines*, para. 141.

[72] Completing the process within 60 days is hardly realistic in practice, where the last submission is filed on day 25, the oral hearing takes place on day 30–40, and the last two weeks at least are devoted to translation.

[73] Appellate Body Report, *US – Lead and Bismuth II*, para. 8; Appellate Body Report, *EC – Asbestos*, para. 8; Appellate Body Report, *Thailand – H-Beams*, para. 7.

[74] Appellate Body Report, *Brazil – Aircraft*, Appellate Body Report, *Canada – Aircraft*.

[75] If a meeting of the DSB is not scheduled during this period, such a meeting must be held to discuss and adopt the report (footnote 8 to Article 17.14 of the DSU).

for a panel report, as explained above.[76] However, the deadline for adoption of an Appellate Body report is only 30 days, possibly because no party needs to make up its mind whether to appeal. Article 17.14 also specifically provides that the parties to the dispute must accept the Appellate Body report "unconditionally", i.e. accept it as resolution of their dispute without further appeal.

Although Article 17.14 does not mention the panel report, it is understood that the Appellate Body report must be adopted *together* with the panel report because one can understand the overall ruling only by reading both reports together. The DSU also provides in Article 16.4 that the DSB will only consider the panel report for adoption after completion of the appeal. Thus, both reports are placed on the DSB agenda for adoption, and the DSB adopts the Appellate Body report together with the panel report, as upheld, modified or reversed by the Appellate Body report. To the extent that the panel's conclusions have not been reversed or modified, or have not been appealed, they are binding on the parties.

The SCM Agreement again provides for a shorter adoption deadline of 20 days in disputes on prohibited and actionable subsidies (Articles 4.9 and 7.7).

IMPLEMENTATION BY THE "LOSING" MEMBER

With the DSB's adoption of the panel (and Appellate Body) report(s), there is now a "recommendation and ruling" by the DSB addressed to the losing party (in the case of a successful violation complaint) to bring itself into compliance with WTO law or (in the case of a successful non-violation complaint) to find a mutually satisfactory adjustment.

Article 3.7 of the DSU states that in the absence of a mutually agreed solution, the first objective of the dispute settlement mechanism is usually to secure the withdrawal of the measures found inconsistent with WTO law. Article 21.1 of the DSU adds that prompt compliance with the recommendations or rulings of the DSB is essential in order to ensure the effective resolution of disputes.

The DSB is the WTO body responsible for supervising the implementation of panel and Appellate Body reports (Article 2 of the DSU). As in the previous stages of the dispute settlement system, it is the WTO Members, whose delegates compose the DSB, who must take the initiative to place items on the DSB agenda (and not the WTO Secretariat).

INTENTIONS OF IMPLEMENTATION

The first duty of the "losing" Member is to inform the DSB, at a meeting within 30 days after the adoption of the report(s), of its intentions to implement the recommendations and rulings of the DSB (Article 21.3 of the DSU).

---

[76] *See* above in the section on the Adoption of panel reports on page 61.

TIME-PERIOD FOR IMPLEMENTATION

It is usually at that same meeting that the Member concerned states whether it is able to comply immediately with the recommendations and rulings. If immediate compliance is not possible, the implementing Member has a reasonable period of time for achieving that compliance (Article 21.3 of the DSU). It is thus clear that the reasonable period of time for complying with the recommendations and rulings is not available unconditionally, but only if immediate compliance is impracticable.[77] In practice, WTO Members very often claim that they cannot immediately comply with the DSB's recommendation and ruling. It is also true that the Member concerned is frequently required to amend its domestic law in order to achieve implementation. Where legislative changes are required, such changes take time.

The reasonable period of time should not be understood as a time during which the WTO Member concerned is acting in accordance with its obligations under the WTO Agreement (assuming a violation complaint that succeeded[78]). It has already been established in the adopted report(s) of the panel (and the Appellate Body) that this is not the case. Rather, the reasonable period of time is a grace period granted to the Member concerned, during which it continues to apply WTO-inconsistent measures,[79] for bringing its measures into compliance. During that period, the Member concerned will not (yet) face the consequences foreseen by the DSU in the event of non-implementation (i.e. the need to offer compensation or face retaliation).

One should also note that the reasonable period of time of Article 21.3 of the DSU does not apply in all cases. In the event of prohibited subsidies, the panel must, pursuant to Article 4.7 of the SCM Agreement "recommend that the subsidizing Member withdraw the subsidy without delay" and must specify the time-period for this withdrawal.[80]

As for the determination of the reasonable period of time, which is counted as of the day of adoption of the report(s), Article 21.3 foresees three different ways. This time-period can be: (i) proposed by the Member concerned and approved by consensus[81] by the DSB; (ii) mutually agreed by the parties to the dispute within 45 days after adoption of the report(s); or (iii) determined by an arbitrator.

The first option, approval by the DSB, has so far never happened. The DSB has, however, on a few occasions approved the implementing Member's request

---

[77] *See* Award of the Arbitrator, *Canada – Pharmaceutical Patents*, para. 45.

[78] In the event of a successful non-violation complaint, the Member concerned is in compliance with WTO law, but it nullifies or impairs benefits accruing to the complainant.

[79] Respectively, to nullify or impair benefits accruing to another Member, in the case of a non-violation complaint.

[80] According to Article 26.2 of the DSU, Article 21.3 of the DSU also would not apply in the event of a situation complaint. According to the view of some Members and trade law experts, Articles 8.2 and 8.3 of the Agreement on Safeguards also provide for a procedure partially departing from Article 21.3 of the DSU, thus bypassing the reasonable period of time.

[81] Article 2.4 of the DSU.

to extend a reasonable period of time that had previously been awarded through arbitration.[82]

Where the DSB has not approved a Member's proposal and both parties cannot agree on the reasonable period of time, the parties may resort to arbitration under Article 21.3(c) of the DSU. This procedure is initiated by one party's request for arbitration, which it communicates to the chairperson of the DSB.[83] Although the arbitrator can be any individual or group of individuals,[84] all arbitrators acting under Article 21.3(c) of the DSU so far have been current or former Appellate Body members. If the parties cannot agree on who should serve as the arbitrator(s) within ten days after referral of the matter to arbitration, the Director-General appoints the arbitrator within another ten days after consulting the parties (footnote 12 to Article 21 of the DSU).

A guideline for the arbitrator is that the reasonable period of time to implement panel or Appellate Body recommendations should not exceed 15 months from the date of adoption of the report(s). However, that time may be shorter or longer, depending upon the particular circumstances (Article 21.3(c) of the DSU). The 15-month period is a "guideline", and not an average or standard period. This guideline is also expressed in the DSU as a maximum period, subject to "particular circumstances".[85] Recognizing the principle of prompt compliance, several arbitrators have held that "the reasonable period of time, as determined under Article 21.3(c), should be the shortest period possible within the legal system of the Member to implement the recommendations and rulings of the DSB".[86] This is not to give an advantage to those Members with a lengthy and cumbersome internal process of law and decision-making, but to give the implementing Member the time it truly needs under its normal procedures, making use of any available flexibility,[87] but "not having to utilize an extraordinary legislative procedure".[88]

The implementing Member bears the burden of proof to show that the duration of any proposed period of implementation constitutes a "reasonable period of time", and the longer the proposed period of implementation, the greater this burden.[89] Suggesting ways and means of implementation or assessing whether the step proposed by the implementing Member brings about conformity with WTO law is not

---

[82] In *US – FSC*, WT/DS108/11, 2 October 2000; *US – Section 110(5) Copyright Act*, WT/DS160/14, 18 July 2001; and *US – 1916 Act*, WT/DS136/13, 18 July 2001.

[83] *See*, for example, Korea's request for arbitration in *US – Line Pipe*, WT/DS202/14, 2 May 2002.

[84] Footnote 13 to Article 21 DSU.

[85] Award of the Arbitrator, *Canada – Pharmaceutical Patents*, para. 45.

[86] Award of the Arbitrator, *EC – Hormones*, para. 26; quoted with approval in Award of the Arbitrator, *Indonesia – Autos*, para. 22; Award of the Arbitrator, *Korea – Alcoholic Beverages*, para. 37; Award of the Arbitrator, *Canada – Pharmaceutical Patents*, para. 47; Award of the Arbitrator, *US – 1916 Act*, para. 32.

[87] See, Award of the Arbitrator, *Canada – Autos*, para. 47; Award of the Arbitrator, *US – Section 110(5) Copyright Act*, para 39; Award of the Arbitrator, *US – 1916 Act*, para. 39; Award of the Arbitrator, *Canada – Patent Term*, para. 64; Award of the Arbitrator, *Canada – Pharmaceutical Patents*, para. 63.

[88] Award of the Arbitrator, *Korea – Alcoholic Beverages*, para. 42.

[89] Award of the Arbitrator, *Canada – Pharmaceutical Patents*, para. 47; quoted with approval in Award of the Arbitrator, *US – 1916 Act*, para. 32.

part of the mandate of the arbitrator under Article 21.3(c) of the DSU. If there are several possible ways to bring about conformity, the implementing Member has the discretion to choose among these options. Whether the chosen option truly achieves full conformity is to be decided according to the procedure of Article 21.5 of the DSU.[90] For those reasons, arbitrators determine the "reasonable period of time" on the basis of the proposal of the implementing Member.[91]

The reasonable periods of time awarded by arbitrators to date have ranged from six to fifteen months. Those that have been agreed between the parties have ranged from four to eighteen months.

In non-violation complaints, Article 26.1(c) of the DSU stipulates that the arbitrator acting under Article 21.3(c) "upon request of either party, may include a determination of the level of benefits which have been nullified or impaired, and may also suggest ways and means of reaching a mutually satisfactory adjustment; such suggestions shall not be binding upon the parties to the dispute".

Article 21.3(c) of the DSU contemplates an arbitration award to be issued within 90 days of the adoption of the panel (and Appellate Body) report(s), but this time-period is nearly always too short, also because the request for arbitration is often made at a late stage.[92] Thus, the parties have mostly agreed to extend the deadline. Parties may also ask the arbitrator to suspend the procedure or withdraw the request for arbitration in view of a mutually agreed solution on the issue of implementation.[93]

TIMELINES

In addition to the specific deadlines of the individual procedural steps, the DSU provides for the period from the establishment of a panel until the date of determination of the reasonable period of time, not to exceed 15 months unless the parties to the dispute agree otherwise. Where either the panel or the Appellate Body has extended their deadlines, the additional time is to be added to the 15 months, but not to exceed 18 months, unless the parties agree that there are exceptional circumstances (Article 21.4 of the DSU).

SURVEILLANCE BY THE DSB

The DSB keeps implementation by a Member of its recommendations or rulings (in other words the implementation of adopted panel (and Appellate Body) reports)

---

[90] Award of the Arbitrator, *Canada – Pharmaceutical Patents*, para. 42.

[91] Award of the Arbitrator, *Canada – Pharmaceutical Patents*, para. 43.

[92] Moreover, these arbitrations have developed from a hardly reasoned time determination of one paragraph length in the first award (Award of the Arbitrator, *Japan – Alcoholic Beverages II*, para. 27) to fully-fledged legal discussions and a detailed reasoning in the more recent awards, which makes more time necessary for deliberation, drafting and translation.

[93] Award of the Arbitrator, *US – Line Pipe*, paras. 6–9.

under surveillance. Any Member can raise the issue of implementation at any time in the DSB. Unless the DSB decides otherwise, the issue of implementation is placed on the agenda of the DSB six months following the date of establishment of the reasonable period of time.[94] The item remains on the DSB's agenda until the issue is resolved.[95] At least ten days before each such DSB meeting, the Member concerned is required to provide the DSB with a written status report of its progress in the implementation (Article 21.6 of the DSU). These status reports ensure transparency, and they may also give an incentive to advance implementation. When the implementing Member delivers these status reports in the DSB, it is common for other Members, particularly the complainant(s), to take the opportunity to demand full and expeditious implementation and to declare that they are following the matter with close attention.

The DSB must continue to keep under surveillance the implementation of the recommendations or rulings it has adopted. This includes cases where compensation has been provided or concessions or other obligations have been suspended but the recommendations to bring a measure into conformity with WTO law have not been implemented (Article 22.8 of the DSU).

COMPLIANCE REVIEW UNDER ARTICLE 21.5 OF THE DSU

When the parties disagree on whether the losing Member has implemented the recommendations and rulings, either of them can request a panel under Article 21.5 of the DSU. Unless the Member required to bring itself into conformity has done nothing at all, such disagreements can easily arise if, for instance, a new regulation or law has been passed and the original respondent believes that this achieves full compliance, but the complainant(s) disagree(s). This procedure is sometimes referred to as the "compliance" panel procedure.

Wherever possible, the DSB will refer the matter to the individuals serving on the original panel, which is supposed to decide in an expedited fashion, normally within 90 days (Article 21.5 of the DSU). It is not yet settled whether consultations are required before this compliance panel procedure. Although not specifically mentioned in Article 21.5 of the DSU, the practice has shown that appeals against compliance panel reports are possible and even quite frequent.

As for the mandate of the Article 21.5 panel, the Appellate Body has clarified that the panel's task is not limited to examining whether the implementing measure fully complies with the recommendations and rulings adopted by the DSB. In other words, the task is not only that of scrutinizing whether the implementing measure remedies the violation or other nullification or impairment as found by

---

[94] "Establishment" means the day on which the duration of the reasonable period of time is determined, not the day on which that period expires.

[95] For example, the *EC – Bananas III* dispute has been on the DSB agenda for years and opened every regular DSB meeting during that time.

the original panel. Rather, compliance panels must consider the new measure in its totality, including its consistency with a covered agreement.[96] This can include, if the complainant raises such claims, any question of WTO consistency of the new measure. Such claims may be new and different from those raised in respect of the original measure in the original panel (and Appellate Body) proceedings.

NON-IMPLEMENTATION

If the losing Member fails to bring its measure into conformity with its WTO obligations within the reasonable period of time, the prevailing complainant is entitled to resort to temporary measures, which can be either compensation or the suspension of WTO obligations, as discussed below. Neither of these temporary measures is preferred to full implementation of DSB recommendations and rulings (Articles 3.7 and 22.1 of the DSU).

COMPENSATION

If the implementing Member does not achieve full compliance by the end of the reasonable period of time, it has to enter into negotiations with the complaining party with a view to agreeing a mutually acceptable compensation (Article 22.2 of the DSU). This compensation does not mean monetary payment; rather, the respondent is supposed to offer a benefit, for example a tariff reduction, which is equivalent to the benefit which the respondent has nullified or impaired by applying its measure.

The parties to the dispute must agree upon the compensation, which must also be consistent with the covered agreements (Article 22.1 of the DSU). This latter requirement is probably one of the reasons why WTO Members have hardly ever been able to work out compensation in cases reaching this stage. Conformity with the covered agreements implies, notably, consistency with the most-favoured-nation obligations (Article I of GATT 1994, among others). Therefore, WTO Members other than the complainant(s) would also benefit, if compensation is offered e.g. in the form of a tariff reduction. This makes compensation less attractive to both the respondent, for whom this raises the "price", and the complainant, who does not get an exclusive benefit. These obstacles could to some extent be overcome, however, if the parties were to select a trade benefit (e.g. tariff reduction) in a sector of particular export interest to the complainant and other Members had little export interest in that sector or product.

---

[96] Appellate Body Report, *Canada – Aircraft (Article 21.5 – Brazil)*, paras. 40–41; Appellate Body Report, *US – Shrimp (Article 21.5 – Malaysia)*, paras. 85–87.

COUNTERMEASURES BY THE PREVAILING MEMBER (SUSPENSION OF OBLIGATIONS)

PREREQUISITES AND OBJECTIVES

If, within 20 days after the expiry of the reasonable period of time, the parties have not agreed on satisfactory compensation, the complainant may ask the DSB for permission to impose trade sanctions against the respondent that has failed to implement. Technically, this is called "suspending concessions or other obligations under the covered agreements" (Article 22.2 of the DSU).

Concessions are, for example, tariff reduction commitments which WTO Members have made in multilateral trade negotiations and are bound under Article II of GATT 1994. These bound concessions are just one form of WTO obligation. "Obligations" is the generic term in Article 22 (concessions or *other* obligations) used in this Guide for the sake of brevity (even though the most typical form practised so far is the suspension of concessions through the imposition of tariff surcharges). Suspending WTO obligations in relation to another Member requires a previous authorization of the DSB. The complainant is thus allowed to impose countermeasures that would otherwise be inconsistent with the WTO Agreement, in response to a violation or to non-violation nullification or impairment. This is informally also called "retaliation" or "sanctions". Such suspension of obligations takes place on a discriminatory basis only against the Member that failed to implement.

Retaliation is the final and most serious consequence a non-implementing Member faces in the WTO dispute settlement system (Article 3.7 of the DSU). Although retaliation requires prior approval by the DSB,[97] the countermeasures are applied selectively by one Member against another.

There is some debate whether the purpose of the suspension of obligations is to enforce recommendations and rulings, or merely to rebalance reciprocal trade benefits (at a new and lower level). Irrespective of the answer, it is clear that the suspension of obligations has the *effect* of rebalancing mutual trade benefits. It is also clear that the complainants who suspend obligations often do so with the intention of inducing compliance. Accordingly, the suspension can have the effect of inducing the respondent to achieve implementation. The DSU also makes clear that the suspension of obligations is temporary and that the DSB is to keep the situation under surveillance as long as there is no implementation. The issue remains on the agenda of the DSB at the request of the complaining party until it is resolved. The suspension must be revoked once the Member concerned has fully complied with the DSB's recommendations and rulings.

---

[97] According to the view of some Members and trade law experts, Articles 8.2 and 8.3 of the Agreement on Safeguards provide for a procedure partially departing from Article 22 of the DSU and allow the suspension of concessions immediately after the adoption of the panel (and Appellate Body) report, without prior DSB authorization.

Most observers agree that suspending obligations in response to the failure of timely implementation is problematic because it usually results in the complainant responding to a (WTO-inconsistent) trade barrier with another trade barrier, which is contrary to the liberalization philosophy underlying the WTO. Also, measures erecting trade barriers come at a price because they are nearly always economically harmful not only for the targeted Member but also for the Member imposing those measures. That said, it is important to note that it is the last resort in the dispute settlement system and is not actually used in most cases. It is clearly the exception, not the rule, for a dispute to go this far and not be resolved at an earlier stage through more constructive means.[98]

RULES GOVERNING THE SUSPENSION OF OBLIGATIONS

The level of suspension of obligations authorized by the DSB must be "equivalent" to the level of nullification or impairment (Article 22.4 of the DSU). This means that the complainant's retaliatory response may not go beyond the level of the harm caused by the respondent. At the same time, the suspension of obligations is prospective rather than retroactive; it covers only the time-period after the DSB has granted authorization, not the whole period during which the measure in question was applied or the entire period of the dispute.

Regarding the type of obligations to be suspended, the DSU imposes certain requirements. In principle, the sanctions should be imposed in the same sector as that in which the violation or other nullification or impairment was found (Article 22.3(a) of the DSU). For this purpose, the multilateral trade agreements are divided into three groups in accordance with the three parts of Annex 1 to the WTO Agreement (Annex 1A comprises the GATT 1994 and the other multilateral trade agreements on trade in goods, Annex 1B the GATS, and Annex 1C the TRIPS Agreement) (Article 22.3(g) of the DSU). Within these agreements, sectors are defined. With regard to TRIPS, the categories of intellectual property rights and the obligations under Part III and those under Part IV of the TRIPS Agreement each constitute separate sectors. In the GATS, each principal sector as identified in the current "Services Sectoral Classification List" is a sector. With respect to goods, all goods belong to the same sector (Article 22.3(f) of the DSU). The general principle is that the complainant should first seek to suspend obligations in the same sector as that in which the violation or other nullification or impairment was found. This means that, for example, the response to a violation in the area of patents should also relate to patents. If the violation occurred in the area of distribution services, then the countermeasure should also be in this area. On the other hand, a WTO-inconsistent tariff on automobiles (a good) can be countered with a tariff surcharge on cheese, furniture or pyjamas (also goods).

---

[98] *See* below the section on Statistics: the first eight years of experience on page 116.

However, if the complainant considers it impracticable or ineffective to remain within the same sector, the sanctions can be imposed in a different sector under the same agreement (Article 22.3(b) of the DSU). This option has no relevance in the area of goods, but, for example, a violation with regard to patents could be countered with countermeasures in the area of trademarks, and a violation in the area of distribution services could be countered in the area of health services.

In turn, if the complainant considers it impracticable or ineffective to remain within the same agreement, and the circumstances are serious enough, the counter-measures can be taken under another agreement (Article 22.3(c) of the DSU). The objective of this hierarchy is to minimize the chances of actions spilling over into unrelated sectors while at the same time allowing the actions to be effective. The possibility of suspending concessions in other sectors or under another agreement is often referred to as "cross-retaliation".

Particularly for smaller and developing country Members, the possibility of sus-pending obligations under a different sector or different agreement can be quite important. First, smaller and developing countries do not always import goods and services or intellectual property rights (in sufficient quantities) in the same sectors as those in which the violation or other nullification or impairment took place.[99] This may make it impossible to suspend obligations at a level equivalent to that of the nullification or impairment committed by the respondent, unless the com-plainant can suspend obligations in a different sector or under a different agreement. Second, the suspension in the same sector or under the same agreement could be ineffective or impracticable because the bilateral trade relationship is asymmetrical in that it is relatively important for the complainant and relatively unimportant for the respondent, particularly if the latter is a big trading nation. In that case, the effects of the suspension of obligations and the imposition of trade barriers might not even be visible in the respondent's trade statistics. Third, it might be economi-cally unaffordable for the developing country complainant to impose trade barriers against imports following the suspension of obligations under GATT 1994 or GATS because this would reduce the supply and/or increase the price of these imports on which the complainant's producers and consumers might depend.

For these reasons, it is important for developing countries to be able to use methods of suspending obligations that do not result in trade barriers. Suspending obligations under the TRIPS Agreement is an example of how to do so.[100]

AUTHORIZATION AND ARBITRATION

The DSB must grant the authorization to suspend obligations within 30 days of the expiry of the reasonable period of time, unless it decides by consensus to reject

---

[99]   This assumes that the violation or other nullification or impairment affected exports of the complainant and that the suspension of obligations would aim to harm imports from the respondent, as is most commonly (but not necessarily) the case.
[100]   Decision by the Arbitrators, *EC – Bananas III (Ecuador) (Article 22.6 – EC)*.

the request. This is the third key situation where the DSB decides by "reverse" or "negative" consensus. In other words, the approval is virtually automatic, because the requesting Member alone could prevent any possible consensus against granting the authorization.

If the parties disagree on the complainant's proposed form of retaliation, arbitration may be requested (Articles 22.6 and 22.7 of the DSU). This disagreement can relate either to the question of whether the level of retaliation is equivalent to the level of nullification or impairment or to the question of whether the principles governing the form of permitted suspension are respected.[101] If the original panelists are available, it is the original panel that carries out this arbitration; otherwise the Director-General appoints an arbitrator. Article 22.6 of the DSU also stipulates that the deadline for completing the arbitration is 60 days after the date of expiry of the reasonable period of time and that the complainant must not proceed with the suspension of obligations during the course of the arbitration.

The arbitrators determine whether the level of the proposed suspension of concessions is equivalent to the level of nullification or impairment. This means that they calculate the approximate value of the trade lost due to the measure found to be WTO-inconsistent or otherwise to nullify or impair benefits. If there is a claim that the principles and procedures for cross-retaliation (Article 22.3 of the DSU)[102] have not been followed, the arbitrator also examines that claim (Article 22.7 of the DSU).

The parties must accept the arbitrator's decision as final and not seek a second arbitration. The DSB is informed promptly of the outcome of the arbitration. Upon request, the DSB grants authorization to suspend obligations provided that the request is consistent with the decision of the arbitrator, except if there is a consensus to reject the request (Article 22.7 of the DSU).

Despite having obtained authorization from the DSB to suspend obligations, a complainant may choose not to proceed with the suspension but rather to use the authorization as a bargaining tool with the implementing Member.

SPECIAL RULES ON COUNTERMEASURES (SCM AGREEMENT)

Again, special rules exist in the SCM Agreement. In the area of prohibited subsidies, where the respondent has not followed the DSB's recommendation within the time-period specified by the panel for the withdrawal of the subsidy, the DSB grants authorization to the complaining Member to take "appropriate countermeasures", unless there is a negative consensus against it (Article 4.10 of the SCM Agreement). The arbitrator under Article 22.6 of the DSU is mandated to determine whether the proposed countermeasures are appropriate (Article 4.11 of the SCM Agreement).

---

[101] *See* above in the section on the Rules governing the suspension of obligations on page 82.
[102] *See* above in the section on the Rules governing the suspension of obligations on page 82.

In dispute settlement practice, the standard of "appropriateness" has been found to permit countermeasures that may be higher rather than strictly "equivalent" to the level of nullification or impairment caused by the prohibited subsidy. This appears to permit countermeasures that have a stronger effect in inducing compliance under the SCM Agreement than under the ordinary rules of the DSU.

On actionable subsidies, Article 7.9 of the SCM Agreement provides that the DSB must (unless there is a consensus to the contrary) grant authorization to the complainant to take countermeasures if the subsidy is not withdrawn or the adverse effects removed within six months from the adoption of the report(s). These countermeasures must be commensurate with the degree and nature of the adverse effects determined to exist. In the arbitration pursuant to Article 22.6 of the DSU, the arbitrator determines whether the countermeasures are commensurate with the degree and nature of the adverse effects (Article 7.10 of the SCM Agreement).

"SEQUENCING"

One of the contentious issues arising in the implementation stage of the dispute settlement system is the relationship between Article 21.5 and Article 22.2 of the DSU. The issue is which of the two procedures, if any, has priority: the compliance proceeding or the suspension of obligations. In other words, the issue is whether the complainant is entitled to request authorization to suspend obligations before a panel (and the Appellate Body) has established pursuant to Article 21.5 of the DSU that there has been a failure to comply with rulings and recommendations of a panel (or the Appellate Body). On the one hand, Article 22.6 of the DSU mandates the DSB to grant the authorization to suspend obligations within 30 days of the expiry of the reasonable period of time (if there is no negative consensus). A possible arbitration on the level or form of retaliation must conclude within 60 days after the expiry of the reasonable period of time. This time is not sufficient to complete the compliance review under Article 21.5 of the DSU (90 days for the panel, plus possible appeal) in order to establish whether there has been full implementation of the DSB recommendations and rulings (i.e. whether there now is WTO-compliance or whether a satisfactory adjustment to a situation of non-violation nullification or impairment has occurred). On the other hand, Article 23 of the DSU prohibits WTO Members from deciding unilaterally whether a measure is inconsistent with the covered agreements or whether it nullifies or impairs benefits.[103]

This conflict came to a head in the *EC – Bananas III* dispute. In subsequent cases, the parties have usually reached an ad hoc agreement on the sequencing of procedures under Article 21.5 and Article 22. In some cases, the parties have agreed to initiate the procedures under Article 21.5 and Article 22 simultaneously and then to suspend the retaliation procedures under Article 22 (the DSB authorization and

---

[103] *See* above in the section on the Prohibition against unilateral determinations on page 7.

the Article 22.6 arbitration) until the completion of the Article 21.5 procedure.[104] In other cases, the parties have agreed to initiate the procedures under Article 21.5 before resorting to the retaliation procedures under Article 22 with the understanding that the respondent would not object to a request for authorization of suspension of concessions under Article 22.6 of the DSU because of the expiry of the 30-day deadline for the DSB to grant this authorization.

Attempts to find a solution to the issue of sequencing through an authoritative interpretation or amendment of the DSU have so far been unsuccessful in both past and current DSU review negotiations.[105]

SURVEILLANCE UNTIL FINAL IMPLEMENTATION

The DSB's surveillance continues (even where compensation has been agreed or obligations have been suspended) as long as the recommendation to bring a measure into conformity with the covered agreements has not yet been implemented (Article 22.8 of the DSU).

SPECIAL PROCEDURES FOR NON-VIOLATION AND SITUATION COMPLAINTS

NON-VIOLATION COMPLAINTS

Although the procedures explained in this chapter, including on implementation, also apply to non-violation complaints, there are several differences. Some relate to those provisions that contain an explicit reference to a measure found inconsistent with the covered agreements, without simultaneously referring to nullification or impairment of benefits caused by WTO-consistent measures. These provisions are not applicable to non-violation complaints. In addition, Article 26.1 of the DSU contains several special provisions applying only to non-violation complaints departing from the normal procedures. These special features have already been referred to in the relevant context, so it is sufficient to briefly summarize the most important procedural aspects:

- there is no obligation to withdraw a WTO-consistent measure found to nullify or impair benefits or to impede the attainment of an objective;
- the panel (and the Appellate Body) accordingly recommends that the Members concerned find a mutually satisfactory adjustment;

---

[104] *See* for example *Canada – Dairy*, WT/DS103/14; and *US – FSC*, WT/DS108/12.
[105] On the negotiations, *see* below the section on Current negotiations on page 118.

– the arbitration under Article 21.3(c) of the DSU on the reasonable period of time may, upon request by either party, include a determination of the level of benefits which have been nullified or impaired, and may also suggest ways and means of reaching a mutually satisfactory adjustment;

– compensation may be part of a mutually satisfactory adjustment as final settlement of the dispute. (Under the general rules, compensation is only temporary pending final implementation. However, in non-violation cases, the obligation of implementation is not that of withdrawing the measure, but to make an adjustment, and this adjustment can notably take the form of compensation.)

SITUATION COMPLAINTS

Situation complaints[106] are quite different in that the general procedures of the DSU apply only up to the point of the circulation of the panel report (Article 26.2 of the DSU). This panel report must in any event be a separate panel report on the situation complaint, even if it is coupled with a simultaneous violation or non-violation complaint (Article 26.2(b) of the DSU).

As regards adoption and surveillance and implementation of recommendations and rulings in situation complaints, the GATT dispute settlement rules and procedures contained in the Decision of 12 April 1989[107] continue to apply. This means that the reverse consensus rule does not apply to the adoption of the panel report and to the authorization of the suspension of obligations in the event of a failure to implement. In other words, any Member, including the "losing" party, can block these decisions in the DSB by opposing a positive consensus. Article 26.2 of the DSU also implicitly excludes the possibility of an appeal against a panel report based on a situation complaint. Similarly, the DSU procedures on the compliance review in Article 21.5 of the DSU, the reasonable period of time to comply with the recommendations and rulings (and accordingly the arbitration on the reasonable period of time) and on the arbitration on the level of suspension of concessions do not automatically apply.

---

[106] *See* above the section on the Situation complaint on page 34.   [107] BISD 36S/61–67.

LEGAL EFFECT OF PANEL AND APPELLATE BODY REPORTS AND DSB RECOMMENDATIONS AND RULINGS

The previous chapters gave an explanation of the various procedures set out in the DSU. This chapter and the following ones will address specific issues of interest. This chapter addresses the legal effect of rulings made by panels, the Appellate Body and the DSB.

LEGAL EFFECTS WITHIN THE CONTEXT OF A PARTICULAR DISPUTE

RECOMMENDATIONS AND RULINGS OF THE DSB

After the DSB adopts a report of a panel (and the Appellate Body), the conclusions and recommendations contained in that report become binding upon the parties to the dispute. The DSU states that, when the parties cannot find a mutually agreeable solution, the first objective is normally to secure the withdrawal of the measure found to be inconsistent with the WTO Agreement (Article 3.7 of the DSU). In a successful violation complaint, the panel (and the Appellate Body) has found an inconsistency with the WTO Agreement and has expressed this finding in its conclusions. The panel (and the Appellate Body) then concludes by recommending that the Member concerned bring its measure into conformity with WTO law (Article 19.1 of the DSU). Article 21.1 of the DSU adds that prompt compliance with the recommendations or rulings of the DSB is essential in order to ensure the effective resolution of disputes.

The DSU clearly stipulates that compensation and suspension of concessions (countermeasures) are only temporary alternatives that fall short of resolving the dispute (Articles 3.7, 21.6 and 22.1 of the DSU). The only permanent remedy is for the losing party to "bring its measure into conformity" with the relevant covered agreements, as provided in Article 19 of the DSU. Moreover, for the reasons explained below, the term "recommendation" in Article 19.1 and the phrase "recommendation and ruling" should not be understood to give the party discretion as to whether to follow the recommendation.

First, it is worth recalling that panels and the Appellate Body only apply WTO law as it is contained in the covered agreements. They cannot add to or diminish the rights and obligations provided in the WTO agreements (Articles 3.2 and 19.2 of the DSU). A panel's or the Appellate Body's conclusion that a certain measure is inconsistent with WTO law therefore merely reflects and declares the legal situation which exists by virtue of the WTO Agreement, independently of the dispute settlement ruling. Because the provisions of the covered agreements constitute binding legal obligations with which all Members must comply,[1] such provisions already contain an obligation to refrain from any inconsistent action. The (adopted) report of a panel or the Appellate Body, therefore, constitutes an obligation for the losing party to put to an end the WTO inconsistency (and is in addition to the primary obligation not to maintain WTO-inconsistent measures in the first place).

Second, the DSU makes clear that a Member that does not bring its WTO-inconsistent measure into conformity with the WTO Agreement risks consequences: it either has to provide compensation with the agreement of the complainant, or it may face retaliatory countermeasures.

Third, the DSU specifically states that there is no obligation to withdraw the WTO-consistent measure in the event of a successful non-violation complaint (Article 26.1(b) of the DSU). This suggests there *is* such an obligation in the event of a successful *violation* complaint.

For these reasons, one can say that the recommendation contained in an adopted panel (and Appellate Body) report – if it concludes that there is a WTO violation – for the respondent to bring its measure into conformity with the WTO Agreement is binding upon the respondent.

The situation is different for non-violation complaints. The adopted panel (and Appellate Body) report is also binding with regard to the panel's or the Appellate Body's conclusion as to whether or not a benefit accruing to the complainant under a covered agreement has been nullified or impaired. However, the DSU specifically states that there is no obligation to withdraw the WTO-consistent measure that resulted in nullification or impairment. The panel or the Appellate Body, therefore, only recommends that the parties find a mutually satisfactory adjustment (Article 26.1(b) of the DSU).

An adopted panel (and Appellate Body) report is also binding on the complainant. This is relevant especially in those cases where the complainant does not prevail with all its claims of violation or of non-violation nullification or impairment. Article 23.2(a) of the DSU prohibits the complainant from determining unilaterally that a violation of the WTO Agreement or that nullification or impairment of a benefit has occurred if this is inconsistent with the findings contained in the panel or Appellate Body report adopted by the DSB.[2]

---

[1] Of course, the WTO Agreement also contains obligations that are of a less binding nature. The WTO rules at issue in violation disputes, however, are rules of a full binding nature.

[2] *See* above the section on the the Prohibition against unilateral determinations on page 7.

OBLIGATIONS IN THE EVENT OF A "REGIONAL OR LOCAL VIOLATION"

A qualification to the above applies when a successful violation complaint relates to a measure taken by regional or local governments or authorities within the territory of a Member. Such measures are attributable to the Member in question and can be the object of a dispute.[3] The difference between such measures and those taken by the authorities belonging to that Member's central government is that the central government, which represents the Member at the WTO (including in the dispute settlement proceedings), might not be able to secure the withdrawal of the measure. The domestic law of that Member, for instance the Constitution, might limit the central government's powers over the regional or local levels of government. This may, for example, be the case in federal States, where the central government is not always entitled to interfere with regional or local legislative or administrative acts.

Accordingly, the implementation obligations of the responsible Member are limited to such reasonable measures as may be available to it to ensure observance of WTO law (Article 22.9 of the DSU). Article XXIV:12 of GATT 1994 contains identical language. This is a specific and limited exception to the principle that subjects of international law are responsible for the activities of all branches of power within their system of governance, *including* all regional levels or other subdivisions of government.

The qualifications of Article 22.9 should not be generalized and extrapolated to other authorities of a Member enjoying a degree of independence, for example, independent judiciaries. Even if a government is unable to remedy a WTO violation because an independent judicial body committed it, the Member in question is fully responsible for this violation in WTO dispute settlement. It is a general principle of international law that it is not possible to invoke domestic law as justification for the failure to carry out international obligations.

Article 22.9 only limits a Member's implementation obligations insofar as the achievement of conformity with the WTO Agreement (by withdrawing the inconsistent measure) is concerned. The dispute settlement provisions relating to compensation and the suspension of obligations fully apply where the Member concerned has not been able to secure the observance of the WTO Agreement in its territory (Article 22.9).

LEGAL STATUS OF ADOPTED/UNADOPTED REPORTS IN OTHER DISPUTES

A dispute relates to a specific matter and takes place between two or more specific Members of the WTO. The report of a panel or the Appellate Body also relates to that specific matter in the dispute between these Members. Even if adopted, the reports of

---

[3] *See* above the section on Measures taken by regional or local subdivisions of a Member on page 40.

panels and the Appellate Body are not binding precedents for other disputes between the same parties on other matters or different parties on the same matter, even though the same questions of WTO law might arise. As in other areas of international law, there is no rule of *stare decisis* in WTO dispute settlement according to which previous rulings bind panels and the Appellate Body in subsequent cases. This means that a panel is not obliged to follow previous Appellate Body reports even if they have developed a certain interpretation of exactly the provisions which are now at issue before the panel. Nor is the Appellate Body obliged to maintain the legal interpretations it has developed in past cases. The Appellate Body has confirmed that conclusions and recommendations in panel reports adopted under GATT 1947 bound the parties to the particular dispute, but that subsequent panels were not legally bound by the details and reasoning of a previous panel report.

If the reasoning developed in the previous report in support of the interpretation given to a WTO rule is persuasive from the perspective of the panel or the Appellate Body in the subsequent case, it is very likely that the panel or the Appellate Body will repeat and follow it. This is also in line with a key objective of the dispute settlement system which is to enhance the security and predictability of the multilateral trading system (Article 3.2 of the DSU). In the words of the Appellate Body, these GATT and WTO panel reports – and equally adopted Appellate Body reports[4] – "create legitimate expectations among WTO Members, and, therefore, should be taken into account where they are relevant to any dispute".[5]

Although *unadopted* panel reports have no formal legal status in the GATT or WTO system, the reasoning contained in an unadopted panel report can nevertheless provide useful guidance to a panel or the Appellate Body in a subsequent case involving the same legal question.[6]

---

[4] Appellate Body Report, *US – Shrimp (Article 21.5 – Malaysia)*, para. 109.
[5] Appellate Body Report, *Japan – Alcoholic Beverages II*, DSR 1996: I, 97 at 107–108.
[6] Panel Report, *Japan – Alcoholic Beverages II*, para. 6.10; Appellate Body Report, *Japan – Alcoholic Beverages II*, DSR 1996: I, 97 at 108.

DISPUTE SETTLEMENT WITHOUT RECOURSE TO PANELS AND THE APPELLATE BODY

The previous chapters have devoted much attention to the involvement of panels and the Appellate Body in the WTO dispute settlement system. However, it is important to stress that panels and the Appellate Body are not always involved in a WTO dispute and there are various other ways to solve disputes within the framework of the WTO. Indeed, the parties often use these other ways and manage to solve their dispute in a cooperative manner and not through recourse to adjudication by panels and the Appellate Body. In this regard, parties can settle a dispute by finding a mutually agreed solution in bilateral negotiations or with the help of dispute resolution mechanisms such as good offices, conciliation or mediation. In addition, they can also agree to refer their dispute to an arbitrator.

In domestic judicial systems, the out-of-court solution of disputes is often referred to as an "alternative" form of dispute resolution. One could also talk about an "alternative" to panels and the Appellate Body in the WTO dispute settlement system, when parties settle their dispute with a mutually agreed solution, or through arbitration. However, these forms of dispute settlement are provided for in the DSU and are therefore formally part of, and not an alternative to, the WTO dispute settlement system.

MUTUALLY AGREED SOLUTIONS

The DSU expresses a preference for the parties to settle their disputes through mutually agreed solutions (Article 3.7 of the DSU). However, unlike many other judicial systems, the DSU does not allow the parties to settle their dispute on whatever terms they wish. Solutions mutually acceptable to the parties to the dispute must also be consistent with the WTO Agreement and must not nullify or impair benefits accruing under the agreement to any other Member (Articles 3.5 and 3.7 of the DSU). If the matter has been formally raised in a request for consultations,[1] the mutually agreed solutions must be notified to the DSB and the relevant Councils and Committees (Article 3.6 of the DSU). This is meant to inform the other WTO Members and to give them an opportunity to raise whatever concern they may have

---

[1] *See* above in the section Legal basis and requirements for a request for consultations on page 45.

with regard to the settlement. Implicit in these rules is an acknowledgement of the danger that the parties to a dispute might be tempted to settle on terms that are detrimental to a third Member not involved in the dispute, or in a way that is not entirely consistent with WTO law. Mutually agreed solutions must therefore be notified to the DSB with sufficient information for other Members.

IN BILATERAL CONSULTATIONS OR AFTERWARDS

Bilateral consultations, which are required to take place at the beginning of any dispute,[2] are intended to provide a setting in which the parties to a dispute should attempt to negotiate a mutually agreed solution. However, even when the consultations have failed to bring about a settlement and the dispute has progressed to the stage of adjudication, the parties are encouraged to continue their efforts to find a mutually agreed solution.

For instance, panels should consult regularly with the parties and give them adequate opportunity to develop a mutually satisfactory solution (Article 11 of the DSU). When panels suspend their work at the request of the complaining party (Article 12.12 of the DSU),[3] this is usually to allow the parties to find a mutually agreed solution. In one case, the parties to the dispute reached a mutually agreed solution prior to the issuance of the interim report.[4] In another case, they did so after the issuance of the interim report, but before the issuance of the final report to the parties.[5] In yet another case, the parties reached a mutually agreed solution after the issuance but prior to the circulation[6] of the panel report to all Members.[7] Where the parties have found a settlement of the matter, the panel issues a report in which it briefly describes the case and reports that the parties have reached a mutually agreed solution (Article 12.7 of the DSU).

At the stage of appellate review, the appellant may withdraw the appeal at any time.[8] One possible reason to do so would be that the parties have found a mutually agreed solution.

MEDIATION, CONCILIATION AND GOOD OFFICES

Sometimes, the involvement of an outside, independent person unrelated to the parties of a dispute can help the parties find a mutually agreed solution. To allow such assistance, the DSU provides for good offices, conciliation and mediation

---

[2] *See* above the section on Consultations on page 43.

[3] *See* above in the section on Deadlines, timetable and suspension on page 59.

[4] Panel Report, *US – DRAMS (Article 21.5 – Korea)*.

[5] Panel Report, *EC – Scallops (Canada)*; Panel Report, *EC – Scallops (Peru and Chile)*.

[6] On the procedural stages of the interim report, the issuance and the circulation of the panel report, *see* above the section on the Interim review on page 58, and the section on the Issuance and circulation of the final report on page 59.

[7] Panel Report, *EC – Butter*.   [8] *See* above the section on the Withdrawal of an appeal on page 73.

on a voluntary basis if the parties to the dispute agree (Article 5.1 of the DSU). Good offices normally consist primarily of providing logistical support to help the parties negotiate in a productive atmosphere. Conciliation additionally involves the direct participation of an outside person in the discussions and negotiations between the parties. In a mediation process, the mediator does not only participate in and contribute to the discussions and negotiations, but may also propose a solution to the parties. The parties would not be obliged to accept this proposal.

Good offices, conciliation and mediation may begin at any time (Article 5.3 of the DSU), but not prior to a request for consultations[9] because that request is necessary to trigger the application of the procedures of the DSU, including Article 5 (Article 1.1 of the DSU). For example, the parties can enter into these procedures during their consultations. If this happens within 60 days after the date of the request for consultations, the complainant must not request a panel before this 60-day period has expired, unless the parties jointly consider that the good offices, conciliation or mediation process has failed to settle the dispute (Article 5.4 of the DSU). However, these procedures can be terminated at any time (Article 5.3 of the DSU). If the parties so agree, these procedures may continue while the panel proceeds with an examination of the matter (Article 5.5 of the DSU).

The proceedings of good offices, conciliation and mediation are strictly confidential, and do not diminish the position of either party in any following dispute settlement procedure (Article 5.2 of the DSU). This is important because, during such negotiations, a party may offer a compromise solution, admit certain facts or divulge to the mediator the outer limit of the terms on which it would be prepared to settle. If no mutually agreed solution emerges from the negotiations and the dispute goes to adjudication, this constructive kind of flexibility and openness must not be detrimental to the parties.

As regards the independent person to be involved, the DSU states that the Director-General of the WTO may offer good offices, conciliation or mediation with a view to assisting Members to settle their dispute (Article 5.6 of the DSU). Due to the absence of recourse to the procedures of Article 5 of the DSU, the Director-General issued a formal communication to the Members of the WTO.[10] In this communication, the Director-General called the Members' attention to his readiness to assist them as contemplated in Article 5.6 of the DSU, with a view to helping settle disputes without recourse to panels and the Appellate Body. The communication also details the procedures to be followed when Members request the Director-General's assistance for good offices, conciliation or mediation.

The communication contemplates that the Director-General or, with the concurrence of the parties, a designated Deputy Director-General would handle the proceedings. Unlike panel and Appellate Body proceedings, the process of good offices, conciliation or mediation should not result in legal conclusions, but assist

---

[9] *See* above the section on Legal basis and requirements for a request for consultations on page 45.
[10] Communication from the Director-General, Article 5 of the DSU, WT/DSB/25, 17 July 2001.

in reaching a mutually agreed solution. The Director-General may involve Secretariat staff to support the process, but these staff members must be insulated from subsequent dispute settlement procedures (i.e. at the panel stage).[11] A request to the Director-General must also identify whether it is for good offices, conciliation and/or mediation, even though the Director-General's role may change during the Article 5 procedure. Finally, the communication stipulates that *ex parte* communications (between one party and the Director-General to the exclusion of the other party) would be permitted, that all communications during the process would remain confidential and that no third party may participate in the process, except if the parties agree.

As already stated, the procedures of Article 5 have so far not been used in WTO dispute settlement. In one instance, three WTO Members jointly requested the Director-General (or a person designated by the Director-General with the requesting Members' agreement) to mediate. The mediator was requested to examine the extent to which a preferential tariff treatment granted to other Members unduly impaired legitimate export interests of two of the requesting Members. The task of the mediator was also possibly to propose a solution.

The requesting Members considered the matter not to be a "dispute" within the terms of the DSU, but agreed that the mediator could be guided by procedures similar to those envisaged for mediation under Article 5 of the DSU. The Director-General nominated a Deputy Director-General to be the mediator,[12] whose conclusions it was agreed by the parties would remain confidential upon completion of the procedure.[13]

The DSU specifically foresees good offices, conciliation and mediation for disputes involving a least-developed country Member. Where the consultations have not resulted in a satisfactory solution and the least-developed country Member so requests, the Director-General or the Chairman of the DSB must offer their good offices, conciliation and mediation. Here as well, the aim is to assist the parties to settle the dispute before the establishment of a panel (Article 24.2 of the DSU).

ARBITRATION PURSUANT TO ARTICLE 25 OF THE DSU

As an alternative to adjudication by panels and the Appellate Body, the parties to a dispute can resort to arbitration (Article 25.1 of the DSU). The parties must agree on the arbitration as well as the procedures to be followed (Article 25.2 of the DSU).

---

[11] On the involvement of Secretariat staff in the panel proceedings, *see* above in the section on Administrative and legal support on page 22.

[12] Communication from the Director-General, Request for Mediation by the Philippines, Thailand and the European Communities, WT/GC/66, 16 October 2002.

[13] Communication from the Director-General, Request for Mediation by the Philippines, Thailand and the European Communities, Addendum, WT/GC/66/Add.1, 23 December 2002.

The parties to the dispute are thus free to depart from the standard procedures of the DSU and to agree on the rules and procedures they deem appropriate for the arbitration, including the selection of the arbitrators. The parties must also clearly define the issues in dispute.

Before the beginning of the arbitration, the parties must notify their agreement to resort to arbitration to all WTO Members. Other Members may become party to an arbitration only with the agreement of the parties engaged in the arbitration. The parties to the arbitration must agree to abide by the arbitration award, which, once issued, must be notified to the DSB and the relevant Councils and Committees overseeing the agreement(s) in question (Articles 25.2 and 25.3 of the DSU). The provisions of Articles 21 and 22 of the DSU on remedies and on the surveillance of implementation of a decision apply to the arbitration award (Article 25.4 of the DSU).

To date, in only one dispute have the parties resorted to arbitration under Article 25 of the DSU. The procedure was not used as an alternative to the panel and Appellate Body procedure, but at the stage of implementation, when the panel report had already been adopted. The parties asked the arbitrators to determine the level of nullification or impairment of benefits caused by the violation established in the panel report. Under the standard procedures of the DSU, parties can obtain a binding determination of the level of nullification or impairment by recourse to arbitration under Article 22.6 of the DSU. A prerequisite for such arbitration is that the complainant has requested the DSB's authorization for the suspension of obligations and that the respondent disagrees with the proposed level of retaliation.[14] In the case where the parties resorted to arbitration under Article 25 of the DSU, they agreed that the award of the arbitrators would be final. Recourse to Articles 21 and 22 of the DSU is available to implement and enforce the conclusions of these arbitration awards.

---

[14] *See* above the section on Authorization and arbitration on page 83.

PARTICIPATION IN DISPUTE SETTLEMENT PROCEEDINGS

PARTIES AND THIRD PARTIES AND PRINCIPLE OF CONFIDENTIALITY

Earlier chapters have already explained that only WTO Member governments have direct access to the dispute settlement system[1] either as parties or as third parties.[2] In addition, the entire procedure is confidential, which covers the consultations (Article 4.6 of the DSU), the panel procedure until the circulation of the report (Articles 14.1 and 18.2 of the DSU and paragraph 3 of the Working Procedures in Appendix 3 to the DSU), and the proceedings of the Appellate Body (Article 17.10 of the DSU).

It is true that Members may make use of their right to disclose their own submissions to the public (Article 18.2 of the DSU and paragraph 3 of the Working Procedures in Appendix 3 to the DSU).[3] The reports of panels and the Appellate Body also give a description of the proceeding, including the positions taken by the various participants. However, this does not give non-participants any opportunity to make a contribution to the dispute settlement proceeding while it is ongoing (i.e. before decisions are made). For that reason, there is a great deal of interest in the question of who can participate in dispute settlement proceedings.

LEGAL REPRESENTATION

A question that arose early in the life of the DSU was whether the parties and third parties to a dispute could only send government officials as their representatives to the meetings with the panel and the oral hearing of the Appellate Body. The DSU does not specifically address the issue of who may represent a party before panels and the Appellate Body.

In *EC – Bananas III*, one party challenged the right of parties or third parties to have independent private legal counsel (i.e. barristers/solicitors/attorneys) as their representatives, even if these individuals are professionals who had been hired for

---

[1] *See* above the section on the Participants in the dispute settlement system one page 9.

[2] For the details of the participation of third parties at the various stages of a dispute settlement proceeding, *see* above the section on Third parties in consultations on page 47, the section on Third parties before the panel on page 50, and the section on Third participants at the appellate stage on page 65.

[3] *See* above in the section on Submissions and oral hearings on page 54.

that specific purpose and were not permanently employed by the government. The practice under GATT 1947 (where private legal counsel was not allowed) was invoked in support of denying such a possibility. The Appellate Body, however, made clear that nothing in the WTO Agreement or in general international law prevents a WTO Member from determining for itself the composition of its delegation in WTO dispute settlement proceedings.[4]

This is valid for hearings of the Appellate Body as well as for the substantive meetings with the panel. It is, therefore, now common practice for private legal counsel to appear in panel and Appellate Body proceedings as part of a Member's delegation and to present arguments on their behalf. Even more common is the involvement of private law firms in the preparation of parties' written submissions, even though this is usually not visible because the party involved would file these submissions with its government's letterhead. This is quite relevant for developing country Members, as it may enable them to take part in dispute settlement proceedings even when they lack human resources with specific expertise in WTO dispute settlement.[5] The Member concerned is of course responsible for these representatives, as for all its governmental delegates, and must ensure that these outside representatives respect the confidentiality of the proceedings.[6]

AMICUS CURIAE SUBMISSIONS

A controversial issue has been whether panels and the Appellate Body may accept and consider unsolicited submissions they receive from entities not a party or third party to the dispute. These submissions are commonly referred to as *amicus curiae* submissions. *Amicus curiae* means "friend of the court". These submissions often come from non-governmental organizations, including industry associations, or university professors. Neither the DSU nor the Working Procedures for Appellate Review[7] specifically address this issue.

AMICUS CURIAE SUBMISSIONS IN PANEL PROCEEDINGS

According to the Appellate Body, the panels' comprehensive authority to seek information from any relevant source (Article 13 of the DSU) and to add to or depart from the Working Procedures in Appendix 3 to the DSU (Article 12.1 of the DSU) permits panels to accept and consider or to reject information and advice, even if submitted in an unsolicited fashion.[8]

---

4   Appellate Body Report, *EC – Bananas III*, para. 10.
5   Appellate Body Report, *EC – Bananas III*, para. 12; *see* further below the section on Representation by private counsel and the Advisory Centre on WTO Law on page 114.
6   *See* Appellate Body Report, *Thailand – H-Beams*, para. 68.
7   *See* above in the section on the Rules on the appellate review on page 63.
8   Appellate Body Report, *US – Shrimp*, paras. 105–108.

The Appellate Body has confirmed this ruling several times, but the issue remains extremely contentious among WTO Members. Many Members are of the strong view that the DSU does not allow panels to accept and consider non-requested *amicus curiae* submissions. They consider WTO disputes as procedures purely between Members and see no role whatsoever for non-parties, particularly non-governmental organizations.[9]

To date, only a few panels have in fact made use of their discretionary right to accept and consider unsolicited briefs. On the basis of the Appellate Body's interpretation, panels have no obligation whatsoever to accept and consider these briefs. Accordingly, interested entities, which are neither parties nor third parties to the dispute, have no legal right to be heard by a panel.

AMICUS CURIAE SUBMISSIONS IN THE APPELLATE PROCEDURE

Amicus curiae submissions have frequently been filed in Appellate Body proceedings. When these briefs are attached to the submission of a participant (appellant or appellee), for instance as exhibits, the Appellate Body considers such material to be an integral part of the submission of that participant who also assumes responsibility for its content.[10]

When the Appellate Body receives unsolicited briefs directly from an *amicus curiae*, the entity filing the brief has no *right* to have it considered.[11] Nonetheless, the Appellate Body maintains that it has the authority to accept and consider any information it considers pertinent and useful in deciding an appeal, including unsolicited *amicus curiae* submissions. The Appellate Body believes such a right flows from its broad authority to adopt procedural rules, provided they do not conflict with the DSU or the covered agreements (Article 17.9 of the DSU).[12]

In one appeal, the Appellate Body foresaw that it might receive a high number of *amicus curiae* briefs and adopted an additional procedure pursuant to Rule 16(1) of the Working Procedures[13] for the purpose of that appeal only. This procedure specified several criteria for such submissions. Persons other than the parties and third parties intending to file such a submission were required to apply for leave to file that submission. Upon review of the applications, however, the Appellate Body denied all applicants leave to file briefs.[14] In reaction to the adoption of these additional procedures, the General Council of the WTO discussed the matter in a special meeting where a majority of WTO Members that spoke

---

[9] The statements of these Members can be found in the minutes of the DSB meetings in which the DSB adopted the respective panel (and Appellate Body) report. *See* also General Council, Minutes of the Meeting of 22 November 2000, WT/GC/M/60.

[10] Appellate Body Report, *US – Shrimp*, paras. 89 and 91.

[11] Appellate Body Report, *US – Lead and Bismuth II*, paras. 40–41.

[12] Appellate Body Report, *US – Lead and Bismuth II*, para. 43.

[13] *See* above in the section on the Rules on the appellate review on page 63.

[14] Appellate Body Report, *EC – Asbestos*, paras. 52–55.

considered it unacceptable for the Appellate Body to accept and consider *amicus curiae* briefs.[15]

Recently, the Appellate Body received an *amicus curiae* submission from a WTO Member that had not been a third party before the panel and, therefore, could not become a third participant in the appellate proceeding.[16] The Appellate Body recalled that it had the authority to receive *amicus curiae* briefs from private individuals or organizations, and concluded that it was equally entitled to accept such a brief from a WTO Member. However, the Appellate Body did not believe it was required to consider the content of that brief.[17]

Despite the controversy surrounding this issue, the Appellate Body has never considered any unsolicited submission to be pertinent or useful, and thus, has never considered any that have been submitted.

---

[15] General Council, Minutes of the Meeting of 22 November 2000, WT/GC/M/60.
[16] *See* above in the section on Third participants at the appellate stage on page 65.
[17] Appellate Body Report, *EC – Sardines*, paras. 164 and 167.

LEGAL ISSUES ARISING IN WTO DISPUTE SETTLEMENT PROCEEDINGS

STANDING

There is no DSU requirement for a complainant to have a "legal interest" as a prerequisite for requesting the establishment of a panel in a dispute.[1] Indeed, complainants have already been allowed to bring complaints against violations of the WTO Agreement, even though such violations were to the detriment of *other* Members.[2] However, the issue of standing (the right to bring a complaint) was not specifically raised in those disputes. In the one case where the respondent specifically challenged the complainant's standing to bring a violation claim under GATT 1994, the Appellate Body was satisfied with the fact that the complainant was a producer and potential exporter of the product in question. Moreover, the claims in that case were interwoven with claims under other covered agreements, for which the complainant's standing had not been challenged. The Appellate Body also relied on a Member's interest in enforcing WTO rules due to the possible direct or indirect economic effects of a WTO violation.[3]

CLAIMS VERSUS ARGUMENTS; AUTONOMOUS REASONING OF A PANEL

By its terms of reference (Article 7 of the DSU), a panel is restricted to addressing only those claims that are specifically set out in a Member's panel request with sufficient precision. The complainant must, therefore, include all the claims it wants the panel to address in the request for the establishment of the panel. If the request does not specify a certain *claim*, then the original request cannot subsequently be "cured" by a complaining party's argumentation in the written submissions or in the oral statements to the panel.[4] The panel would be precluded from ruling on such a subsequent claim.

---

[1] Appellate Body Report, *EC – Bananas III*, para. 132.
[2] E.g. Appellate Body Report, *US – Section 211 Omnibus Appropriations Act*, paras. 275–281, 309; Appellate Body Report, *US – Line Pipe*, paras. 120–122, 130–133.
[3] Appellate Body Report, *EC – Bananas III*, paras. 136–138.
[4] *See* above in the section on the Establishment of a panel on page 48.

However, there is a significant difference between the *claims* identified in the panel request, and the *arguments* supporting those claims.[5] "Claim" means an assertion that the respondent has violated, nullified or impaired benefits accruing under an identified provision of a covered agreement. "Arguments" are put forward by the complainant to demonstrate that the respondent has indeed infringed the identified provision or otherwise nullified or impaired benefits.[6] Arguments are not required to be included in the request for the establishment of the panel. Rather, the parties usually develop extensive legal arguments only in the further stages of the proceedings (i.e. in their written submissions and oral statements to the panel).

A panel is not limited to using the parties' arguments. Rather, a panel is free to accept or reject such arguments and has the discretion to develop its own legal reasoning to support its findings and conclusions. In other words, a panel can develop its own autonomous reasoning.[7]

NECESSITY FOR THE RESPONDENT TO INVOKE EXCEPTIONS

There is one important deviation from the principle that panels and the Appellate Body are free autonomously to apply WTO law in reviewing the complainant's claims and to develop their own legal reasoning. It relates to the application of WTO legal exceptions. When the respondent intends to rely on a legal exception to the obligation, a violation of which the complainant has claimed, the respondent must expressly invoke such an exception. Examples of such exceptions are Article XX of GATT 1994[8] or Article 5.7 of the SPS Agreement.[9] A panel and the Appellate Body cannot apply such exceptions if they have not been invoked by the respondent.

JUDICIAL ECONOMY

Under its terms of reference,[10] a panel has a mandate to address all the complainant's claims. However, complainants often allege that the challenged measure violates simultaneously a number of different WTO provisions in either the same or various covered agreements.

In such cases, panels are not required to address all the legal claims that the complainant makes. It is sufficient for a panel to deal with the claims that are

---

[5] Appellate Body Report, *India – Patents (US)*, para. 88; Appellate Body Report, *EC – Hormones*, para. 156.
[6] Appellate Body Report, *Korea – Dairy*, para. 139.
[7] Appellate Body Report, *EC – Hormones*, para. 156; Appellate Body Report, *Korea – Dairy*, para. 139; Appellate Body Report, *US – Certain EC Products*, para. 123.
[8] Appellate Body Report, *US – Shrimp*, paras. 125 and 146.
[9] Appellate Body Report, *EC – Hormones*, paras. 120–125.
[10] *See* above in the section on the Establishment of a panel on page 48 and the section on Claims versus arguments on page 101.

necessary to resolve the matter at issue in the dispute. If the panel has already found that the challenged measure is inconsistent with a particular provision of a covered agreement, it is generally not necessary to go on and to examine whether the same measure is also inconsistent with other provisions the complainant invokes.[11] Panels have the *discretion* to decline to rule on these further claims,[12] but they must do so explicitly.[13]

There is a limit to this discretion, however, since the principle of judicial economy must be applied consistently with the objective of the dispute settlement system: to resolve the matter at issue and "to secure a positive solution to a dispute" (Article 3.7 of the DSU). The Appellate Body has cautioned that it would be false judicial economy to provide only a partial resolution of the matter at issue. A panel must, therefore, address all those claims on which a finding is necessary in order to enable the DSB to make sufficiently precise recommendations and rulings so as to allow for prompt compliance by a Member "in order to ensure effective resolution of disputes to the benefit of all Members" (Article 21.1 of the DSU).[14]

Where a panel dismisses a complaint, there is obviously no scope for the application of judicial economy. Each and every claim cited in the complaint must be addressed and rejected in such a case. Sometimes, complainants make several claims of violation, but some of them only in a conditional manner: "If the panel does not find a violation of Article Y, we assert that the measure in dispute violates Article Z." This is also not a situation where a panel has any discretion to apply judicial economy. It would first examine Article Y and address Article Z if, and only if, it has found no violation of Article Y.

STANDARD OF REVIEW

THE GENERAL RULE IN ARTICLE 11 OF THE DSU

A panel's standard of review is stipulated in Article 11 of the DSU. A panel has to "make an objective assessment of the matter before it, including an objective assessment of the facts of the case and the applicability of and conformity with the relevant covered agreements, and make such other findings as will assist the DSB in making the recommendations or in giving the rulings provided for in the covered agreements".

As to the establishment of the facts in a case, this "objective assessment" has been understood as mandating neither a *de novo* review (i.e. the complete repetition of

---

[11] Appellate Body Report, *US – Wool Shirts and Blouses*, DSR 1997: I, 323 at 339–340.
[12] Appellate Body Report, *US – Lead and Bismuth II*, paras. 71 and 73; Appellate Body Report, *Canada – Autos*, para. 116.
[13] Appellate Body Report, *Canada – Autos*, para. 117.
[14] Appellate Body Report, *Australia – Salmon*, para. 223.

the fact-finding conducted by national authorities) nor "total deference" to domestic authorities (i.e. the simple acceptance of their determination).[15]

In the area of safeguard measures,[16] this has been considered to mean that a panel must assess whether the national authorities have examined all the relevant facts and provided a reasoned explanation of how the facts support their determination.[17] National authorities must look for and evaluate relevant information, irrespective of whether any interested party involved in the national proceedings has relied upon it.[18] Panels must critically examine the competent authorities' explanation as to whether it fully addresses the nature, and the complexities, of the data, and responds to other plausible interpretations of that data.[19] However, panels must not consider evidence which did not exist at the time when the Member made its determination.[20]

THE SPECIAL STANDARD OF REVIEW IN ARTICLE 17.6 OF THE ANTI-DUMPING AGREEMENT

One covered agreement, the Anti-Dumping Agreement, sets out a special standard of review (Article 17.6 of the Anti-Dumping Agreement). This special provision is intended to give a greater margin of deference to the Member's anti-dumping determination than would Article 11 of the DSU.

In its assessment of the facts of the matter in an anti-dumping dispute, a panel must determine whether the establishment of the facts by the anti-dumping authorities was proper and whether their evaluation of those facts was unbiased and objective. If that is the case, the panel must accept the anti-dumping determination, even though it might have reached a different conclusion about those facts.

As regards the standard of *legal* review, Article 17.6(ii) confirms that the panel must interpret the relevant provisions of the Anti-Dumping Agreement in accordance with customary rules of interpretation of public international law.[21] Where a relevant provision can have more than one permissible interpretation, the panel must find the anti-dumping measure to be in conformity with the Anti-Dumping Agreement if it is based upon one of those permissible interpretations.[22]

---

[15] Appellate Body Report, *EC – Hormones*, para. 117.
[16] Adopted pursuant to Article XIX of GATT 1994 and the Agreement on Safeguards.
[17] Appellate Body Report, *Argentina – Footwear (EC)*, para. 121.
[18] Appellate Body Report, *US – Wheat Gluten*, para. 55.
[19] Appellate Body Report, *US – Lamb*, paras. 103 and 106.
[20] Appellate Body Report, *US – Cotton Yarn*, paras. 73 and 78.
[21] *See* Article 3.2 DSU and above the section on Clarification of rights and obligations through interpretation on page 3.
[22] As regards the interpretation of Article 17.6(ii), *see* Appellate Body Report, *US – Hot-Rolled Steel*, paras. 57–62, 172; Appellate Body Report, *EC – Bed Linen*, paras. 63–65 and 85.

BURDEN OF PROOF

The DSU does not include any express rule concerning the burden of proof in panel proceedings. The concept of the burden of proof generally has two important aspects in any judicial or quasi-judicial system: (i) Who should "lose" the dispute if the facts remain unclear? In whose favour should a panel decide if, based on the available evidence, it cannot establish the facts necessary to determine whether or not the respondent has violated a certain provision of the covered agreements? For example, Article 11.3 of the Agreement on Safeguards prohibits WTO Members from encouraging or supporting non-governmental measures equivalent to a voluntary import or export restraint. How should the panel rule, if the available evidence leaves open whether an alleged act of governmental support has taken place or not? (ii) What level of proof suffices for a panel to establish a fact? Above this level, the panel would consider the fact at issue as established and would base its decision, among other things, upon this fact. In turn, below this level, the panel cannot consider the fact as established; if it is a fact that is necessary to satisfy the legal provision, the panel would rule against the party bearing the burden of proof.

The Appellate Body has recognized that the concept of a burden of proof is implicit in the WTO dispute settlement system. The mere assertion of a claim does not amount to proof. In line with the practice of various international tribunals, the Appellate Body has endorsed the rule that the party who asserts a fact, whether the complainant or the respondent, is responsible for providing proof thereof. The burden of proof rests upon the party, whether complaining or defending, who asserts the affirmative of a particular claim or defence.[23]

This means that the party claiming a violation of a provision of the WTO Agreement (i.e. the complainant) must assert and prove its claim. In turn, the party invoking in defence a provision that is an exception to the allegedly violated obligation (i.e. the respondent) bears the burden of proof that the conditions set out in the exception are met.[24] Such exceptions are, for example, Articles XX and XI:2(c)(i) of GATT 1994.

As regards the required level of proof, the Appellate Body has clarified that the party bearing the burden of proof must put forward evidence sufficient to make a prima facie case (a presumption) that what is claimed is true. When that prima facie case is made, the onus shifts to the other party, who will fail unless it submits sufficient evidence to disprove the claim, thus rebutting the presumption.[25] Precisely

---

[23] Appellate Body Report, *US – Wool Shirts and Blouses*, p. 335.

[24] Appellate Body Report, *US – Wool Shirts and Blouses*, p. 337.

[25] This does not impose a requirement on panels to make an explicit ruling on whether the complainant has established a prima facie case of violation before a panel may proceed to examine the respondent's defence and evidence (*see* Appellate Body Report, *Korea – Dairy*, para. 145). The panel's task is to balance all evidence on record and decide whether the complainant, as party bearing the original burden of proof, has convinced the panel of the validity of its claims (*see* Panel Report, *US – Section 301 Trade Act*, para. 7.14).

how much and precisely what kind of evidence will be required to establish a presumption that what is claimed is true (i.e. what is required to establish a prima facie case) varies from measure to measure, provision to provision, and case to case.[26]

THE PANEL'S RIGHT TO SEEK INFORMATION

Article 13 of the DSU entitles panels to seek information from any appropriate source for the exploration and establishment of the facts necessary to adjudicate in a dispute. This right is broad and comprehensive and its exercise is left to the discretion of the panel.[27] One aspect of Article 13 is the panel's right to resort to experts.[28] In addition, Article 13 has been understood as an unconditional right which includes the panel's right to request and obtain information from the Members who are party to the dispute.[29]

Despite the language in Article 13.1, third sentence, that a Member "should respond promptly and fully" to any request for information, the Appellate Body has ruled that Members, including the parties to the dispute, are under a full legal obligation to surrender the requested information.[30] If a Member violates this obligation by refusing to submit the requested information, the panel has the discretionary right to draw negative inferences from the attitude of the non-cooperating Member.[31] This means it may interpret the factual matter in doubt to the disadvantage of that Member.

THE NATURE OF DOMESTIC LEGISLATION AS AN OBJECT OF A DISPUTE

The characterization of domestic legislation, which becomes the object of dispute settlement, is an interesting aspect relating to the distinction between questions of law and questions of facts. This distinction is relevant, among other things, for the scope of the appellate review.[32]

Domestic law is frequently at issue in disputes. Article XVI:4 of the WTO Agreement provides that "[e]ach Member shall ensure the conformity of its laws, regulations and administrative procedures with its obligations as provided in the annexed Agreements". For example, often in a dispute, a complaint will not address

---

[26] Appellate Body Report, *US – Wool Shirts and Blouses*, p. 335.
[27] Appellate Body Report, *US – Shrimp*, paras. 104 and 106.
[28] *See* above the section on Experts on page 25.
[29] Appellate Body Report, *Canada – Aircraft*, para. 185.
[30] Appellate Body Report, *Canada – Aircraft*, paras. 188 and 189.
[31] Appellate Body Report, *Canada – Aircraft*, paras. 198–203.
[32] *See* above the section on the Object of an appeal on page 66.

whether an internal tax imposed by the respondent on a certain shipment of imports, say imported vodka, was consistent with Article III:2 of GATT 1994. Rather, the complainant will directly challenge the internal tax law as such as being inconsistent with Article III:2 of GATT 1994 where different internal taxes are imposed under the law on two different kinds of "like" products, say shochu and on vodka. In other words, the complaint is directed at the existence of the law rather than a specific application of the law. In such cases, several issues relating to the domestic legislation must be reviewed before the question of its WTO conformity can be decided.

Probably the most important of these issues is whether the domestic legislation in question is mandatory or discretionary in providing for an act in contravention of WTO law. As has already been discussed, Members can successfully challenge laws as such (i.e. the existence of the law itself) only if such laws are mandatory.[33] However, it is not always clear whether a particular domestic law is mandatory or discretionary with respect to WTO-inconsistent acts. The question could depend on a host of factors such as the domestic legal framework, how the law in question operates together with other domestic legal provisions, the relationship between the different branches of government and how the authorities and courts interpret domestic law. A panel would then have to make a determination in light of these factors of whether the law is mandatory or discretionary in the WTO sense. Under domestic law, such determination would certainly be a legal question. However, is it also a legal question within the framework of WTO dispute settlement? If so, the panel's assessment of whether or not the domestic law is mandatory would be subject to appellate review. However, if it is a question of fact, it would not be subject to appellate review. There are other issues relating to the nature, content, and structure of challenged domestic laws or measures that raise the same question: is this a question of law or a question of fact from the perspective of WTO law? The Appellate Body has had an opportunity to express itself on the question of how to qualify, for purposes of WTO law, domestic legal characterizations.

In *India – Patents (US)*, for example, the Appellate Body insisted that it was the panel's task to determine whether India's "administrative instructions" were in conformity with its obligations under the TRIPS Agreement. For that purpose, the panel was entitled to and even obliged to seek a detailed understanding of the operation of the domestic provisions in question. From this, the Appellate Body concluded that it was also necessary for the Appellate Body to review the panel's examination of the same Indian domestic law.[34] In *US – Section 211 Appropriations Act*, the Appellate Body concluded on the basis of its own prior jurisprudence that "municipal law of WTO Members may serve not only as evidence of facts, but also as evidence of compliance or non-compliance with international obligations. . . . Such an assessment is a legal characterization by a panel. And, therefore, a panel's

---

[33] *See* above in the section on Discretionary and mandatory legislation on page 41.
[34] Appellate Body Report, *India – Patents (US)*, paras. 66 and 68.

assessment of municipal law as to its consistency with WTO obligations is subject to appellate review under Article 17.6 of the DSU."[35]

In contrast, the panel in *US – Section 301 Trade Act* stated that it was "called upon to establish the meaning of Sections 301–310 as *factual* elements and to check whether these factual elements constitute conduct by the US contrary to its WTO obligations".[36] Under this approach, it would seem that the panel's establishment of these factual elements would not be a question of law subject to appellate review.

---

[35] Appellate Body Report, *US – Section 211 Appropriations Act*, para. 105.
[36] Panel Report, *US – Section 301 Trade Act*, para. 7.18 (emphasis added).

DEVELOPING COUNTRIES IN WTO DISPUTE SETTLEMENT

Previous chapters have addressed at least in part where the DSU specifically refers to developing country Members and provides for special rules applicable to disputes involving a developing country Member. Nevertheless, these rules providing special and differential treatment are the subject of this separate chapter in order to examine the subject in more detail. This chapter also addresses other aspects of the developing countries' role in the dispute settlement system.

DEVELOPING COUNTRY MEMBERS IN DISPUTE SETTLEMENT – THEORY AND PRACTICE

It is generally agreed that the very existence of a compulsory multilateral dispute settlement system is itself a particular benefit for developing countries and small Members. Such a system, to which all Members have equal access and in which decisions are made on the basis of rules rather than on the basis of economic power, empowers developing countries and smaller economies by placing "the weak" on a more equal footing with "the strong". In this sense, any judicial law enforcement system benefits the weak more than the strong because the strong would always have other means to defend and impose their interests in the absence of a law enforcement system.

Such a view has been challenged by some as being overly formal and theoretical. Nonetheless, it must be noted that, in practice, the WTO dispute settlement system has already offered many examples of developing country Members prevailing in dispute settlement over large trading nations, including the withdrawal of the WTO–inconsistent measures the developing country Member had challenged.

At the same time, it is clear that developing country Members wanting to avail themselves of the benefits of the dispute settlement system face considerable burdens. For example, developing countries, especially the smaller ones, often do not have a sufficient number of specialized human resources who are experts in the intricacies of the substance of WTO law or the dispute settlement procedure. The growing body of jurisprudence developed by panels and the Appellate Body makes it increasingly difficult for trade officials around the globe to master both the substance and the procedural aspects of WTO law, including the latest developments. In addition, it is often difficult for a small trade administration to be able to assign one of its few officials – who already face the challenge of keeping up with the whole breadth of WTO matters – to a dispute. A single dispute could well keep an official busy for large periods of time – up to two years. It may also be difficult for a developing country Member to endure the economic harm arising from another Member's trade barrier for the entire period of the dispute settlement proceedings. If such a trade barrier undermines the export opportunities of the developing country and is found to be inconsistent with the WTO, its withdrawal may not occur until two or three years after the filing of a WTO dispute settlement complaint.

Despite these difficulties, developing country Members have been active participants in the dispute settlement system over the past eight years. Since 1995, they have been the complainants in over one third of all disputes[1] and respondents in roughly two-fifths of all cases. Developing countries initiate disputes against developed country Members as well as against other developing country Members. In one year, 2001, developing country Members accounted for 75 per cent of all complaints. Least-developed country Members have so far been neither complainant nor respondent in any WTO dispute. Third party participation of developing country Members is quite frequent and provides a valuable experience for Members not regularly involved in dispute settlement proceedings.

On the other hand, it is true that in the majority of WTO disputes so far, the complainant has been a developed country Member, and the same is true as far as respondents are concerned. Taking account of the fact that the majority of WTO Members are developing countries, one could conclude that the developed countries make a disproportionate use of the dispute settlement system. Jumping to this conclusion, however, would disregard the fact that these Members, who are complainants and respondents in a majority of WTO disputes, account for most of world-wide trade. They often have trade relationships that are very broad (in all sectors of goods and services) and deep (in terms of the volume of trade in quantity or value). Such trade relationships significantly increase the probability of frictions arising as a result of trade barriers, which the exporting Member may be willing to challenge in dispute settlement.

This, in turn, reveals a problematic reality from the perspective of developing country Members. The moderate trade volume affected by a possibly WTO-incompatible trade barrier maintained by another Member might not always justify the considerable investment of time and money necessary for a WTO dispute. There is thus no question that developing country Members are in a special situation which, to some extent, the current dispute settlement system also addresses. There is also no question that the ability of developing country Members to make effective use of the dispute settlement system is essential for them to be able to reap the full benefits they are entitled to under the WTO Agreement. The tools to address the particular situation of developing country Members are the rules of

---

[1] Every case in which one Member addresses a formal request for consultations to another Member (*see* above the section on the Legal basis and requirements for a request for consultations on page 45) is counted as "dispute" in the sense of the DSU.

special and differential treatment[2] and legal assistance as elaborated in the following sections.

SPECIAL AND DIFFERENTIAL TREATMENT

Special and differential treatment takes a different form in the DSU than in the other covered agreements, which contain the substantive rules governing international trade. The DSU recognizes the special situation of developing and least-developed country Members by making available to them, for example, additional or privileged procedures and legal assistance.

Developing countries may choose a faster procedure, request longer time-limits, or request legal assistance. WTO Members are encouraged to give special consideration to the situation of developing country Members. These rules will be specifically addressed below. Some are applied very frequently, but others have not yet had any practical relevance. A general criticism is that several of these rules are not very specific.

SPECIAL AND DIFFERENTIAL TREATMENT IN CONSULTATIONS

During consultations, Members should give special attention to the particular problems and interests of developing country Members (Article 4.10 of the DSU). If the object of the consultations is a measure taken by a developing country Member, the parties may agree to extend the regular periods of consultation. If, at the end of the consultation period, the parties cannot agree that the consultations have concluded, the DSB chairperson can extend the time-period for consultations (Article 12.10 of the DSU).

SPECIAL AND DIFFERENTIAL TREATMENT AT THE PANEL STAGE

Special and differential treatment is also available at the panel stage. When a dispute is between a developing country Member and a developed country Member the panel must, upon request by the developing country Member, include at least one panelist from a developing country Member (Article 8.10 of the DSU).

If a developing country Member is the respondent, the panel must accord it sufficient time to prepare and present its defence. However, this must not affect the overall time period for the panel to complete the dispute settlement procedure (Article 12.10 of the DSU). One panel has already applied this provision by granting the responding developing country Member, upon request, an additional period of

---

[2] "Special and differential treatment" is a technical term used throughout the WTO Agreement to designate those provisions that are applicable only to developing country Members.

ten days to prepare its first written submission to the panel, despite the complainant's objection.[3]

When a developing country Member is party to a dispute and raises rules on special and differential treatment of the DSU or other covered agreements, the panel report must explicitly indicate the form in which these rules have been taken into account (Article 12.11 of the DSU). This is meant to make transparent how effective these rules have been in a given case and to show how they have actually been applied.

SPECIAL AND DIFFERENTIAL TREATMENT IN IMPLEMENTATION

At the stage of implementation, the DSU mandates that particular attention be paid to matters affecting the interests of developing country Members (Article 21.2 of the DSU). This provision has already been applied repeatedly by arbitrators acting under Article 21.3(c) of the DSU[4] in their determination of the reasonable period of time for implementation.[5] One arbitrator has, relying on Article 21.2 of the DSU, explicitly granted an additional period of six months for implementation in the particular circumstances of the case.[6]

In the framework of supervising the implementation, the DSB must consider what further and appropriate action it might take in addition to surveillance and status reports,[7] if a developing country Member has raised the matter (Article 21.7 of the DSU). In considering what appropriate action to take in a case brought by a developing country Member, the DSB has to consider not only the trade coverage of the challenged measures, but also their impact on the economy of developing country Members concerned (Article 21.8 of the DSU).

ACCELERATED PROCEDURE AT THE REQUEST OF A DEVELOPING COUNTRY MEMBER – DECISION OF 5 APRIL 1966

If a developing country Member brings a complaint against a developed country Member, the complaining party has the discretionary right to invoke, as an alternative to the provisions in Articles 4, 5, 6 and 12 of the DSU, the accelerated procedures of the Decision of 5 April 1966.[8] The rules and procedures of the 1966 Decision prevail over the corresponding rules and procedures of Articles 4, 5, 6 and 12 of the DSU to the extent that there is a difference (Article 3.12 of the DSU).

---

[3] Panel Report, *India – Quantitative Restrictions*, para. 5.10.
[4] *See* above in the section on the Time-period for implementation on page 76.
[5] Award of the Arbitrator, *Indonesia – Autos (Article 21.3)*, para. 24; Award of the Arbitrator on *Chile – Alcoholic Beverages (Article 21.3)*, para. 45; Award of the Arbitrator, *Argentina – Hides and Leather*.
[6] Award of the Arbitrator, *Indonesia – Autos (Article 21.3)*, para. 24.
[7] *See* above in the section on the Surveillance by the DSB on page 78.
[8] BISD 14S/18. The Decision of 1966 is also reproduced in the Annex on page 185.

This Decision provides, first, that the Director-General may use his good offices, and conduct consultations at the request of the developing country with a view to facilitating a solution to the dispute, where the consultations between the parties have failed. Second, if these consultations conducted by the Director-General do not bring about a mutually satisfactory solution within two months, the Director-General submits, at the request of one of the parties, a report on his action. The DSB then establishes the panel with the approval of the parties. Third, the panel must take due account of all circumstances and considerations relating to the application of the challenged measures, and their impact on the trade and economic development of the affected Members. Fourth, the Decision provides for only 60 days for the panel to submit its findings from the date the matter was referred to it. Where the Panel considers this time-frame insufficient it may extend it with the agreement of the complaining party.

The time-frames of the Decision were applied only once under GATT 1947,[9] but have not yet been applied in the WTO. In practice, developing country Members tend to prefer to have more time to prepare their submissions. However, they often insist that the panel respect the overall time-frames for the completion of the procedure.

LEAST-DEVELOPED COUNTRY MEMBERS INVOLVED IN A DISPUTE

All of the above rules of special and differential treatment apply to least-developed country Members, which are included in the group of developing country Members. In addition, the DSU sets out a few particular rules applicable only to least-developed country Members.

Where a least-developed country Member is involved in a dispute, particular consideration must be given to the special situation of that Member at all stages of the dispute. Members must exercise due restraint in bringing disputes against a least-developed country Member and in asking for compensation or seeking authorization to suspend obligations against a least-developed country Member that has "lost" a dispute (Article 24.1 of the DSU).

For disputes involving a least-developed country Member, the DSU also specifically foresees good offices, conciliation and mediation. Where consultations have not resulted in a satisfactory solution and the least-developed country Member so requests, the Director-General or the Chairman of the DSB must offer their good offices, conciliation and mediation. The aim is to assist the parties to settle the dispute before the establishment of a panel. In providing such assistance, the Director-General or the Chairman of the DSB, may consult any source either considers appropriate (Article 24.2 of the DSU).

---

[9] Panel Report, *EEC (Member States) – Bananas I.*

LEGAL ASSISTANCE

The WTO Secretariat assists all Members in respect of dispute settlement at their request, but it provides additional legal advice and assistance to developing country Members. To this end, the Secretariat is required to make available a qualified legal expert from the WTO technical cooperation services to any developing country member which so requests (Article 27.2 of the DSU).

The Institute for Training and Technical Cooperation, a division in the WTO Secretariat, currently employs one full-time official and, on a permanent part-time basis, two independent consultants for this purpose. These experts must assist the developing country Member in a way that respects the continued impartiality of the Secretariat (Article 27.2 of the DSU).

The WTO Secretariat also runs technical cooperation activities in Geneva and in the capitals of Members by conducting special training courses concerning the dispute settlement system (Article 27.3 of the DSU). The courses that take place in Geneva are also accessible for representatives of developed country Members.

REPRESENTATION BY PRIVATE COUNSEL AND THE ADVISORY CENTRE ON WTO LAW

As already mentioned,[10] private legal counsel may appear before panels and the Appellate Body as part of a party's delegation. Also, private law firms often participate in the preparation of the parties' written submissions to a panel or the Appellate Body. This is important for developing country Members, as it may enable them to take part in dispute settlement proceedings even when they lack human resources with specific expertise in WTO dispute settlement.[11] Resorting to private law firms, however, is costly, especially because lawyers specialized and experienced in WTO law are mostly established in the capitals of developed countries (e.g. Washington, Brussels, Geneva, Paris and London).

Developing country Members can receive effective assistance in dispute settlement from the recently established, Geneva-based Advisory Centre on WTO Law. The Advisory Centre is a "legal aid" centre in the form of an independent intergovernmental organization. It is separate and independent from the WTO. It was established by an international agreement signed by 29 Members of the WTO in Seattle on 1 December 1999, the "Agreement Establishing the Advisory Centre on WTO Law". This Agreement entered into force on 15 June 2001 and the official opening of the Advisory Centre took place on 5 October 2001. There are currently some 30 members. Every WTO Member, whether a developing country or not, as well as countries and independent customs territories in the process of accession to the WTO, can become members of the Advisory Centre.

---

[10] *See* above in the section on Legal representation on page 97.
[11] Appellate Body Report, *EC – Bananas III*, para. 12.

The Advisory Centre functions essentially as a law office specializing in WTO law. It provides legal services and training to developing countries or countries with economies in transition, as well as to all least-developed countries that are WTO Members or accession candidates. The legal services fall into two categories. First, the Advisory Centre provides legal assistance in WTO dispute settlement proceedings. This means representing WTO Members throughout dispute settlement proceedings (e.g. by drafting documents addressed to the DSB, submissions to panels and the Appellate Body and by appearing on behalf of those Members before panels and the Appellate Body). Since July 2001, the Advisory Centre has regularly represented developing country Members in WTO disputes. For these services, the "clients" pay (discounted) rates at varying levels that depend on the level of economic development and on whether they are members of the Advisory Centre.

Second, the Advisory Centre provides legal advice on matters that are not or not yet the subject of a WTO dispute settlement proceeding. These services are free of charge for all least-developed countries and members of the Advisory Centre that are developing countries or countries with economies in transition up to a certain amount of hours. The Advisory Centre also provides legal assistance, at a commercial rate, to developing countries that are not its members. The Advisory Centre also provides training on WTO dispute settlement and plans to offer paid internships in order to contribute to capacity building (by enhancing the WTO expertise of developing country officials). The staff of the Advisory Centre is small, but comprises legal experts, some with long experience in matters of WTO law in general and WTO dispute settlement in particular.

EVALUATION OF THE WTO DISPUTE SETTLEMENT SYSTEM: RESULTS TO DATE

STATISTICS: THE FIRST EIGHT YEARS OF EXPERIENCE

The first eight and a half years of the operation of the WTO dispute settlement system (from January 1995 to June 2003) have produced the following numbers. In total, Members have filed 295 requests for consultations over that period. In 124 of those 295 disputes, or in 42 per cent of the cases, a developing country Member was the complainant. Since 2000, developing country Members were the complainants in nearly two-thirds of all complaints (69 out of 110). In one year, 2001, developing country Members filed three quarters of all requests for consultations.

The annual number of requests for consultations peaked in 1997 with 50 requests, then fell to 40 in 1998 and, since then, has fluctuated between 23 and 37. The covered agreement most frequently invoked by complainants has been the GATT 1994. In a distant second place are the SCM Agreement, the Agreement on Agriculture and the Anti-Dumping Agreement. So far, the TRIPS Agreement and the GATS have rarely been invoked as the basis of a dispute. Very often, complainants invoke more than one agreement in their request for consultations.

The DSB established 110 panels between January 1995 and June 2003, which shows that consultations are often able to settle the disputes. In the same period, the DSB adopted 71 panel reports and 47 Appellate Body reports. While the parties appealed nearly every single panel report in the early years of the dispute settlement system, the appeal rate has significantly decreased over the past few years.

There have been 14 compliance disputes under Article 21.5 of the DSU.[1] Only seven times has the DSB granted authorization to a complainant to suspend obligations, and in all seven cases, arbitration took place because the respondent disagreed with the complainant's proposal for the suspension.

ACHIEVEMENT OF THE OBJECTIVES?

The above statistics support the conclusion that, on the whole, the operation of the dispute settlement system has been a success. The large number of cases in which parties invoked the dispute settlement system in the first eight and a half years of

---

[1] *See* above the section on Compliance review under Article 21.5 of the DSU on page 79.

the WTO (which is already significantly larger than the number of disputes brought under GATT 1947 during a period of nearly 50 years) suggests that Members have faith in the system. It appears that the WTO dispute settlement system has fulfilled its main function: to contribute to the settlement of trade disputes. Moreover, the reports of panels and the Appellate Body have served to provide clarification of the rights and obligations contained in the covered agreements (Article 3.2 of the DSU).

The fact that many cases do not go through all stages of the process – as one moves forward in the dispute settlement procedure from consultations to panels and the Appellate Body to compliance reviews and finally to the authorization of suspension – is to some extent a positive sign. In most cases, it is not necessary to have recourse to retaliation in the dispute settlement system because most cases are resolved at earlier stages.

STRENGTHS AND WEAKNESSES

The system has both strengths and weaknesses. For example, with respect to its weaknesses, despite the deadlines, a full dispute settlement procedure still takes a considerable amount of time, during which the complainant suffers continued economic harm if the challenged measure is indeed WTO-inconsistent. No provisional measures (interim relief) are available to protect the economic and trade interests of the successful complainant during the dispute settlement procedure. Moreover, even after prevailing in dispute settlement, a successful complainant will receive no compensation for the harm suffered during the time given to the respondent to implement the ruling. Nor does the "winning party" receive any reimbursement from the other side for its legal expenses. In the event of non-implementation, not all Members have the same practical ability to resort to the suspension of obligations.[2] Lastly, in a few cases, a suspension of concessions has been ineffective in bringing about implementation. However, these cases are the exception rather than the rule.

How successful one considers the dispute settlement system to have been depends on the benchmark one applies. If one compares the WTO dispute settlement system with the previous dispute settlement system of GATT 1947, the current system has been far more effective. Moreover, its quasi-judicial and quasi-automatic character enables it to handle more difficult cases. These features also provide greater guarantees for Members that wish to defend their rights. Compared with other multilateral systems of dispute resolution in international law, the compulsory nature and the enforcement mechanism of the WTO dispute settlement system certainly stand out.

---

[2] *See* above in the section on Prerequisites for Countermeasures by the prevailing Member (suspension of obligations) on page 81.

CURRENT NEGOTIATIONS

Although there is broad consensus that the current WTO dispute settlement system has worked reasonably well, there is also a widely shared view that improvements are desirable. Since the new WTO dispute settlement system was substantially different from the old system, the ministers of the WTO Members called for a full review of the DSU within four years after the entry into force of the WTO Agreement when they concluded the Uruguay Round.[3] This review started in 1997 but did not result in any agreed outcomes.

Building "on the work done thus far", the Doha Ministerial Declaration contained a mandate for "negotiations on improvements and clarifications" of the DSU.[4] Despite intensive negotiations over the past year and a half[5] and significant progress in many areas, Members were unable to conclude negotiations by the end of the deadline stipulated in the Doha Ministerial Declaration (end of May 2003). A proposal to extend the deadline until May 2004 was agreed by the General Council at its meeting in July 2003.[6]

---

[3] Marrakesh Ministerial *Decision on the Application and Review of the Understanding on Rules and Procedures Governing the Settlement of Disputes* of 14 April 1994.

[4] World Trade Organization, *Ministerial Declaration, Fourth Session of the Ministerial Conference*, WT/MIN(01)/DEC/1, 9–14 November 2001, para. 30.

[5] The Members' reform proposals tabled to date are accessible at http://www.wto.org/english/tratop_e/dispu_e/dispu_e.htm.

[6] WT/GC/M/81.

FURTHER INFORMATION

GLOSSARY

All documents produced in the WTO dispute settlement system (with the exception of the parties' submissions) are public. They are accessible via the dispute settlement gateway of the WTO's website: http://www.wto.org/english/ tratop_e/dispu_e/dispu_e.htm.

This section will briefly explain the symbols of the most important WTO dispute settlement documents. The main categories of documents are:

WT/DSB	Documents of the Dispute Settlement Body (minutes of meetings, indicative list of panelists, annual reports etc.)
WT/AB	Documents of the Appellate Body outside of the framework of disputes (Working Procedures for Appellate Review)
WT/DS	WTO dispute settlement documents (from the requests for consultations to the authorization of the suspension of obligations)

WTO dispute settlement (WT/DS) documents can be looked for and recognized as follows:

WT/DSnumber/1	Requests for consultations
WT/DSnumber/##	Requests for the establishment of a panel, requests for arbitration, status reports, notification of appeals, decision of arbitrators under Article 21.3(c) of the DSU etc.
WT/DSnumber/R/	Panel reports
WT/DSnumber/RW	Panel reports in compliance reviews under Article 21.5 of the DSU
WT/DSnumber/AB/R/	Appellate Body reports
WT/DSnumber/AB/RW/	Appellate Body reports in compliance reviews under Article 21.5 of the DSU
WT/DSnumber/ARB	Decisions of the Arbitrators under Article 22.6 of the DSU
WT/DS/OV/##	Update of WTO dispute settlement cases

INFORMATION AND DOCUMENTS ON THE WTO WEBSITE

The above documents are accessible on the WTO website. The following sites are particularly relevant for the dispute settlement system:

Dispute settlement gateway	http://www.wto.org/english/tratop_e/dispu_e/dispu_e.htm
Panel and Appellate Body report	http://www.wto.org/english/tratop_e/dispu_e/dispu_status_e.htm
Legal Texts (WTO agreements)	http://www.wto.org/english/docs_e/legal_e/legal_e.htm
GATT panel reports	http://www.wto.org/english/tratop_e/dispu_e/gt47ds_e.htm
Official Documents of the WTO	http://docsonline.wto.org/gen_home.asp

The WTO's Documents Online database (http://docsonline.wto.org) allows users to search for all WTO documents. One can search for documents using their documents symbols, numbers, key words, or by date.

REFERENCE BOOKS

The first edition of the WTO Analytical Index[1] has recently been published. The WTO Analytical Index contains excerpts from documents relating to the application of the entire WTO Agreement and the development of WTO law. It includes a chapter on the DSU containing extracts from panel and Appellate Body reports relating to the various articles of the DSU.

For the dispute settlement practice under GATT 1947, the GATT Analytical Index[2] remains relevant.

CONTACTING THE WTO

At the WTO Secretariat, the Legal Affairs Division has general responsibility for administration of the dispute settlement system. Disputes under the Anti-Dumping Agreement and the SCM Agreement fall within the particular responsibility of the Rules Division.[3] The Appellate Body, which handles the appellate review of panel reports, has its own Secretariat.[4] These divisions can be reached as follows:

---

[1] *WTO Analytical Index: Guide to WTO Law and Practice*, 1st edition (2003).
[2] World Trade Organization, *Analytical Index: Guide to GATT Law and Practice*, Vols. 1 and 2 (6th ed., 1995).
[3] *See* above in the section on Administrative and legal support on page 22.
[4] *See* above in the section on Appellate Body on page 22.

Legal Affairs Division: Tel: (+41)/(0) 22 739 52 48
Fax: (+41)/(0) 22 739 57 88
Rules Division: Tel: (+41)/(0) 22 739 51 09
Fax: (+41)/(0) 22 739 55 05
Appellate Body Secretariat: Tel: (+41)/(0) 22 739 51 30
Fax: (+41)/(0) 22 739 57 86
Information and Media   Tel: (+41)/(0) 22 739 50 07/51 90
Relations Division: Fax: (+41)/(0) 22 739 54 58
E-mail: enquiries@wto.org
WTO Publications: Tel: (+41)/(0) 22 739 52 08/53 08
Fax: (+41)/(0) 22 739 57 92
E-mail: publications@wto.org
Mailing address of the WTO: 154 rue de Lausanne, 1211 Geneva 21,
Switzerland

ANNEX
LEGAL TEXTS

Provisions on consultation and dispute settlement in GATT 1994, GATS and the TRIPS Agreement

THE GENERAL AGREEMENT ON TARIFFS AND TRADE 1994

Article XXII

Consultation

1.   Each contracting party shall accord sympathetic consideration to, and shall afford adequate opportunity for consultation regarding, such representations as may be made by another contracting party with respect to any matter affecting the operation of this Agreement.

2.   The CONTRACTING PARTIES may, at the request of a contracting party, consult with any contracting party or parties in respect of any matter for which it has not been possible to find a satisfactory solution through consultation under paragraph 1.

Article XXIII

Nullification or Impairment

1.   If any contracting party should consider that any benefit accruing to it directly or indirectly under this Agreement is being nullified or impaired or that the attainment of any objective of the Agreement is being impeded as the result of

   (a) the failure of another contracting party to carry out its obligations under this Agreement, or
   (b) the application by another contracting party of any measure, whether or not it conflicts with the provisions of this Agreement, or
   (c) the existence of any other situation,

the contracting party may, with a view to the satisfactory adjustment of the matter, make written representations or proposals to the other contracting party or parties which it considers to be concerned. Any contracting party thus approached shall give sympathetic consideration to the representations or proposals made to it.

2.   If no satisfactory adjustment is effected between the Contracting Parties concerned within a reasonable time, or if the difficulty is of the type described in paragraph 1 (*c*) of this Article, the matter may be referred to the CONTRACTING PARTIES. The CONTRACTING PARTIES shall promptly investigate any matter

so referred to them and shall make appropriate recommendations to the Contracting Parties which they consider to be concerned, or give a ruling on the matter, as appropriate. The CONTRACTING PARTIES may consult with Contracting Parties, with the Economic and Social Council of the United Nations and with any appropriate inter-governmental organization in cases where they consider such consultation necessary. If the CONTRACTING PARTIES consider that the circumstances are serious enough to justify such action, they may authorize a contracting party or parties to suspend the application to any other contracting party or parties of such concessions or other obligations under this Agreement as they determine to be appropriate in the circumstances. If the application to any contracting party of any concession or other obligation is in fact suspended, that contracting party shall then be free, not later than sixty days after such action is taken, to give written notice to the Executive Secretary[1] to the Contracting Parties of its intention to withdraw from this Agreement and such withdrawal shall take effect upon the sixtieth day following the day on which such notice is received by him.

GENERAL AGREEMENT ON TRADE IN SERVICES

Article XXII

Consultation

1. Each Member shall accord sympathetic consideration to, and shall afford adequate opportunity for, consultation regarding such representations as may be made by any other Member with respect to any matter affecting the operation of this Agreement. The Dispute Settlement Understanding (DSU) shall apply to such consultations.

2. The Council for Trade in Services or the Dispute Settlement Body (DSB) may, at the request of a Member, consult with any Member or Members in respect of any matter for which it has not been possible to find a satisfactory solution through consultation under paragraph 1.

3. A Member may not invoke Article XVII, either under this Article or Article XXIII, with respect to a measure of another Member that falls within the scope of an international agreement between them relating to the avoidance of double taxation. In case of disagreement between Members as to whether a measure falls within the scope of such an agreement between them, it shall be open to either Member to bring this matter before the Council for Trade in Services.[2] The Council shall refer the matter to arbitration. The decision of the arbitrator shall be final and binding on the Members.

---

[1] (footnote original) By the Decision of 23 March 1965, the CONTRACTING PARTIES changed the title of the head of the GATT secretariat from "Executive Secretary" to "Director-General".

[2] (footnote original) With respect to agreements on the avoidance of double taxation which exist on the date of entry into force of the WTO Agreement, such a matter may be brought before the Council for Trade in Services only with the consent of both parties to such an agreement.

Article XXIII

Dispute Settlement and Enforcement

1.   If any Member should consider that any other Member fails to carry out its obligations or specific commitments under this Agreement, it may with a view to reaching a mutually satisfactory resolution of the matter have recourse to the DSU.

2.   If the DSB considers that the circumstances are serious enough to justify such action, it may authorize a Member or Members to suspend the application to any other Member or Members of obligations and specific commitments in accordance with Article 22 of the DSU.

3.   If any Member considers that any benefit it could reasonably have expected to accrue to it under a specific commitment of another Member under Part III of this Agreement is being nullified or impaired as a result of the application of any measure which does not conflict with the provisions of this Agreement, it may have recourse to the DSU. If the measure is determined by the DSB to have nullified or impaired such a benefit, the Member affected shall be entitled to a mutually satisfactory adjustment on the basis of paragraph 2 of Article XXI, which may include the modification or withdrawal of the measure. In the event an agreement cannot be reached between the Members concerned, Article 22 of the DSU shall apply.

AGREEMENT ON TRADE-RELATED ASPECTS OF
INTELLECTUAL PROPERTY RIGHTS

Article 64

Dispute Settlement

1.   The provisions of Articles XXII and XXIII of GATT 1994 as elaborated and applied by the Dispute Settlement Understanding shall apply to consultations and the settlement of disputes under this Agreement except as otherwise specifically provided herein.

2.   Subparagraphs 1(b) and 1(c) of Article XXIII of GATT 1994 shall not apply to the settlement of disputes under this Agreement for a period of five years from the date of entry into force of the WTO Agreement.

3.   During the time period referred to in paragraph 2, the Council for TRIPS shall examine the scope and modalities for complaints of the type provided for under subparagraphs 1(b) and 1(c) of Article XXIII of GATT 1994 made pursuant to this Agreement, and submit its recommendations to the Ministerial Conference for approval. Any decision of the Ministerial Conference to approve such recommendations or to extend the period in paragraph 2 shall be made only by consensus, and approved recommendations shall be effective for all Members without further formal acceptance process.

Understanding on Rules and Procedures Governing the Settlement of Disputes

Members hereby *agree* as follows:

Article 1

Coverage and Application

1. The rules and procedures of this Understanding shall apply to disputes brought pursuant to the consultation and dispute settlement provisions of the agreements listed in Appendix 1 to this Understanding (referred to in this Understanding as the "covered agreements"). The rules and procedures of this Understanding shall also apply to consultations and the settlement of disputes between Members concerning their rights and obligations under the provisions of the Agreement Establishing the World Trade Organization (referred to in this Understanding as the "WTO Agreement") and of this Understanding taken in isolation or in combination with any other covered agreement.

2. The rules and procedures of this Understanding shall apply subject to such special or additional rules and procedures on dispute settlement contained in the covered agreements as are identified in Appendix 2 to this Understanding. To the extent that there is a difference between the rules and procedures of this Understanding and the special or additional rules and procedures set forth in Appendix 2, the special or additional rules and procedures in Appendix 2 shall prevail. In disputes involving rules and procedures under more than one covered agreement, if there is a conflict between special or additional rules and procedures of such agreements under review, and where the parties to the dispute cannot agree on rules and procedures within 20 days of the establishment of the panel, the Chairman of the Dispute Settlement Body provided for in paragraph 1 of Article 2 (referred to in this Understanding as the "DSB"), in consultation with the parties to the dispute, shall determine the rules and procedures to be followed within ten days after a request by either Member. The Chairman shall be guided by the principle that special or additional rules and procedures should be used where possible, and the rules and procedures set out in this Understanding should be used to the extent necessary to avoid conflict.

Article 2

Administration

1. The Dispute Settlement Body is hereby established to administer these rules and procedures and, except as otherwise provided in a covered agreement, the consultation and dispute settlement provisions of the covered agreements. Accordingly, the DSB shall have the authority to establish panels, adopt panel and Appellate Body reports, maintain surveillance of implementation of rulings and recommendations,

and authorize suspension of concessions and other obligations under the covered agreements. With respect to disputes arising under a covered agreement which is a Plurilateral Trade Agreement, the term "Member" as used herein shall refer only to those Members that are parties to the relevant Plurilateral Trade Agreement. Where the DSB administers the dispute settlement provisions of a Plurilateral Trade Agreement, only those Members that are parties to that Agreement may participate in decisions or actions taken by the DSB with respect to that dispute.

2.   The DSB shall inform the relevant WTO Councils and Committees of any developments in disputes related to provisions of the respective covered agreements.

3.   The DSB shall meet as often as necessary to carry out its functions within the time-frames provided in this Understanding.

4.   Where the rules and procedures of this Understanding provide for the DSB to take a decision, it shall do so by consensus.[1]

Article 3

General Provisions

1.   Members affirm their adherence to the principles for the management of disputes heretofore applied under Articles XXII and XXIII of GATT 1947, and the rules and procedures as further elaborated and modified herein.

2.   The dispute settlement system of the WTO is a central element in providing security and predictability to the multilateral trading system. The Members recognize that it serves to preserve the rights and obligations of Members under the covered agreements, and to clarify the existing provisions of those agreements in accordance with customary rules of interpretation of public international law. Recommendations and rulings of the DSB cannot add to or diminish the rights and obligations provided in the covered agreements.

3.   The prompt settlement of situations in which a Member considers that any benefits accruing to it directly or indirectly under the covered agreements are being impaired by measures taken by another Member is essential to the effective functioning of the WTO and the maintenance of a proper balance between the rights and obligations of Members.

4.   Recommendations or rulings made by the DSB shall be aimed at achieving a satisfactory settlement of the matter in accordance with the rights and obligations under this Understanding and under the covered agreements.

5.   All solutions to matters formally raised under the consultation and dispute settlement provisions of the covered agreements, including arbitration awards, shall be consistent with those agreements and shall not nullify or impair benefits accruing

---

[1]   (footnote original) The DSB shall be deemed to have decided by consensus on a matter submitted for its consideration, if no Member, present at the meeting of the DSB when the decision is taken, formally objects to the proposed decision.

to any Member under those agreements, nor impede the attainment of any objective of those agreements.

6.   Mutually agreed solutions to matters formally raised under the consultation and dispute settlement provisions of the covered agreements shall be notified to the DSB and the relevant Councils and Committees, where any Member may raise any point relating thereto.

7.   Before bringing a case, a Member shall exercise its judgement as to whether action under these procedures would be fruitful. The aim of the dispute settlement mechanism is to secure a positive solution to a dispute. A solution mutually acceptable to the parties to a dispute and consistent with the covered agreements is clearly to be preferred. In the absence of a mutually agreed solution, the first objective of the dispute settlement mechanism is usually to secure the withdrawal of the measures concerned if these are found to be inconsistent with the provisions of any of the covered agreements. The provision of compensation should be resorted to only if the immediate withdrawal of the measure is impracticable and as a temporary measure pending the withdrawal of the measure which is inconsistent with a covered agreement. The last resort which this Understanding provides to the Member invoking the dispute settlement procedures is the possibility of suspending the application of concessions or other obligations under the covered agreements on a discriminatory basis vis-à-vis the other Member, subject to authorization by the DSB of such measures.

8.   In cases where there is an infringement of the obligations assumed under a covered agreement, the action is considered *prima facie* to constitute a case of nullification or impairment. This means that there is normally a presumption that a breach of the rules has an adverse impact on other Members parties to that covered agreement, and in such cases, it shall be up to the Member against whom the complaint has been brought to rebut the charge.

9.   The provisions of this Understanding are without prejudice to the rights of Members to seek authoritative interpretation of provisions of a covered agreement through decision-making under the WTO Agreement or a covered agreement which is a Plurilateral Trade Agreement.

10.   It is understood that requests for conciliation and the use of the dispute settlement procedures should not be intended or considered as contentious acts and that, if a dispute arises, all Members will engage in these procedures in good faith in an effort to resolve the dispute. It is also understood that complaints and counter-complaints in regard to distinct matters should not be linked.

11.   This Understanding shall be applied only with respect to new requests for consultations under the consultation provisions of the covered agreements made on or after the date of entry into force of the WTO Agreement. With respect to disputes for which the request for consultations was made under GATT 1947 or under any other predecessor agreement to the covered agreements before the date of entry into force of the WTO Agreement, the relevant dispute settlement rules

and procedures in effect immediately prior to the date of entry into force of the WTO Agreement shall continue to apply.[2]

12. Notwithstanding paragraph 11, if a complaint based on any of the covered agreements is brought by a developing country Member against a developed country Member, the complaining party shall have the right to invoke, as an alternative to the provisions contained in Articles 4, 5, 6 and 12 of this Understanding, the corresponding provisions of the Decision of 5 April 1966 (BISD 14S/18), except that where the Panel considers that the time-frame provided for in paragraph 7 of that Decision is insufficient to provide its report and with the agreement of the complaining party, that time-frame may be extended. To the extent that there is a difference between the rules and procedures of Articles 4, 5, 6 and 12 and the corresponding rules and procedures of the Decision, the latter shall prevail.

Article 4

Consultations

1. Members affirm their resolve to strengthen and improve the effectiveness of the consultation procedures employed by Members.

2. Each Member undertakes to accord sympathetic consideration to and afford adequate opportunity for consultation regarding any representations made by another Member concerning measures affecting the operation of any covered agreement taken within the territory of the former.[3]

3. If a request for consultations is made pursuant to a covered agreement, the Member to which the request is made shall, unless otherwise mutually agreed, reply to the request within ten days after the date of its receipt and shall enter into consultations in good faith within a period of no more than 30 days after the date of receipt of the request, with a view to reaching a mutually satisfactory solution. If the Member does not respond within ten days after the date of receipt of the request, or does not enter into consultations within a period of no more than 30 days, or a period otherwise mutually agreed, after the date of receipt of the request, then the Member that requested the holding of consultations may proceed directly to request the establishment of a panel.

4. All such requests for consultations shall be notified to the DSB and the relevant Councils and Committees by the Member which requests consultations. Any request for consultations shall be submitted in writing and shall give the reasons for the request, including identification of the measures at issue and an indication of the legal basis for the complaint.

---

[2] (footnote original) This paragraph shall also be applied to disputes on which panel reports have not been adopted or fully implemented.

[3] (footnote original) Where the provisions of any other covered agreement concerning measures taken by regional or local governments or authorities within the territory of a Member contain provisions different from the provisions of this paragraph, the provisions of such other covered agreement shall prevail.

5.   In the course of consultations in accordance with the provisions of a covered agreement, before resorting to further action under this Understanding, Members should attempt to obtain satisfactory adjustment of the matter.

6.   Consultations shall be confidential, and without prejudice to the rights of any Member in any further proceedings.

7.   If the consultations fail to settle a dispute within 60 days after the date of receipt of the request for consultations, the complaining party may request the establishment of a panel. The complaining party may request a panel during the 60-day period if the consulting parties jointly consider that consultations have failed to settle the dispute.

8.   In cases of urgency, including those which concern perishable goods, Members shall enter into consultations within a period of no more than ten days after the date of receipt of the request. If the consultations have failed to settle the dispute within a period of 20 days after the date of receipt of the request, the complaining party may request the establishment of a panel.

9.   In cases of urgency, including those which concern perishable goods, the parties to the dispute, panels and the Appellate Body shall make every effort to accelerate the proceedings to the greatest extent possible.

10.   During consultations Members should give special attention to the particular problems and interests of developing country Members.

11.   Whenever a Member other than the consulting Members considers that it has a substantial trade interest in consultations being held pursuant to paragraph 1 of Article XXII of GATT 1994, paragraph 1 of Article XXII of GATS, or the corresponding provisions in other covered agreements,[4] such Member may notify the consulting Members and the DSB, within ten days after the date of the circulation of the request for consultations under said Article, of its desire to be joined in the consultations. Such Member shall be joined in the consultations, provided that the Member to which the request for consultations was addressed agrees that the claim of substantial interest is well-founded. In that event they shall so inform the DSB. If the request to be joined in the consultations is not accepted, the applicant Member shall be free to request consultations under paragraph 1 of Article XXII or paragraph 1 of Article XXIII of GATT 1994, paragraph 1 of Article XXII or

---

[4]   (footnote original) The corresponding consultation provisions in the covered agreements are listed hereunder: Agreement on Agriculture, Article 19; Agreement on the Application of Sanitary and Phytosanitary Measures, paragraph 1 of Article 11; Agreement on Textiles and Clothing, paragraph 4 of Article 8; Agreement on Technical Barriers to Trade, paragraph 1 of Article 14; Agreement on Trade-Related Investment Measures, Article 8; Agreement on Implementation of Article VI of GATT 1994, paragraph 2 of Article 17; Agreement on Implementation of Article VII of GATT 1994, paragraph 2 of Article 19; Agreement on Preshipment Inspection, Article 7; Agreement on Rules of Origin, Article 7; Agreement on Import Licensing Procedures, Article 6; Agreement on Subsidies and Countervailing Measures, Article 30; Agreement on Safeguards, Article 14; Agreement on Trade-Related Aspects of Intellectual Property Rights, Article 64.1; and any corresponding consultation provisions in Plurilateral Trade Agreements as determined by the competent bodies of each Agreement and as notified to the DSB.

paragraph 1 of Article XXIII of GATS, or the corresponding provisions in other covered agreements.

Article 5

Good Offices, Conciliation and Mediation

1.   Good offices, conciliation and mediation are procedures that are undertaken voluntarily if the parties to the dispute so agree.

2.   Proceedings involving good offices, conciliation and mediation, and in particular positions taken by the parties to the dispute during these proceedings, shall be confidential, and without prejudice to the rights of either party in any further proceedings under these procedures.

3.   Good offices, conciliation or mediation may be requested at any time by any party to a dispute. They may begin at any time and be terminated at any time. Once procedures for good offices, conciliation or mediation are terminated, a complaining party may then proceed with a request for the establishment of a panel.

4.   When good offices, conciliation or mediation are entered into within 60 days after the date of receipt of a request for consultations, the complaining party must allow a period of 60 days after the date of receipt of the request for consultations before requesting the establishment of a panel. The complaining party may request the establishment of a panel during the 60-day period if the parties to the dispute jointly consider that the good offices, conciliation or mediation process has failed to settle the dispute.

5.   If the parties to a dispute agree, procedures for good offices, conciliation or mediation may continue while the panel process proceeds.

6.   The Director-General may, acting in an *ex officio* capacity, offer good offices, conciliation or mediation with the view to assisting Members to settle a dispute.

Article 6

Establishment of Panels

1.   If the complaining party so requests, a panel shall be established at the latest at the DSB meeting following that at which the request first appears as an item on the DSB's agenda, unless at that meeting the DSB decides by consensus not to establish a panel.[5]

2.   The request for the establishment of a panel shall be made in writing. It shall indicate whether consultations were held, identify the specific measures at issue and provide a brief summary of the legal basis of the complaint sufficient to present the problem clearly. In case the applicant requests the establishment of a panel

---

[5]   (footnote original) If the complaining party so requests, a meeting of the DSB shall be convened for this purpose within 15 days of the request, provided that at least ten days' advance notice of the meeting is given.

with other than standard terms of reference, the written request shall include the proposed text of special terms of reference.

Article 7

Terms of Reference of Panels

1.   Panels shall have the following terms of reference unless the parties to the dispute agree otherwise within 20 days from the establishment of the panel:

> "To examine, in the light of the relevant provisions in (name of the covered agreement(s) cited by the parties to the dispute), the matter referred to the DSB by (name of party) in document ... and to make such findings as will assist the DSB in making the recommendations or in giving the rulings provided for in that/those agreement(s)."

2.   Panels shall address the relevant provisions in any covered agreement or agreements cited by the parties to the dispute.

3.   In establishing a panel, the DSB may authorize its Chairman to draw up the terms of reference of the panel in consultation with the parties to the dispute, subject to the provisions of paragraph 1. The terms of reference thus drawn up shall be circulated to all Members. If other than standard terms of reference are agreed upon, any Member may raise any point relating thereto in the DSB.

Article 8

Composition of Panels

1.   Panels shall be composed of well-qualified governmental and/or non-governmental individuals, including persons who have served on or presented a case to a panel, served as a representative of a Member or of a contracting party to GATT 1947 or as a representative to the Council or Committee of any covered agreement or its predecessor agreement, or in the Secretariat, taught or published on international trade law or policy, or served as a senior trade policy official of a Member.

2.   Panel members should be selected with a view to ensuring the independence of the members, a sufficiently diverse background and a wide spectrum of experience.

3.   Citizens of Members whose governments[6] are parties to the dispute or third parties as defined in paragraph 2 of Article 10 shall not serve on a panel concerned with that dispute, unless the parties to the dispute agree otherwise.

4.   To assist in the selection of panelists, the Secretariat shall maintain an indicative list of governmental and non-governmental individuals possessing the qualifications

---

[6]   (footnote original) In the case where customs unions or common markets are parties to a dispute, this provision applies to citizens of all member countries of the customs unions or common markets.

outlined in paragraph 1, from which panelists may be drawn as appropriate. That list shall include the roster of non-governmental panelists established on 30 November 1984 (BISD 31S/9), and other rosters and indicative lists established under any of the covered agreements, and shall retain the names of persons on those rosters and indicative lists at the time of entry into force of the WTO Agreement. Members may periodically suggest names of governmental and non-governmental individuals for inclusion on the indicative list, providing relevant information on their knowledge of international trade and of the sectors or subject matter of the covered agreements, and those names shall be added to the list upon approval by the DSB. For each of the individuals on the list, the list shall indicate specific areas of experience or expertise of the individuals in the sectors or subject matter of the covered agreements.

5.   Panels shall be composed of three panelists unless the parties to the dispute agree, within ten days from the establishment of the panel, to a panel composed of five panelists. Members shall be informed promptly of the composition of the panel.

6.   The Secretariat shall propose nominations for the panel to the parties to the dispute. The parties to the dispute shall not oppose nominations except for compelling reasons.

7.   If there is no agreement on the panelists within 20 days after the date of the establishment of a panel, at the request of either party, the Director-General, in consultation with the Chairman of the DSB and the Chairman of the relevant Council or Committee, shall determine the composition of the panel by appointing the panelists whom the Director-General considers most appropriate in accordance with any relevant special or additional rules or procedures of the covered agreement or covered agreements which are at issue in the dispute, after consulting with the parties to the dispute. The Chairman of the DSB shall inform the Members of the composition of the panel thus formed no later than ten days after the date the Chairman receives such a request.

8.   Members shall undertake, as a general rule, to permit their officials to serve as panelists.

9.   Panelists shall serve in their individual capacities and not as government representatives, nor as representatives of any organization. Members shall therefore not give them instructions nor seek to influence them as individuals with regard to matters before a panel.

10.   When a dispute is between a developing country Member and a developed country Member the panel shall, if the developing country Member so requests, include at least one panelist from a developing country Member.

11.   Panelists' expenses, including travel and subsistence allowance, shall be met from the WTO budget in accordance with criteria to be adopted by the General Council, based on recommendations of the Committee on Budget, Finance and Administration.

Article 9

Procedures for Multiple Complainants

1. Where more than one Member requests the establishment of a panel related to the same matter, a single panel may be established to examine these complaints taking into account the rights of all Members concerned. A single panel should be established to examine such complaints whenever feasible.

2. The single panel shall organize its examination and present its findings to the DSB in such a manner that the rights which the parties to the dispute would have enjoyed had separate panels examined the complaints are in no way impaired. If one of the parties to the dispute so requests, the panel shall submit separate reports on the dispute concerned. The written submissions by each of the complainants shall be made available to the other complainants, and each complainant shall have the right to be present when any one of the other complainants presents its views to the panel.

3. If more than one panel is established to examine the complaints related to the same matter, to the greatest extent possible the same persons shall serve as panelists on each of the separate panels and the timetable for the panel process in such disputes shall be harmonized.

Article 10

Third Parties

1. The interests of the parties to a dispute and those of other Members under a covered agreement at issue in the dispute shall be fully taken into account during the panel process.

2. Any Member having a substantial interest in a matter before a panel and having notified its interest to the DSB (referred to in this Understanding as a "third party") shall have an opportunity to be heard by the panel and to make written submissions to the panel. These submissions shall also be given to the parties to the dispute and shall be reflected in the panel report.

3. Third parties shall receive the submissions of the parties to the dispute to the first meeting of the panel.

4. If a third party considers that a measure already the subject of a panel proceeding nullifies or impairs benefits accruing to it under any covered agreement, that Member may have recourse to normal dispute settlement procedures under this Understanding. Such a dispute shall be referred to the original panel wherever possible.

Article 11

Function of Panels

The function of panels is to assist the DSB in discharging its responsibilities under this Understanding and the covered agreements. Accordingly, a panel should make an objective assessment of the matter before it, including an objective assessment of the facts of the case and the applicability of and conformity with the relevant covered agreements, and make such other findings as will assist the DSB in making the recommendations or in giving the rulings provided for in the covered agreements. Panels should consult regularly with the parties to the dispute and give them adequate opportunity to develop a mutually satisfactory solution.

Article 12

Panel Procedures

1.   Panels shall follow the Working Procedures in Appendix 3 unless the panel decides otherwise after consulting the parties to the dispute.

2.   Panel procedures should provide sufficient flexibility so as to ensure high-quality panel reports, while not unduly delaying the panel process.

3.   After consulting the parties to the dispute, the panelists shall, as soon as practicable and whenever possible within one week after the composition and terms of reference of the panel have been agreed upon, fix the timetable for the panel process, taking into account the provisions of paragraph 9 of Article 4, if relevant.

4.   In determining the timetable for the panel process, the panel shall provide sufficient time for the parties to the dispute to prepare their submissions.

5.   Panels should set precise deadlines for written submissions by the parties and the parties should respect those deadlines.

6.   Each party to the dispute shall deposit its written submissions with the Secretariat for immediate transmission to the panel and to the other party or parties to the dispute. The complaining party shall submit its first submission in advance of the responding party's first submission unless the panel decides, in fixing the timetable referred to in paragraph 3 and after consultations with the parties to the dispute, that the parties should submit their first submissions simultaneously. When there are sequential arrangements for the deposit of first submissions, the panel shall establish a firm time-period for receipt of the responding party's submission. Any subsequent written submissions shall be submitted simultaneously.

7.   Where the parties to the dispute have failed to develop a mutually satisfactory solution, the panel shall submit its findings in the form of a written report to the DSB. In such cases, the report of a panel shall set out the findings of fact, the applicability of relevant provisions and the basic rationale behind any findings and recommendations that it makes. Where a settlement of the matter among the parties to the dispute has been found, the report of the panel shall be confined to a brief description of the case and to reporting that a solution has been reached.

8.   In order to make the procedures more efficient, the period in which the panel shall conduct its examination, from the date that the composition and terms of reference of the panel have been agreed upon until the date the final report is issued

to the parties to the dispute, shall, as a general rule, not exceed six months. In cases of urgency, including those relating to perishable goods, the panel shall aim to issue its report to the parties to the dispute within three months.

9.   When the panel considers that it cannot issue its report within six months, or within three months in cases of urgency, it shall inform the DSB in writing of the reasons for the delay together with an estimate of the period within which it will issue its report. In no case should the period from the establishment of the panel to the circulation of the report to the Members exceed nine months.

10.   In the context of consultations involving a measure taken by a developing country Member, the parties may agree to extend the periods established in paragraphs 7 and 8 of Article 4. If, after the relevant period has elapsed, the consulting parties cannot agree that the consultations have concluded, the Chairman of the DSB shall decide, after consultation with the parties, whether to extend the relevant period and, if so, for how long. In addition, in examining a complaint against a developing country Member, the panel shall accord sufficient time for the developing country Member to prepare and present its argumentation. The provisions of paragraph 1 of Article 20 and paragraph 4 of Article 21 are not affected by any action pursuant to this paragraph.

11.   Where one or more of the parties is a developing country Member, the panel's report shall explicitly indicate the form in which account has been taken of relevant provisions on differential and more-favourable treatment for developing country Members that form part of the covered agreements which have been raised by the developing country Member in the course of the dispute settlement procedures.

12.   The panel may suspend its work at any time at the request of the complaining party for a period not to exceed 12 months. In the event of such a suspension, the time-frames set out in paragraphs 8 and 9 of this Article, paragraph 1 of Article 20, and paragraph 4 of Article 21 shall be extended by the amount of time that the work was suspended. If the work of the panel has been suspended for more than 12 months, the authority for establishment of the panel shall lapse.

Article 13

Right to Seek Information

1.   Each panel shall have the right to seek information and technical advice from any individual or body which it deems appropriate. However, before a panel seeks such information or advice from any individual or body within the jurisdiction of a Member it shall inform the authorities of that Member. A Member should respond promptly and fully to any request by a panel for such information as the panel considers necessary and appropriate. Confidential information which is provided shall not be revealed without formal authorization from the individual, body, or authorities of the Member providing the information.

2.   Panels may seek information from any relevant source and may consult experts to obtain their opinion on certain aspects of the matter. With respect to a factual issue concerning a scientific or other technical matter raised by a party to a dispute, a panel may request an advisory report in writing from an expert review group. Rules for the establishment of such a group and its procedures are set forth in Appendix 4.

Article 14

Confidentiality

1.   Panel deliberations shall be confidential.

2.   The reports of panels shall be drafted without the presence of the parties to the dispute in the light of the information provided and the statements made.

3.   Opinions expressed in the panel report by individual panelists shall be anonymous.

Article 15

Interim Review Stage

1.   Following the consideration of rebuttal submissions and oral arguments, the panel shall issue the descriptive (factual and argument) sections of its draft report to the parties to the dispute. Within a period of time set by the panel, the parties shall submit their comments in writing.

2.   Following the expiration of the set period of time for receipt of comments from the parties to the dispute, the panel shall issue an interim report to the parties, including both the descriptive sections and the panel's findings and conclusions. Within a period of time set by the panel, a party may submit a written request for the panel to review precise aspects of the interim report prior to circulation of the final report to the Members. At the request of a party, the panel shall hold a further meeting with the parties on the issues identified in the written comments. If no comments are received from any party within the comment period, the interim report shall be considered the final panel report and circulated promptly to the Members.

3.   The findings of the final panel report shall include a discussion of the arguments made at the interim review stage. The interim review stage shall be conducted within the time-period set out in paragraph 8 of Article 12.

Article 16

Adoption of Panel Reports

1.   In order to provide sufficient time for the Members to consider panel reports, the reports shall not be considered for adoption by the DSB until 20 days after the date they have been circulated to the Members.

2. Members having objections to a panel report shall give written reasons to explain their objections for circulation at least ten days prior to the DSB meeting at which the panel report will be considered.

3. The parties to a dispute shall have the right to participate fully in the consideration of the panel report by the DSB, and their views shall be fully recorded.

4. Within 60 days after the date of circulation of a panel report to the Members, the report shall be adopted at a DSB meeting[7] unless a party to the dispute formally notifies the DSB of its decision to appeal or the DSB decides by consensus not to adopt the report. If a party has notified its decision to appeal, the report by the panel shall not be considered for adoption by the DSB until after completion of the appeal. This adoption procedure is without prejudice to the right of Members to express their views on a panel report.

Article 17

Appellate Review: Standing Appellate Body

1. A standing Appellate Body shall be established by the DSB. The Appellate Body shall hear appeals from panel cases. It shall be composed of seven persons, three of whom shall serve on any one case. Persons serving on the Appellate Body shall serve in rotation. Such rotation shall be determined in the working procedures of the Appellate Body.

2. The DSB shall appoint persons to serve on the Appellate Body for a four-year term, and each person may be reappointed once. However, the terms of three of the seven persons appointed immediately after the entry into force of the WTO Agreement shall expire at the end of two years, to be determined by lot. Vacancies shall be filled as they arise. A person appointed to replace a person whose term of office has not expired shall hold office for the remainder of the predecessor's term.

3. The Appellate Body shall comprise persons of recognized authority, with demonstrated expertise in law, international trade and the subject matter of the covered agreements generally. They shall be unaffiliated with any government. The Appellate Body membership shall be broadly representative of membership in the WTO. All persons serving on the Appellate Body shall be available at all times and on short notice, and shall stay abreast of dispute settlement activities and other relevant activities of the WTO. They shall not participate in the consideration of any disputes that would create a direct or indirect conflict of interest.

4. Only parties to the dispute, not third parties, may appeal a panel report. Third parties which have notified the DSB of a substantial interest in the matter pursuant to paragraph 2 of Article 10 may make written submissions to, and be given an opportunity to be heard by, the Appellate Body.

---

[7] (footnote original) If a meeting of the DSB is not scheduled within this period at a time that enables the requirements of paragraphs 1 and 4 of Article 16 to be met, a meeting of the DSB shall be held for this purpose.

5.   As a general rule, the proceedings shall not exceed 60 days from the date a party to the dispute formally notifies its decision to appeal to the date the Appellate Body circulates its report. In fixing its timetable the Appellate Body shall take into account the provisions of paragraph 9 of Article 4, if relevant. When the Appellate Body considers that it cannot provide its report within 60 days, it shall inform the DSB in writing of the reasons for the delay together with an estimate of the period within which it will submit its report. In no case shall the proceedings exceed 90 days.

6.   An appeal shall be limited to issues of law covered in the panel report and legal interpretations developed by the panel.

7.   The Appellate Body shall be provided with appropriate administrative and legal support as it requires.

8.   The expenses of persons serving on the Appellate Body, including travel and subsistence allowance, shall be met from the WTO budget in accordance with criteria to be adopted by the General Council, based on recommendations of the Committee on Budget, Finance and Administration.

Procedures for Appellate Review

9.   Working procedures shall be drawn up by the Appellate Body in consultation with the Chairman of the DSB and the Director-General, and communicated to the Members for their information.

10.   The proceedings of the Appellate Body shall be confidential. The reports of the Appellate Body shall be drafted without the presence of the parties to the dispute and in the light of the information provided and the statements made.

11.   Opinions expressed in the Appellate Body report by individuals serving on the Appellate Body shall be anonymous.

12.   The Appellate Body shall address each of the issues raised in accordance with paragraph 6 during the appellate proceeding.

13.   The Appellate Body may uphold, modify or reverse the legal findings and conclusions of the panel.

Adoption of Appellate Body Reports

14.   An Appellate Body report shall be adopted by the DSB and unconditionally accepted by the parties to the dispute unless the DSB decides by consensus not to adopt the Appellate Body report within 30 days following its circulation to the Members.[8] This adoption procedure is without prejudice to the right of Members to express their views on an Appellate Body report.

---

[8]   (footnote original) If a meeting of the DSB is not scheduled during this period, such a meeting of the DSB shall be held for this purpose.

Article 18

Communications with the Panel or Appellate Body

1.   There shall be no *ex parte* communications with the panel or Appellate Body concerning matters under consideration by the panel or Appellate Body.

2.   Written submissions to the panel or the Appellate Body shall be treated as confidential, but shall be made available to the parties to the dispute. Nothing in this Understanding shall preclude a party to a dispute from disclosing statements of its own positions to the public. Members shall treat as confidential information submitted by another Member to the panel or the Appellate Body which that Member has designated as confidential. A party to a dispute shall also, upon request of a Member, provide a non-confidential summary of the information contained in its written submissions that could be disclosed to the public.

Article 19

Panel and Appellate Body Recommendations

1.   Where a panel or the Appellate Body concludes that a measure is inconsistent with a covered agreement, it shall recommend that the Member concerned[9] bring the measure into conformity with that agreement.[10] In addition to its recommendations, the panel or Appellate Body may suggest ways in which the Member concerned could implement the recommendations.

2.   In accordance with paragraph 2 of Article 3, in their findings and recommendations, the panel and Appellate Body cannot add to or diminish the rights and obligations provided in the covered agreements.

Article 20

Time-frame for DSB Decisions

Unless otherwise agreed to by the parties to the dispute, the period from the date of establishment of the panel by the DSB until the date the DSB considers the panel or appellate report for adoption shall as a general rule not exceed nine months where the panel report is not appealed or 12 months where the report is appealed. Where either the panel or the Appellate Body has acted, pursuant to paragraph 9 of Article 12 or paragraph 5 of Article 17, to extend the time for providing its report, the additional time taken shall be added to the above periods.

---

[9]   (footnote original) The "Member concerned" is the party to the dispute to which the panel or Appellate Body recommendations are directed.

[10]   (footnote original) With respect to recommendations in cases not involving a violation of GATT 1994 or any other covered agreement, see Article 26.

Article 21

Surveillance of Implementation of Recommendations and Rulings

1. Prompt compliance with recommendations or rulings of the DSB is essential in order to ensure effective resolution of disputes to the benefit of all Members.

2. Particular attention should be paid to matters affecting the interests of developing country Members with respect to measures which have been subject to dispute settlement.

3. At a DSB meeting held within 30 days[11] after the date of adoption of the panel or Appellate Body report, the Member concerned shall inform the DSB of its intentions in respect of implementation of the recommendations and rulings of the DSB. If it is impracticable to comply immediately with the recommendations and rulings, the Member concerned shall have a reasonable period of time in which to do so. The reasonable period of time shall be:

> (a) the period of time proposed by the Member concerned, provided that such period is approved by the DSB; or, in the absence of such approval,
>
> (b) a period of time mutually agreed by the parties to the dispute within 45 days after the date of adoption of the recommendations and rulings; or, in the absence of such agreement,
>
> (c) a period of time determined through binding arbitration within 90 days after the date of adoption of the recommendations and rulings.[12] In such arbitration, a guideline for the arbitrator[13] should be that the reasonable period of time to implement panel or Appellate Body recommendations should not exceed 15 months from the date of adoption of a panel or Appellate Body report. However, that time may be shorter or longer, depending upon the particular circumstances.

4. Except where the panel or the Appellate Body has extended, pursuant to paragraph 9 of Article 12 or paragraph 5 of Article 17, the time of providing its report, the period from the date of establishment of the panel by the DSB until the date of determination of the reasonable period of time shall not exceed 15 months unless the parties to the dispute agree otherwise. Where either the panel or the Appellate Body has acted to extend the time of providing its report, the additional time taken shall be added to the 15-month period; provided that unless the parties to the dispute agree that there are exceptional circumstances, the total time shall not exceed 18 months.

---

[11] (footnote original) If a meeting of the DSB is not scheduled during this period, such a meeting of the DSB shall be held for this purpose.

[12] (footnote original) If the parties cannot agree on an arbitrator within ten days after referring the matter to arbitration, the arbitrator shall be appointed by the Director-General within ten days, after consulting the parties.

[13] (footnote original) The expression "arbitrator" shall be interpreted as referring either to an individual or a group.

5.   Where there is disagreement as to the existence or consistency with a covered agreement of measures taken to comply with the recommendations and rulings such dispute shall be decided through recourse to these dispute settlement procedures, including wherever possible resort to the original panel. The panel shall circulate its report within 90 days after the date of referral of the matter to it. When the panel considers that it cannot provide its report within this time frame, it shall inform the DSB in writing of the reasons for the delay together with an estimate of the period within which it will submit its report.

6.   The DSB shall keep under surveillance the implementation of adopted recommendations or rulings. The issue of implementation of the recommendations or rulings may be raised at the DSB by any Member at any time following their adoption. Unless the DSB decides otherwise, the issue of implementation of the recommendations or rulings shall be placed on the agenda of the DSB meeting after six months following the date of establishment of the reasonable period of time pursuant to paragraph 3 and shall remain on the DSB's agenda until the issue is resolved. At least ten days prior to each such DSB meeting, the Member concerned shall provide the DSB with a status report in writing of its progress in the implementation of the recommendations or rulings.

7.   If the matter is one which has been raised by a developing country Member, the DSB shall consider what further action it might take which would be appropriate to the circumstances.

8.   If the case is one brought by a developing country Member, in considering what appropriate action might be taken, the DSB shall take into account not only the trade coverage of measures complained of, but also their impact on the economy of developing country Members concerned.

Article 22

Compensation and the Suspension of Concessions

1.   Compensation and the suspension of concessions or other obligations are temporary measures available in the event that the recommendations and rulings are not implemented within a reasonable period of time. However, neither compensation nor the suspension of concessions or other obligations is preferred to full implementation of a recommendation to bring a measure into conformity with the covered agreements. Compensation is voluntary and, if granted, shall be consistent with the covered agreements.

2.   If the Member concerned fails to bring the measure found to be inconsistent with a covered agreement into compliance therewith or otherwise comply with the recommendations and rulings within the reasonable period of time determined pursuant to paragraph 3 of Article 21, such Member shall, if so requested, and no later than the expiry of the reasonable period of time, enter into negotiations with any party having invoked the dispute settlement procedures, with a view to developing mutually acceptable compensation. If no satisfactory compensation has been agreed

within 20 days after the date of expiry of the reasonable period of time, any party having invoked the dispute settlement procedures may request authorization from the DSB to suspend the application to the Member concerned of concessions or other obligations under the covered agreements.

3. In considering what concessions or other obligations to suspend, the complaining party shall apply the following principles and procedures:

(a) the general principle is that the complaining party should first seek to suspend concessions or other obligations with respect to the same sector(s) as that in which the panel or Appellate Body has found a violation or other nullification or impairment;

(b) if that party considers that it is not practicable or effective to suspend concessions or other obligations with respect to the same sector(s), it may seek to suspend concessions or other obligations in other sectors under the same agreement;

(c) if that party considers that it is not practicable or effective to suspend concessions or other obligations with respect to other sectors under the same agreement, and that the circumstances are serious enough, it may seek to suspend concessions or other obligations under another covered agreement;

(d) in applying the above principles, that party shall take into account:

    (i) the trade in the sector or under the agreement under which the panel or Appellate Body has found a violation or other nullification or impairment, and the importance of such trade to that party;

    (ii) the broader economic elements related to the nullification or impairment and the broader economic consequences of the suspension of concessions or other obligations;

(e) if that party decides to request authorization to suspend concessions or other obligations pursuant to subparagraphs (b) or (c), it shall state the reasons therefor in its request. At the same time as the request is forwarded to the DSB, it also shall be forwarded to the relevant Councils and also, in the case of a request pursuant to subparagraph (b), the relevant sectoral bodies;

(f) for purposes of this paragraph, "sector" means:

    (i) with respect to goods, all goods;

    (ii) with respect to services, a principal sector as identified in the current "Services Sectoral Classification List" which identifies such sectors;[14]

    (iii) with respect to trade-related intellectual property rights, each of the categories of intellectual property rights covered in Section 1, or Section 2, or Section 3, or Section 4, or Section 5, or Section 6, or

---

[14] (footnote original) The list in document MTN.GNS/W/120 identifies eleven sectors.

Section 7 of Part II, or the obligations under Part III, or Part IV of the Agreement on TRIPS;

(g) for purposes of this paragraph, "agreement" means:

(i) with respect to goods, the agreements listed in Annex 1A of the WTO Agreement, taken as a whole as well as the Plurilateral Trade Agreements in so far as the relevant parties to the dispute are parties to these agreements;

(ii) with respect to services, the GATS;

(iii) with respect to intellectual property rights, the Agreement on TRIPS.

4.   The level of the suspension of concessions or other obligations authorized by the DSB shall be equivalent to the level of the nullification or impairment.

5.   The DSB shall not authorize suspension of concessions or other obligations if a covered agreement prohibits such suspension.

6.   When the situation described in paragraph 2 occurs, the DSB, upon request, shall grant authorization to suspend concessions or other obligations within 30 days of the expiry of the reasonable period of time unless the DSB decides by consensus to reject the request. However, if the Member concerned objects to the level of suspension proposed, or claims that the principles and procedures set forth in paragraph 3 have not been followed where a complaining party has requested authorization to suspend concessions or other obligations pursuant to paragraph 3(b) or (c), the matter shall be referred to arbitration. Such arbitration shall be carried out by the original panel, if members are available, or by an arbitrator[15] appointed by the Director-General and shall be completed within 60 days after the date of expiry of the reasonable period of time. Concessions or other obligations shall not be suspended during the course of the arbitration.

7.   The arbitrator[16] acting pursuant to paragraph 6 shall not examine the nature of the concessions or other obligations to be suspended but shall determine whether the level of such suspension is equivalent to the level of nullification or impairment. The arbitrator may also determine if the proposed suspension of concessions or other obligations is allowed under the covered agreement. However, if the matter referred to arbitration includes a claim that the principles and procedures set forth in paragraph 3 have not been followed, the arbitrator shall examine that claim. In the event the arbitrator determines that those principles and procedures have not been followed, the complaining party shall apply them consistent with paragraph 3. The parties shall accept the arbitrator's decision as final and the parties concerned shall not seek a second arbitration. The DSB shall be informed promptly of the decision of the arbitrator and shall upon request, grant authorization to suspend

---

[15] (footnote original) The expression "arbitrator" shall be interpreted as referring either to an individual or a group.

[16] (footnote original) The expression "arbitrator" shall be interpreted as referring either to an individual or a group or to the members of the original panel when serving in the capacity of arbitrator.

concessions or other obligations where the request is consistent with the decision of the arbitrator, unless the DSB decides by consensus to reject the request.

8.   The suspension of concessions or other obligations shall be temporary and shall only be applied until such time as the measure found to be inconsistent with a covered agreement has been removed, or the Member that must implement recommendations or rulings provides a solution to the nullification or impairment of benefits, or a mutually satisfactory solution is reached. In accordance with paragraph 6 of Article 21, the DSB shall continue to keep under surveillance the implementation of adopted recommendations or rulings, including those cases where compensation has been provided or concessions or other obligations have been suspended but the recommendations to bring a measure into conformity with the covered agreements have not been implemented.

9.   The dispute settlement provisions of the covered agreements may be invoked in respect of measures affecting their observance taken by regional or local governments or authorities within the territory of a Member. When the DSB has ruled that a provision of a covered agreement has not been observed, the responsible Member shall take such reasonable measures as may be available to it to ensure its observance. The provisions of the covered agreements and this Understanding relating to compensation and suspension of concessions or other obligations apply in cases where it has not been possible to secure such observance.[17]

Article 23

Strengthening of the Multilateral System

1.   When Members seek the redress of a violation of obligations or other nullification or impairment of benefits under the covered agreements or an impediment to the attainment of any objective of the covered agreements, they shall have recourse to, and abide by, the rules and procedures of this Understanding.

2.   In such cases, Members shall:

   (a) not make a determination to the effect that a violation has occurred, that benefits have been nullified or impaired or that the attainment of any objective of the covered agreements has been impeded, except through recourse to dispute settlement in accordance with the rules and procedures of this Understanding, and shall make any such determination consistent with the findings contained in the panel or Appellate Body report adopted by the DSB or an arbitration award rendered under this Understanding;

   (b) follow the procedures set forth in Article 21 to determine the reasonable period of time for the Member concerned to implement the recommendations and rulings; and

---

[17]   (footnote original) Where the provisions of any covered agreement concerning measures taken by regional or local governments or authorities within the territory of a Member contain provisions different from the provisions of this paragraph, the provisions of such covered agreement shall prevail.

(c) follow the procedures set forth in Article 22 to determine the level of suspension of concessions or other obligations and obtain DSB authorization
in accordance with those procedures before suspending concessions or
other obligations under the covered agreements in response to the failure
of the Member concerned to implement the recommendations and rulings
within that reasonable period of time.

Article 24

Special Procedures Involving Least-Developed Country Members

1. At all stages of the determination of the causes of a dispute and of dispute settlement procedures involving a least-developed country Member, particular consideration shall be given to the special situation of least-developed country Members.
In this regard, Members shall exercise due restraint in raising matters under these
procedures involving a least-developed country Member. If nullification or impairment is found to result from a measure taken by a least-developed country
Member, complaining parties shall exercise due restraint in asking for compensation or seeking authorization to suspend the application of concessions or other
obligations pursuant to these procedures.

2. In dispute settlement cases involving a least-developed country Member, where
a satisfactory solution has not been found in the course of consultations the Director-
General or the Chairman of the DSB shall, upon request by a least-developed
country Member offer their good offices, conciliation and mediation with a view to
assisting the parties to settle the dispute, before a request for a panel is made. The
Director-General or the Chairman of the DSB, in providing the above assistance,
may consult any source which either deems appropriate.

Article 25

Arbitration

1. Expeditious arbitration within the WTO as an alternative means of dispute
settlement can facilitate the solution of certain disputes that concern issues that are
clearly defined by both parties.

2. Except as otherwise provided in this Understanding, resort to arbitration shall
be subject to mutual agreement of the parties which shall agree on the procedures
to be followed. Agreements to resort to arbitration shall be notified to all Members
sufficiently in advance of the actual commencement of the arbitration process.

3. Other Members may become party to an arbitration proceeding only upon the
agreement of the parties which have agreed to have recourse to arbitration. The
parties to the proceeding shall agree to abide by the arbitration award. Arbitration
awards shall be notified to the DSB and the Council or Committee of any relevant
agreement where any Member may raise any point relating thereto.

4.   Articles 21 and 22 of this Understanding shall apply *mutatis mutandis* to arbitration awards.

Article 26

1. Non-Violation Complaints of the Type Described in Paragraph 1(b) of Article XXIII of GATT 1994

Where the provisions of paragraph 1(b) of Article XXIII of GATT 1994 are applicable to a covered agreement, a panel or the Appellate Body may only make rulings and recommendations where a party to the dispute considers that any benefit accruing to it directly or indirectly under the relevant covered agreement is being nullified or impaired or the attainment of any objective of that Agreement is being impeded as a result of the application by a Member of any measure, whether or not it conflicts with the provisions of that Agreement. Where and to the extent that such party considers and a panel or the Appellate Body determines that a case concerns a measure that does not conflict with the provisions of a covered agreement to which the provisions of paragraph 1(b) of Article XXIII of GATT 1994 are applicable, the procedures in this Understanding shall apply, subject to the following:

(a)   the complaining party shall present a detailed justification in support of any complaint relating to a measure which does not conflict with the relevant covered agreement;

(b)   where a measure has been found to nullify or impair benefits under, or impede the attainment of objectives, of the relevant covered agreement without violation thereof, there is no obligation to withdraw the measure. However, in such cases, the panel or the Appellate Body shall recommend that the Member concerned make a mutually satisfactory adjustment;

(c)   notwithstanding the provisions of Article 21, the arbitration provided for in paragraph 3 of Article 21, upon request of either party, may include a determination of the level of benefits which have been nullified or impaired, and may also suggest ways and means of reaching a mutually satisfactory adjustment; such suggestions shall not be binding upon the parties to the dispute;

(d)   notwithstanding the provisions of paragraph 1 of Article 22, compensation may be part of a mutually satisfactory adjustment as final settlement of the dispute.

2. Complaints of the Type Described in Paragraph 1(c) of Article XXIII of GATT 1994

Where the provisions of paragraph 1(c) of Article XXIII of GATT 1994 are applicable to a covered agreement, a panel may only make rulings and recommendations where a party considers that any benefit accruing to it directly or indirectly under the relevant covered agreement is being nullified or impaired or the attainment of any objective of that Agreement is being impeded as a result of the existence of any situation other than those to which the provisions of paragraphs 1(a) and 1(b) of Article XXIII of GATT 1994 are applicable. Where and to the extent that such party considers and a panel determines that the matter is covered by this paragraph, the procedures of this Understanding shall apply only up to and including the point in the proceedings where the panel report has been circulated to the Members. The dispute settlement rules and procedures contained in the Decision of 12 April 1989 (BISD 36S/61–67) shall apply to consideration for adoption, and surveillance and implementation of recommendations and rulings. The following shall also apply:

(a) the complaining party shall present a detailed justification in support of any argument made with respect to issues covered under this paragraph;

(b) in cases involving matters covered by this paragraph, if a panel finds that cases also involve dispute settlement matters other than those covered by this paragraph, the panel shall circulate a report to the DSB addressing any such matters and a separate report on matters falling under this paragraph.

Article 27

Responsibilities of the Secretariat

1.   The Secretariat shall have the responsibility of assisting panels, especially on the legal, historical and procedural aspects of the matters dealt with, and of providing secretarial and technical support.

2.   While the Secretariat assists Members in respect of dispute settlement at their request, there may also be a need to provide additional legal advice and assistance in respect of dispute settlement to developing country Members. To this end, the Secretariat shall make available a qualified legal expert from the WTO technical cooperation services to any developing country Member which so requests. This expert shall assist the developing country Member in a manner ensuring the continued impartiality of the Secretariat.

3.   The Secretariat shall conduct special training courses for interested Members concerning these dispute settlement procedures and practices so as to enable Members' experts to be better informed in this regard.

APPENDIX 1

AGREEMENTS COVERED BY THE UNDERSTANDING

(A)   Agreement Establishing the World Trade Organization

(B)   Multilateral Trade Agreements

Annex 1A: Multilateral Agreements on Trade in Goods

Annex 1B: General Agreement on Trade in Services

Annex 1C: Agreement on Trade-Related Aspects of Intellectual Property Rights

    Annex 2:   Understanding on Rules and Procedures Governing the
                      Settlement of Disputes
(C)   Plurilateral Trade Agreements
    Annex 4:   Agreement on Trade in Civil Aircraft
                      Agreement on Government Procurement
                      International Dairy Agreement
                      International Bovine Meat Agreement

The applicability of this Understanding to the Plurilateral Trade Agreements shall be subject to the adoption of a decision by the parties to each agreement setting out the terms for the application of the Understanding to the individual agreement, including any special or additional rules or procedures for inclusion in Appendix 2, as notified to the DSB.

APPENDIX 2

SPECIAL OR ADDITIONAL RULES AND PROCEDURES CONTAINED IN THE COVERED AGREEMENTS

Agreement	*Rules and Procedures*
Agreement on the Application of Sanitary and Phytosanitary Measures	11.2
Agreement on Textiles and Clothing	2.14, 2.21, 4.4, 5.2, 5.4, 5.6, 6.9, 6.10, 6.11, 8.1 through 8.12
Agreement on Technical Barriers to Trade	14.2 through 14.4, Annex 2
Agreement on Implementation of Article VI of GATT 1994	17.4 through 17.7
Agreement on Implementation of Article VII of GATT 1994	19.3 through 19.5, Annex II.2(f), 3, 9, 21
Agreement on Subsidies and Countervailing Measures	4.2 through 4.12, 6.6, 7.2 through 7.10, 8.5, footnote 35, 24.4, 27.7, Annex V
General Agreement on Trade in Services	XXII:3, XXIII:3
Annex on Financial Services	4
Annex on Air Transport Services	4
Decision on Certain Dispute Settlement Procedures for the GATS	1 through 5

The list of rules and procedures in this Appendix includes provisions where only a part of the provision may be relevant in this context.

    Any special or additional rules or procedures in the Plurilateral Trade Agreements as determined by the competent bodies of each agreement and as notified to the DSB.

APPENDIX 3

WORKING PROCEDURES

1. In its proceedings the panel shall follow the relevant provisions of this Understanding. In addition, the following working procedures shall apply.

2. The panel shall meet in closed session. The parties to the dispute, and interested parties, shall be present at the meetings only when invited by the panel to appear before it.

3. The deliberations of the panel and the documents submitted to it shall be kept confidential. Nothing in this Understanding shall preclude a party to a dispute from disclosing statements of its own positions to the public. Members shall treat as confidential information submitted by another Member to the panel which that Member has designated as confidential. Where a party to a dispute submits a confidential version of its written submissions to the panel, it shall also, upon request of a Member, provide a non-confidential summary of the information contained in its submissions that could be disclosed to the public.

4. Before the first substantive meeting of the panel with the parties, the parties to the dispute shall transmit to the panel written submissions in which they present the facts of the case and their arguments.

5. At its first substantive meeting with the parties, the panel shall ask the party which has brought the complaint to present its case. Subsequently, and still at the same meeting, the party against which the complaint has been brought shall be asked to present its point of view.

6. All third parties which have notified their interest in the dispute to the DSB shall be invited in writing to present their views during a session of the first substantive meeting of the panel set aside for that purpose. All such third parties may be present during the entirety of this session.

7. Formal rebuttals shall be made at a second substantive meeting of the panel. The party complained against shall have the right to take the floor first to be followed by the complaining party. The parties shall submit, prior to that meeting, written rebuttals to the panel.

8. The panel may at any time put questions to the parties and ask them for explanations either in the course of a meeting with the parties or in writing.

9. The parties to the dispute and any third party invited to present its views in accordance with Article 10 shall make available to the panel a written version of their oral statements.

10. In the interest of full transparency, the presentations, rebuttals and statements referred to in paragraphs 5 to 9 shall be made in the presence of the parties. Moreover, each party's written submissions, including any comments on the descriptive part of the report and responses to questions put by the panel, shall be made available to the other party or parties.

11.   Any additional procedures specific to the panel.

12.   Proposed timetable for panel work:

    (a)   Receipt of first written submissions of the parties:
        (1)   complaining Party: —   3–6 weeks
        (2)   Party complained against: —   2–3 weeks
    (b)   Date, time and place of first substantive meeting with
        the parties; third party session: —   1–2 weeks
    (c)   Receipt of written rebuttals of the parties: —   2–3 weeks
    (d)   Date, time and place of second substantive meeting
        with the parties: —   1–2 weeks
    (e)   Issuance of descriptive part of the report to the
        parties: —   2–4 weeks
    (f)   Receipt of comments by the parties on the
        descriptive part of the report: —   2 weeks
    (g)   Issuance of the interim report, including the findings
        and conclusions, to the parties: —   2–4 weeks
    (h)   Deadline for party to request review of part(s) of
        report: —   1 week
    (i)   Period of review by panel, including possible
        additional meeting with parties: —   2 weeks
    (j)   Issuance of final report to parties to dispute: —   2 weeks
    (k)   Circulation of the final report to the Members: —   3 weeks

The above calendar may be changed in the light of unforeseen developments. Additional meetings with the parties shall be scheduled if required.

APPENDIX 4

EXPERT REVIEW GROUPS

The following rules and procedures shall apply to expert review groups established in accordance with the provisions of paragraph 2 of Article 13.

1.   Expert review groups are under the panel's authority. Their terms of reference and detailed working procedures shall be decided by the panel, and they shall report to the panel.

2.   Participation in expert review groups shall be restricted to persons of professional standing and experience in the field in question.

3.   Citizens of parties to the dispute shall not serve on an expert review group without the joint agreement of the parties to the dispute, except in exceptional circumstances when the panel considers that the need for specialized scientific expertise cannot be fulfilled otherwise. Government officials of parties to the dispute shall not serve on an expert review group. Members of expert review groups shall serve in their individual capacities and not as government representatives, nor as

representatives of any organization. Governments or organizations shall therefore not give them instructions with regard to matters before an expert review group.

4.   Expert review groups may consult and seek information and technical advice from any source they deem appropriate. Before an expert review group seeks such information or advice from a source within the jurisdiction of a Member, it shall inform the government of that Member. Any Member shall respond promptly and fully to any request by an expert review group for such information as the expert review group considers necessary and appropriate.

5.   The parties to a dispute shall have access to all relevant information provided to an expert review group, unless it is of a confidential nature. Confidential information provided to the expert review group shall not be released without formal authorization from the government, organization or person providing the information. Where such information is requested from the expert review group but release of such information by the expert review group is not authorized, a non-confidential summary of the information will be provided by the government, organization or person supplying the information.

6.   The expert review group shall submit a draft report to the parties to the dispute with a view to obtaining their comments, and taking them into account, as appropriate, in the final report, which shall also be issued to the parties to the dispute when it is submitted to the panel. The final report of the expert review group shall be advisory only.

DSB Practices

WORKING PRACTICES CONCERNING DISPUTE SETTLEMENT
PROCEDURES AS AGREED BY THE DISPUTE SETTLEMENT BODY
(WT/DSB/6) 6 JUNE 1996

For practical purposes the working practices agreed by the Dispute Settlement Body concerning dispute settlement procedures since the entry into force of the WTO are compiled in this document. The working practices pertain to:

1. "Date of circulation" in the DSU and its additional and special rules.
2. Communications under the DSU.
3. Time-periods under the DSU and other covered agreements.
4. Notifications of requests for consultations.

"DATE OF CIRCULATION" IN THE DSU AND ITS ADDITIONAL AND SPECIAL RULES[1]

When there is a reference to the terms "date of circulation" or "issuance to all Members" or "issuance to the Members" in the DSU and its additional and special rules, the date to be used is the date printed on the WTO document to be circulated with the assurance of the Secretariat that the date printed on the document is the date on which this document is effectively put in the pigeon holes of delegations in all three working languages. This practice will be used on a trial basis and be subject to revision when necessary.

COMMUNICATIONS UNDER THE DSU[2]

Where there is a requirement under the DSU or any other covered agreements that communications by delegations be addressed to the DSB Chairman such communications should always be sent to the WTO Secretariat with a copy to the DSB Chairman. Members are invited to contact the Council Division in the WTO Secretariat, to inform it that a communication is being sent in order to enable an expeditious processing and circulation of communications.

Note: In addition to notification to the DSB, Notice of Appeal must be sent to the Appellate Body Secretariat in accordance with the Working Procedures for Appellate Review (WT/AB/WP/1). All other communications to the Appellate Body are required to be submitted to the Appellate Body Secretariat as provided for in the above-mentioned Working Procedures.

---

[1] See Minutes of the DSB meeting on 29 March 1995 (WT/DSB/M/2).
[2] See Minutes of the DSB meeting on 31 May 1995 (WT/DSB/M/5).

TIME-PERIODS UNDER THE DSU AND OTHER COVERED AGREEMENTS[3]

When, under the DSU and its special or additional rules and procedures, a time-period within which a communication must be made or action taken by a Member to exercise or preserve its rights expires on a non-working day of the WTO Secretariat, any such communication or action will be deemed to have been made or taken on the WTO non-working day if lodged on the first working day of the WTO Secretariat following the day on which such time-period would normally expire.[4]

NOTIFICATIONS OF REQUESTS FOR CONSULTATIONS[5]

All requests for consultations under Article 4.4 of the DSU which should be notified to the DSB and the relevant Councils and Committees by a Member should be sent to the Secretariat (Council Division) specifying in the notifications the other relevant Councils or Committees to which they wished the notification to be addressed. The Secretariat would then distribute it to the specified relevant bodies.

ARTICLE 4.11 OF THE DSU – REPLIES TO REQUESTS TO BE JOINED
IN ONGOING CONSULTATIONS

COMMUNICATION FROM THE CHAIRMAN OF THE DISPUTE
SETTLEMENT BODY
(WT/DS200/13)
3 AUGUST 2000

. . .

With reference to your comments regarding the need to circulate not only requests for consultations (Article 4.3 of the DSU) and requests to be joined in consultations (Article 4.11 of the DSU), but also the various responses to such requests to be joined into consultations, I have looked into the matter and advised the Secretariat that it should resort to its previous practice of circulating a Note identifying Members accepted to participate in consultations pursuant to Article 4.11 of the DSU, where such information has been made available to the Secretariat. . . .

---

[3] See Minutes of the DSB meeting on 27 September 1995 (WT/DSB/M/7).
[4] See also WT/DSB/W/10/Add.1 containing an illustrative list of DSU provisions which refer to time-periods and WT/DSB/W/16 indicating the WTO non-working days in 1996.
[5] See Minutes of the DSB meeting on 19 July 1995 (WT/DSB/M/6).

Example of Panel Working Procedures

PANEL REPORT, *US – STEEL SAFEGUARDS*, WT/DS248/R, WT/DS249/R, WT/DS251/R, WT/DS252/R, WT/DS253/R, WT/DS254/R, WT/DS258/R, WT/DS259/R, CIRCULATED 11 JULY 2003, PARA. 6.1:

1. In its proceedings the Panel shall follow the relevant provisions of the DSU. In addition, the following working procedures shall apply.

2. The panel shall meet in closed session. The parties to the dispute, and interested third parties, shall be present at the meetings only when invited by the Panel to appear before it.

3. The deliberations of the Panel and the documents submitted to it shall be kept confidential. Nothing in the DSU shall preclude a party to a dispute from disclosing statements of its own positions to the public. Members shall treat as confidential information submitted by another Member to the Panel which that Member has designated as confidential. Where a party to a dispute submits a confidential version of its written submissions to the Panel, it shall also, upon request of a Member, provide a non-confidential summary of the information contained in its submissions that could be disclosed to the public.

4. Before the first substantive meeting of the Panel with the parties, the parties to the dispute shall transmit to the Panel written submissions in which they present the facts of the case and their arguments. Third parties may transmit to the Panel written submissions after the first written submissions of the parties have been submitted.

5. Within seven days following the date for filing a submission, each of the parties and third parties is invited to provide the Panel with an executive summary of their submissions. The executive summaries will be used only for the purpose of assisting the Panel in drafting a concise factual and arguments section of the Panel report to the Members. They shall not in any way serve as a substitute for the submissions of the parties in the Panel's examination of the case. The executive summary to be provided by each party should not exceed 15 pages in length and shall summarize the content of the written submissions. In relation to the executive summaries to be provided by the United States, it is allowed an additional 15 pages to address issues that have been raised in the submissions of one or more of the other parties that are specific to those parties and which are not common to the other parties. The summary to be provided by each third party shall summarize their written submissions, as applicable, and should not exceed 5 pages in length.

6. At its first substantive meeting with the parties, the Panel shall ask the Complaining Parties to present their cases. Subsequently, and still at the same meeting, the United States will be asked to present its point of view. The parties will then be allowed an opportunity for final statements, with the Complaining Parties presenting their statements first.

7.   All third parties which have notified their interest in the dispute to the Dispute Settlement Body shall be invited in writing to present their views during a session of the first substantive meeting of the Panel set aside for that purpose. All such third parties may be present during the entirety of this session.

8.   Formal rebuttals shall be made at a second substantive meeting of the Panel. The United States shall have the right to take the floor first, to be followed by the Complaining Parties. The parties shall submit, prior to that meeting, written rebuttals and executive summaries to the Panel.

9.   The Panel may at any time put questions to the parties and to the third parties and ask them for explanations either in the course of a meeting or in writing. Answers to questions shall be submitted in writing by the date(s) specified by the Panel. Answers to questions after the first meeting shall be submitted in writing, at a date to be determined by the Panel.

10.   A party shall submit any request for a preliminary ruling not later than its first submission to the Panel. If the Complaining Parties request such a ruling, the United States shall submit its response to the request in its first submission. If the United States requests such a ruling, the Complaining Parties shall submit their responses to the request prior to the first substantive meeting of the Panel, at a time to be determined by the Panel in light of the request. Exceptions to this procedure will be granted upon a showing of good cause.

11.   Parties shall submit all factual evidence to the Panel no later than during the first substantive meeting, except with respect to evidence necessary for purposes of rebuttal submissions, or answers to questions or provided that good cause is shown. In all cases, the other party(ies) shall be accorded a period of time for comment, as appropriate.

12.   The parties to the dispute have the right to determine the composition of their own delegations. The parties shall have the responsibility for all members of their delegations and shall ensure that all members of the delegation act in accordance with the rules of the DSU and the Working Procedures of this Panel, particularly in regard to confidentiality of the proceedings.

13.   The parties to the dispute and any third party invited to present its views shall make available to the Panel and the parties to the dispute a written version of their oral statements, preferably at the end of the meeting, and in any event not later than the day following the meeting. Parties and third parties are encouraged to provide the Panel and other participants in the meeting with a provisional written version of their oral statements at the time the oral statement is presented.

14.   In the interest of full transparency, the presentations, rebuttals and statements shall be made in the presence of the parties. Moreover, each party's written submissions, including responses to questions put by the Panel, shall be made available to the other party or parties.

15.   To facilitate the maintenance of the record of the dispute, and to maximize the clarity of submissions, in particular the references to exhibits submitted by parties,

parties shall sequentially number their exhibits throughout the course of the dispute. For example, exhibits submitted by the United States could be numbered USA-1, USA-2, etc. If the last exhibit in connection with the first submission was numbered USA-5, the first exhibit of the next submission thus would be numbered USA-6.

16. Following issuance of the interim report, the parties shall have one week to submit written requests to review precise aspects of the interim report – unless the Panel decides otherwise at the second substantive meeting of the parties and/or to request a further meeting with the Panel. The right to request such a meeting must be exercised no later than at that time. Following receipt of any written requests for review, if no further meeting with the Panel is requested, the parties shall have the opportunity, within 2 weeks, to submit written comments on the other party's written requests for review. Such comments shall be strictly limited to responding to the other party's or parties' written request for review.

17. The following procedures regarding service of documents shall apply:

a. Each party shall serve its submissions directly on the other party. Each party shall, in addition, serve its first written submission on third parties. Each third party shall serve its submissions on the parties and other third parties. Parties and third parties shall confirm, at the time a submission is provided to the Panel, that copies have been served as required.

b. The parties and the third parties shall provide their written submissions to the Dispute Settlement Registrar by 5:30 p.m. on the deadlines established by the Panel and by 5:00 p.m. if the deadline falls on a Friday. If, due to exceptional circumstances, it is not possible for submissions to be provided to the Registrar by the times stipulated, parties should agree otherwise with the Secretary to the Panel, Ms Dariel De Sousa. The parties and the third parties shall provide the Panel with 10 paper copies of their written submissions. All these copies must be filed with the Dispute Settlement Registrar, Mr. Ferdinand Ferranco (Office 3154).

c. Ten copies of all submissions (oral and written), exhibits and other documents relating to this dispute must be submitted to the Panel through the WTO Secretariat when the original documents are filed with the Secretariat.

d. At the time they provide paper copies of their submissions, the parties and third parties shall also provide the Panel with an electronic copy of the submissions on a diskette or as an e-mail attachment, in a format compatible with the Secretariat's software (e-mail to the Dispute Settlement Registrar . . . , with a copy to the Secretary to the Panel, . . .).

Working Procedures for Appellate Review

DATED 1 MAY 2003 (WT/AB/WP/7)

Definitions

1. In these *Working Procedures for Appellate Review*,
"appellant"

> means any party to the dispute that has filed a Notice of Appeal pursuant to Rule 20 or has filed a submission pursuant to paragraph 1 of Rule 23;

"appellate report"

> means an Appellate Body report as described in Article 17 of the DSU;

"appellee"

> means any party to the dispute that has filed a submission pursuant to Rule 22 or paragraph 3 of Rule 23;

"consensus"

> a decision is deemed to be made by consensus if no Member formally objects to it;

"covered agreements"

> has the same meaning as "covered agreements" in paragraph 1 of Article 1 of the DSU;

"division"

> means the three Members who are selected to serve on any one appeal in accordance with paragraph 1 of Article 17 of the DSU and paragraph 2 of Rule 6;

"documents"

> means the Notice of Appeal and the submissions and other written statements presented by the participants;

"DSB"

> means the Dispute Settlement Body established under Article 2 of the DSU;

"DSU"

> means the *Understanding on Rules and Procedures Governing the Settlement of Disputes* which is Annex 2 to the *WTO Agreement*;

"Member"

> means a Member of the Appellate Body who has been appointed by the DSB in accordance with Article 17 of the DSU;

"participant"

> means any party to the dispute that has filed a Notice of Appeal pursuant to Rule 20 or a submission pursuant to Rule 22 or paragraphs 1 or 3 of Rule 23;

"party to the dispute"

> means any WTO Member who was a complaining or defending party in the panel dispute, but does not include a third party;

"proof of service"

> means a letter or other written acknowledgement that a document has been delivered, as required, to the parties to the dispute, participants, third parties or third participants, as the case may be;

"Rules"

> means these *Working Procedures for Appellate Review*;

"*Rules of Conduct*"

> means the *Rules of Conduct for the Understanding on Rules and Procedures Governing the Settlement of Disputes* as attached in Annex II to these Rules;

"*SCM Agreement*"

> means the *Agreement on Subsidies and Countervailing Measures* which is in Annex 1A to the *WTO Agreement*;

"Secretariat"

> means the Appellate Body Secretariat;

"service address"

> means the address of the party to the dispute, participant, third party or third participant as generally used in WTO dispute settlement proceedings, unless the party to the dispute, participant, third party or third participant has clearly indicated another address;

"third participant"

> means any third party that has filed a written submission pursuant to Rule 24(1); or any third party that appears at the oral hearing, whether or not it makes an oral statement at that hearing;

"third party"

> means any WTO Member who has notified the DSB of its substantial interest in the matter before the panel pursuant to paragraph 2 of Article 10 of the DSU;

"WTO"

> means the World Trade Organization;

"*WTO Agreement*"
>means the *Marrakesh Agreement Establishing the World Trade Organization*, done at Marrakesh, Morocco on 15 April 1994;

"WTO Member"
>means any State or separate customs territory possessing full autonomy in the conduct of its external commercial relations that has accepted or acceded to the WTO in accordance with Articles XI, XII or XIV of the *WTO Agreement*; and

"WTO Secretariat"
>means the Secretariat of the World Trade Organization.

PART I MEMBERS

Duties and Responsibilities

2. (1) A Member shall abide by the terms and conditions of the DSU, these Rules and any decisions of the DSB affecting the Appellate Body.
    (2) During his/her term, a Member shall not accept any employment nor pursue any professional activity that is inconsistent with his/her duties and responsibilities.
    (3) A Member shall exercise his/her office without accepting or seeking instructions from any international, governmental, or non-governmental organization or any private source.
    (4) A Member shall be available at all times and on short notice and, to this end, shall keep the Secretariat informed of his/her whereabouts at all times.

Decision-Making

3. (1) In accordance with paragraph 1 of Article 17 of the DSU, decisions relating to an appeal shall be taken solely by the division assigned to that appeal. Other decisions shall be taken by the Appellate Body as a whole.
    (2) The Appellate Body and its divisions shall make every effort to take their decisions by consensus. Where, nevertheless, a decision cannot be arrived at by consensus, the matter at issue shall be decided by a majority vote.

Collegiality

4. (1) To ensure consistency and coherence in decision-making, and to draw on the individual and collective expertise of the Members, the Members shall convene on a regular basis to discuss matters of policy, practice and procedure.

(2) The Members shall stay abreast of dispute settlement activities and other relevant activities of the WTO and, in particular, each Member shall receive all documents filed in an appeal.

(3) In accordance with the objectives set out in paragraph 1, the division responsible for deciding each appeal shall exchange views with the other Members before the division finalizes the appellate report for circulation to the WTO Members. This paragraph is subject to paragraphs 2 and 3 of Rule 11.

(4) Nothing in these Rules shall be interpreted as interfering with a division's full authority and freedom to hear and decide an appeal assigned to it in accordance with paragraph 1 of Article 17 of the DSU.

Chairman

5. (1) There shall be a Chairman of the Appellate Body who shall be elected by the Members.

(2) The term of office of the Chairman of the Appellate Body shall be one year. The Appellate Body Members may decide to extend the term of office for an additional period of up to one year. However, in order to ensure rotation of the Chairmanship, no Member shall serve as Chairman for more than two consecutive terms.

(3) The Chairman shall be responsible for the overall direction of the Appellate Body business, and in particular, his/her responsibilities shall include:

(a) the supervision of the internal functioning of the Appellate Body; and

(b) any such other duties as the Members may agree to entrust to him/her.

(4) Where the office of the Chairman becomes vacant due to permanent incapacity as a result of illness or death or by resignation or expiration of his/her term, the Members shall elect a new Chairman who shall serve a full term in accordance with paragraph 2.

(5) In the event of a temporary absence or incapacity of the Chairman, the Appellate Body shall authorize another Member to act as Chairman *ad interim*, and the Member so authorized shall temporarily exercise all the powers, duties and functions of the Chairman until the Chairman is capable of resuming his/her functions.

Divisions

6. (1) In accordance with paragraph 1 of Article 17 of the DSU, a division consisting of three Members shall be established to hear and decide an appeal.

(2) The Members constituting a division shall be selected on the basis of rotation, while taking into account the principles of random selection, unpredictability and opportunity for all Members to serve regardless of their national origin.

(3) A Member selected pursuant to paragraph 2 to serve on a division shall serve on that division, unless:

   (i) he/she is excused from that division pursuant to Rules 9 or 10;

   (ii) he/she has notified the Chairman and the Presiding Member that he/she is prevented from serving on the division because of illness or other serious reasons pursuant to Rule 12; or

   (iii) he/she has notified his/her intentions to resign pursuant to Rule 14.

Presiding Member of the Division

7. (1) Each division shall have a Presiding Member, who shall be elected by the Members of that division.

   (2) The responsibilities of the Presiding Member shall include:

   (a) coordinating the overall conduct of the appeal proceeding;

   (b) chairing all oral hearings and meetings related to that appeal; and

   (c) coordinating the drafting of the appellate report.

   (3) In the event that a Presiding Member becomes incapable of performing his/her duties, the other Members serving on that division and the Member selected as a replacement pursuant to Rule 13 shall elect one of their number to act as the Presiding Member.

Rules of Conduct

8. (1) On a provisional basis, the Appellate Body adopts those provisions of the *Rules of Conduct for the Understanding on Rules and Procedures Governing the Settlement of Disputes*, attached in Annex II to these Rules, which are applicable to it, until *Rules of Conduct* are approved by the DSB.

   (2) Upon approval of *Rules of Conduct* by the DSB, such *Rules of Conduct* shall be directly incorporated and become part of these Rules and shall supersede Annex II.

9. (1) Upon the filing of a Notice of Appeal, each Member shall take the steps set out in Article VI:4(b)(i) of Annex II, and a Member may consult with the other Members prior to completing the disclosure form.

   (2) Upon the filing of a Notice of Appeal, the professional staff of the Secretariat assigned to that appeal shall take the steps set out in Article VI:4(b)(ii) of Annex II.

   (3) Where information has been submitted pursuant to Article VI:4(b)(i) or (ii) of Annex II, the Appellate Body shall consider whether further action is necessary.

   (4) As a result of the Appellate Body's consideration of the matter pursuant to paragraph 3, the Member or the professional staff member concerned may continue to be assigned to the division or may be excused from the division.

10. (1) Where evidence of a material violation is filed by a participant pursuant to Article VIII of Annex II, such evidence shall be confidential and shall be supported by affidavits made by persons having actual knowledge or a reasonable belief as to the truth of the facts stated.

    (2) Any evidence filed pursuant to Article VIII:1 of Annex II shall be filed at the earliest practicable time: that is, forthwith after the participant submitting it knew or reasonably could have known of the facts supporting it. In no case shall such evidence be filed after the appellate report is circulated to the WTO Members.

    (3) Where a participant fails to submit such evidence at the earliest practicable time, it shall file an explanation in writing of the reasons why it did not do so earlier, and the Appellate Body may decide to consider or not to consider such evidence, as appropriate.

    (4) While taking fully into account paragraph 5 of Article 17 of the DSU, where evidence has been filed pursuant to Article VIII of Annex II, an appeal shall be suspended for fifteen days or until the procedure referred to in Article VIII:14–16 of Annex II is completed, whichever is earlier.

    (5) As a result of the procedure referred to in Article VIII:14–16 of Annex II, the Appellate Body may decide to dismiss the allegation, to excuse the Member or professional staff member concerned from being assigned to the division or make such other order as it deems necessary in accordance with Article VIII of Annex II.

11. (1) A Member who has submitted a disclosure form with information attached pursuant to Article VI:4(b)(i) or is the subject of evidence of a material violation pursuant to Article VIII:1 of Annex II, shall not participate in any decision taken pursuant to paragraph 4 of Rule 9 or paragraph 5 of Rule 10.

    (2) A Member who is excused from a division pursuant to paragraph 4 of Rule 9 or paragraph 5 of Rule 10 shall not take part in the exchange of views conducted in that appeal pursuant to paragraph 3 of Rule 4.

    (3) A Member who, had he/she been a Member of a division, would have been excused from that division pursuant to paragraph 4 of Rule 9, shall not take part in the exchange of views conducted in that appeal pursuant to paragraph 3 of Rule 4.

Incapacity

12. (1) A Member who is prevented from serving on a division by illness or for other serious reasons shall give notice and duly explain such reasons to the Chairman and to the Presiding Member.

    (2) Upon receiving such notice, the Chairman and the Presiding Member shall forthwith inform the Appellate Body.

Replacement

13.   Where a Member is unable to serve on a division for a reason set out in paragraph 3 of Rule 6, another Member shall be selected forthwith pursuant to paragraph 2 of Rule 6 to replace the Member originally selected for that division.

Resignation

14.   (1) A Member who intends to resign from his/her office shall notify his/her intentions in writing to the Chairman of the Appellate Body who shall immediately inform the Chairman of the DSB, the Director-General and the other Members of the Appellate Body.

(2) The resignation shall take effect 90 days after the notification has been made pursuant to paragraph 1, unless the DSB, in consultation with the Appellate Body, decides otherwise.

Transition

15.   A person who ceases to be a Member of the Appellate Body may, with the authorization of the Appellate Body and upon notification to the DSB, complete the disposition of any appeal to which that person was assigned while a Member, and that person shall, for that purpose only, be deemed to continue to be a Member of the Appellate Body.

PART II   PROCESS

General Provisions

16.   (1) In the interests of fairness and orderly procedure in the conduct of an appeal, where a procedural question arises that is not covered by these Rules, a division may adopt an appropriate procedure for the purposes of that appeal only, provided that it is not inconsistent with the DSU, the other covered agreements and these Rules. Where such a procedure is adopted, the division shall immediately notify the parties to the dispute, participants, third parties and third participants as well as the other Members of the Appellate Body.

(2) In exceptional circumstances, where strict adherence to a time period set out in these Rules would result in a manifest unfairness, a party to the dispute, a participant, a third party or a third participant may request that a division modify a time period set out in these Rules for the filing of documents or the date set out in the working schedule for the oral hearing. Where such a request is granted by a division, any modification of time shall be notified to the parties to the dispute, participants, third parties and third participants in a revised working schedule.

17. (1) Unless the DSB decides otherwise, in computing any time period stipulated in the DSU or in the special or additional provisions of the covered agreements, or in these Rules, within which a communication must be made or an action taken by a WTO Member to exercise or preserve its rights, the day from which the time period begins to run shall be excluded and, subject to paragraph 2, the last day of the time-period shall be included.

(2) The DSB Decision on "Expiration of Time-Periods in the DSU", WT/DSB/M/7, shall apply to appeals heard by divisions of the Appellate Body.

Documents

18. (1) No document is considered filed with the Appellate Body unless the document is received by the Secretariat within the time period set out for filing in accordance with these Rules.

(2) Except as otherwise provided in these Rules, every document filed by a party to the dispute, a participant, a third party or a third participant shall be served on each of the other parties to the dispute, participants, third parties and third participants in the appeal.

(3) A proof of service on the other parties to the dispute, participants, third parties and third participants shall appear on, or be affixed to, each document filed with the Secretariat under paragraph 1 above.

(4) A document shall be served by the most expeditious means of delivery or communication available, including by:

(a) delivering a copy of the document to the service address of the party to the dispute, participant, third party or third participant; or

(b) sending a copy of the document to the service address of the party to the dispute, participant, third party or third participant by facsimile transmission, expedited delivery courier or expedited mail service.

(5) Upon authorization by the division, a participant or a third participant may correct clerical errors in any of its submissions. Such correction shall be made within 3 days of the filing of the original submission and a copy of the revised version shall be filed with the Secretariat and served upon the other parties to the dispute, participants, third parties and third participants.

Ex Parte Communications

19. (1) Neither a division nor any of its Members shall meet with or contact one party to the dispute, participant, third party or third participant in the absence of the other parties to the dispute, participants, third parties and third participants.

(2) No Member of the division may discuss any aspect of the subject matter of an appeal with any party to the dispute, participant, third party or third participant in the absence of the other Members of the division.

(3) A Member who is not assigned to the division hearing the appeal shall not discuss any aspect of the subject matter of the appeal with any party to the dispute, participant, third party or third participant.

Commencement of Appeal

20. (1) An appeal shall be commenced by notification in writing to the DSB in accordance with paragraph 4 of Article 16 of the DSU and simultaneous filing of a Notice of Appeal with the Secretariat.

(2) A Notice of Appeal shall include the following information:

(a) the title of the panel report under appeal;

(b) the name of the party to the dispute filing the Notice of Appeal;

(c) the service address, telephone and facsimile numbers of the party to the dispute; and

(d) a brief statement of the nature of the appeal, including the allegations of errors in the issues of law covered in the panel report and legal interpretations developed by the panel.

Appellant's Submission

21. (1) The appellant shall, within ten days after the date of the filing of the Notice of Appeal, file with the Secretariat a written submission prepared in accordance with paragraph 2 and serve a copy of the submission on the other parties to the dispute and third parties.

(2) A written submission referred to in paragraph 1 shall

(a) be dated and signed by the appellant; and

(b) set out

(i) a precise statement of the grounds for the appeal, including the specific allegations of errors in the issues of law covered in the panel report and legal interpretations developed by the panel, and the legal arguments in support thereof;

(ii) a precise statement of the provisions of the covered agreements and other legal sources relied on; and

(iii) the nature of the decision or ruling sought.

Appellee's Submission

22. (1) Any party to the dispute that wishes to respond to allegations raised in an appellant's submission filed pursuant to Rule 21 may, within 25 days after the date of the filing of the Notice of Appeal, file with the Secretariat a written submission prepared in accordance with paragraph 2 and serve a

copy of the submission on the appellant, other parties to the dispute and third parties.

(2) A written submission referred to in paragraph 1 shall

    (a) be dated and signed by the appellee; and

    (b) set out

        (i) a precise statement of the grounds for opposing the specific allegations of errors in the issues of law covered in the panel report and legal interpretations developed by the panel raised in the appellant's submission, and the legal arguments in support thereof;

        (ii) an acceptance of, or opposition to, each ground set out in the appellant's submission;

        (iii) a precise statement of the provisions of the covered agreements and other legal sources relied on; and

        (iv) the nature of the decision or ruling sought.

Multiple Appeals

23. (1) Within 15 days after the date of the filing of the Notice of Appeal, a party to the dispute other than the original appellant may join in that appeal or appeal on the basis of other alleged errors in the issues of law covered in the panel report and legal interpretations developed by the panel.

(2) Any written submission made pursuant to paragraph 1 shall be in the format required by paragraph 2 of Rule 21.

(3) The appellant, any appellee and any other party to the dispute that wishes to respond to a submission filed pursuant to paragraph 1 may file a written submission within 25 days after the date of the filing of the Notice of Appeal, and any such submission shall be in the format required by paragraph 2 of Rule 22.

(4) This Rule does not preclude a party to the dispute which has not filed a submission under Rule 21 or paragraph 1 of this Rule from exercising its right of appeal pursuant to paragraph 4 of Article 16 of the DSU.

(5) Where a party to the dispute which has not filed a submission under Rule 21 or paragraph 1 of this Rule exercises its right to appeal as set out in paragraph 4, a single division shall examine the appeals.

Third Participants

24. (1) Any third party may file a written submission containing the grounds and legal arguments in support of its position. Such submission shall be filed within 25 days after the date of the filing of the Notice of Appeal.

(2) A third party not filing a written submission shall, within the same period of 25 days, notify the Secretariat in writing if it intends to appear at the oral hearing, and, if so, whether it intends to make an oral statement.

(3) Third participants are encouraged to file written submissions to facilitate their positions being taken fully into account by the division hearing the appeal and in order that participants and other third participants will have notice of positions to be taken at the oral hearing.

(4) Any third party that has neither filed a written submission pursuant to paragraph (1), nor notified the Secretariat pursuant to paragraph (2), may notify the Secretariat that it intends to appear at the oral hearing, and may request to make an oral statement at the hearing. Such notifications and requests should be notified to the Secretariat in writing at the earliest opportunity.

Transmittal of Record

25. (1) Upon the filing of a Notice of Appeal, the Director-General of the WTO shall transmit forthwith to the Appellate Body the complete record of the panel proceeding.

(2) The complete record of the panel proceeding includes, but is not limited to:

    (i) written submissions, rebuttal submissions, and supporting evidence attached thereto by the parties to the dispute and the third parties;

    (ii) written arguments submitted at the panel meetings with the parties to the dispute and the third parties, the recordings of such panel meetings, and any written answers to questions posed at such panel meetings;

    (iii) the correspondence relating to the panel dispute between the panel or the WTO Secretariat and the parties to the dispute or the third parties; and

    (iv) any other documentation submitted to the panel.

Working Schedule

26. (1) Forthwith after the commencement of an appeal, the division shall draw up an appropriate working schedule for that appeal in accordance with the time periods stipulated in these Rules.

(2) The working schedule shall set forth precise dates for the filing of documents and a timetable for the division's work, including where possible, the date for the oral hearing.

(3) In accordance with paragraph 9 of Article 4 of the DSU, in appeals of urgency, including those which concern perishable goods, the Appellate Body shall make every effort to accelerate the appellate proceedings to the greatest extent possible. A division shall take this into account in drawing up its working schedule for that appeal.

(4) The Secretariat shall serve forthwith a copy of the working schedule on the appellant, the parties to the dispute and any third parties.

Oral Hearing

27. (1) A division shall hold an oral hearing, which shall be held, as a general rule, 30 days after the date of the filing of the Notice of Appeal.

    (2) Where possible in the working schedule or otherwise at the earliest possible date, the Secretariat shall notify all parties to the dispute, participants, third parties and third participants of the date for the oral hearing.

    (3) (a) Any third party that has filed a submission pursuant to Rule 24(1), or has notified the Secretariat pursuant to Rule 24(2) that it intends to appear at the oral hearing, may appear at the oral hearing, make an oral statement at the hearing, and respond to questions posed by the division.

    (b) Any third party that has notified the Secretariat pursuant to Rule 24(4) that it intends to appear at the oral hearing may appear at the oral hearing.

    (c) Any third party that has made a request pursuant to Rule 24(4) may, at the discretion of the division hearing the appeal, taking into account the requirements of due process, make an oral statement at the hearing, and respond to questions posed by the division.

    (4) The Presiding Member may, as necessary, set time-limits for oral arguments and presentations.

Written Responses

28. (1) At any time during the appellate proceeding, including, in particular, during the oral hearing, the division may address questions orally or in writing to, or request additional memoranda from, any participant or third participant, and specify the time periods by which written responses or memoranda shall be received.

    (2) Any such questions, responses or memoranda shall be made available to the other participants and third participants in the appeal, who shall be given an opportunity to respond.

    (3) When the questions or requests for memoranda are made prior to the oral hearing, then the questions or requests, as well as the responses or memoranda, shall also be made available to the third parties, who shall also be given an opportunity to respond.

Failure to Appear

29. Where a participant fails to file a submission within the required time periods or fails to appear at the oral hearing, the division shall, after hearing the views of the participants, issue such order, including dismissal of the appeal, as it deems appropriate.

Withdrawal of Appeal

30. (1) At any time during an appeal, the appellant may withdraw its appeal by notifying the Appellate Body, which shall forthwith notify the DSB.

(2) Where a mutually agreed solution to a dispute which is the subject of an appeal has been notified to the DSB pursuant to paragraph 6 of Article 3 of the DSU, it shall be notified to the Appellate Body.

Prohibited Subsidies

31. (1) Subject to Article 4 of the *SCM Agreement*, the general provisions of these Rules shall apply to appeals relating to panel reports concerning prohibited subsidies under Part II of that *Agreement*.

(2) The working schedule for an appeal involving prohibited subsidies under Part II of the *SCM Agreement* shall be as set out in Annex I to these Rules.

Entry into Force and Amendment

32. (1) These Rules shall enter into force on 15 February 1996.

(2) The Appellate Body may amend these Rules in compliance with the procedures set forth in paragraph 9 of Article 17 of the DSU.

(3) Whenever there is an amendment to the DSU or to the special or additional rules and procedures of the covered agreements, the Appellate Body shall examine whether amendments to these Rules are necessary.

ANNEX I

TIMETABLE FOR APPEALS

	General Appeals Day	Prohibited Subsidies Appeals Day
Notice of Appeal[1]	0	0
Appellant's Submission[2]	10	5
Other Appellant(s) Submission(s)[3]	15	7
Appellee(s) Submission(s)[4]	25	12
Third Participant(s) Submission(s)[5]	25	12
Third Participant(s) Notification(s)[6]	25	12
Oral Hearing[7]	30	15
Circulation of Appellate Report	60–90[8]	30–60[9]
DSB Meeting for Adoption	90–120[10]	50–80[11]

---

[1] (footnote original) Rule 20.   [2] (footnote original) Rule 21.   [3] (footnote original) Rule 23(1).

[4] (footnote original) Rules 22 and 23(3).   [5] (footnote original) Rule 24(1).

[6] (footnote original) Rule 24(2).   [7] (footnote original) Rule 27.

[8] (footnote original) Article 17:5, DSU.   [9] (footnote original) Article 4:9, *SCM Agreement*.

[10] (footnote original) Article 17:14, DSU.   [11] (footnote original) Article 4:9, *SCM Agreement*.

ANNEX II

RULES OF CONDUCT FOR THE UNDERSTANDING ON RULES AND PROCEDURES GOVERNING THE SETTLEMENT OF DISPUTES

ADOPTED BY THE DSB ON 3 DECEMBER 1996
(WT/DSB/RC/1)

I. Preamble

Members,

Recalling that on 15 April 1994 in Marrakesh, Ministers welcomed the stronger and clearer legal framework they had adopted for the conduct of international trade, including a more effective and reliable dispute settlement mechanism;

Recognizing the importance of full adherence to the Understanding on Rules and Procedures Governing the Settlement of Disputes ("DSU") and the principles for the management of disputes applied under Articles XXII and XXIII of GATT 1947, as further elaborated and modified by the DSU;

Affirming that the operation of the DSU would be strengthened by rules of conduct designed to maintain the integrity, impartiality and confidentiality of proceedings conducted under the DSU thereby enhancing confidence in the new dispute settlement mechanism;

Hereby establish the following Rules of Conduct.

II. Governing Principle

1.   Each person covered by these Rules (as defined in paragraph 1 of Section IV below and hereinafter called "covered person") shall be independent and impartial, shall avoid direct or indirect conflicts of interest and shall respect the confidentiality of proceedings of bodies pursuant to the dispute settlement mechanism, so that through the observance of such standards of conduct the integrity and impartiality of that mechanism are preserved. These Rules shall in no way modify the rights and obligations of Members under the DSU nor the rules and procedures therein.

III. Observance of the Governing Principle

1.   To ensure the observance of the Governing Principle of these Rules, each covered person is expected (1) to adhere strictly to the provisions of the DSU; (2) to disclose the existence or development of any interest, relationship or matter that that person could reasonably be expected to know and that is likely to affect, or give rise to justifiable doubts as to, that person's independence or impartiality; and (3) to take due care in the performance of their duties to fulfil these expectations, including through avoidance of any direct or indirect conflicts of interest in respect of the subject matter of the proceedings.

2.   Pursuant to the Governing Principle, each covered person, shall be independent and impartial, and shall maintain confidentiality. Moreover, such persons shall consider only issues raised in, and necessary to fulfil their responsibilities within, the dispute settlement proceeding and shall not delegate this responsibility to any other person. Such person shall not incur any obligation or accept any benefit that would in any way interfere with, or which could give rise to, justifiable doubts as to the proper performance of that person's dispute settlement duties.

IV. Scope

1.   These Rules shall apply, as specified in the text, to each person serving: (a) on a panel; (b) on the Standing Appellate Body; (c) as an arbitrator pursuant to the provisions mentioned in Annex "1a"; or (d) as an expert participating in the dispute settlement mechanism pursuant to the provisions mentioned in Annex "1b". These Rules shall also apply, as specified in this text and the relevant provisions of the Staff Regulations, to those members of the Secretariat called upon to assist the panel in accordance with Article 27.1 of the DSU or to assist in formal arbitration proceedings pursuant to Annex "1a"; to the Chairman of the Textiles Monitoring Body (hereinafter called "TMB") and other members of the TMB Secretariat called upon to assist the TMB in formulating recommendations, findings or observations pursuant to the WTO Agreement on Textiles and Clothing; and to Standing Appellate Body support staff called upon to provide the Standing Appellate Body with administrative or legal support in accordance with Article 17.7 of the DSU (hereinafter "Member of the Secretariat or Standing Appellate Body support staff"), reflecting their acceptance of established norms regulating the conduct of such persons as international civil servants and the Governing Principle of these Rules.

2.   The application of these Rules shall not in any way impede the Secretariat's discharge of its responsibility to continue to respond to Members' requests for assistance and information.

3.   These Rules shall apply to the members of the TMB to the extent prescribed in Section V.

V. Textiles Monitoring Body

1.   Members of the TMB shall discharge their functions on an *ad personam* basis, in accordance with the requirement of Article 8.1 of the Agreement on Textiles and Clothing, as further elaborated in the working procedures of the TMB, so as to preserve the integrity and impartiality of its proceedings.[*]

---

[*]   (footnote original) These working procedures, as adopted by the TMB on 26 July 1995 (G/TMB/R/1), currently include, *inter alia*, the following language in paragraph 1.4: "In discharging their functions in accordance with paragraph 1.1 above, the TMB members and alternates shall undertake not to solicit, accept or act upon instructions from governments, nor to be influenced by any other organisations or undue extraneous factors. They shall disclose to the Chairman any information that they may consider likely to impede their capacity to

VI. Self-Disclosure Requirements by Covered Persons

1. (a) Each person requested to serve on a panel, on the Standing Appellate Body, as an arbitrator, or as an expert shall, at the time of the request, receive from the Secretariat these Rules, which include an Illustrative List (Annex 2) of examples of the matters subject to disclosure.

    (b) Any member of the Secretariat described in paragraph IV:1, who may expect to be called upon to assist in a dispute, and Standing Appellate Body support staff, shall be familiar with these Rules.

2. As set out in paragraph VI:4 below, all covered persons described in paragraph VI.1(a) and VI.1(b) shall disclose any information that could reasonably be expected to be known to them at the time which, coming within the scope of the Governing Principle of these Rules, is likely to affect or give rise to justifiable doubts as to their independence or impartiality. These disclosures include the type of information described in the Illustrative List, if relevant.

3. These disclosure requirements shall not extend to the identification of matters whose relevance to the issues to be considered in the proceedings would be insignificant. They shall take into account the need to respect the personal privacy of those to whom these Rules apply and shall not be so administratively burdensome as to make it impracticable for otherwise qualified persons to serve on panels, the Standing Appellate Body, or in other dispute settlement roles.

4. (a) All panelists, arbitrators and experts, prior to confirmation of their appointment, shall complete the form at Annex 3 of these Rules. Such information would be disclosed to the Chair of the Dispute Settlement Body ("DSB") for consideration by the parties to the dispute.

    (b) (i) Persons serving on the Standing Appellate Body who, through rotation, are selected to hear the appeal of a particular panel case, shall review the factual portion of the Panel report and complete the form at Annex 3. Such information would be disclosed to the Standing Appellate Body for its consideration whether the member concerned should hear a particular appeal.

    (ii) Standing Appellate Body support staff shall disclose any relevant matter to the Standing Appellate Body, for its consideration in deciding on the assignment of staff to assist in a particular appeal.

    (c) When considered to assist in a dispute, members of the Secretariat shall disclose to the Director-General of the WTO the information required under paragraph VI:2 of these Rules and any other relevant information

---

discharge their functions on an *ad personam* basis. Should serious doubts arise during the deliberations of the TMB regarding the ability of a TMB member to act on an *ad personam* basis, they shall be communicated to the Chairman. The Chairman shall deal with the particular matter as necessary."

required under the Staff Regulations, including the information described in the footnote.[**]

5.   During a dispute, each covered person shall also disclose any new information relevant to paragraph VI:2 above at the earliest time they become aware of it.

6.   The Chair of the DSB, the Secretariat, parties to the dispute, and other individuals involved in the dispute settlement mechanism shall maintain the confidentiality of any information revealed through this disclosure process, even after the panel process and its enforcement procedures, if any, are completed.

VII. Confidentiality

1.   Each covered person shall at all times maintain the confidentiality of dispute settlement deliberations and proceedings together with any information identified by a party as confidential. No covered person shall at any time use such information acquired during such deliberations and proceedings to gain personal advantage or advantage for others.

2.   During the proceedings, no covered person shall engage in *ex parte* contacts concerning matters under consideration. Subject to paragraph VII:1, no covered person shall make any statements on such proceedings or the issues in dispute in which that person is participating, until the report of the panel or the Standing Appellate Body has been derestricted.

VIII. Procedures Concerning Subsequent Disclosure and Possible Material Violations

1.   Any party to a dispute, conducted pursuant to the WTO Agreement, who possesses or comes into possession of evidence of a material violation of the obligations of independence, impartiality or confidentiality or the avoidance of direct or indirect

---

[**] (footnote original) Pending adoption of the Staff Regulations, members of the Secretariat shall make disclosures to the Director-General in accordance with the following draft provision to be included in the Staff Regulations:

"When paragraph VI:4(c) of the Rules of Conduct for the DSU is applicable, members of the Secretariat would disclose to the Director-General of the WTO the information required in paragraph VI:2 of those Rules, as well as any information regarding their participation in earlier formal consideration of the specific measure at issue in a dispute under any provisions of the WTO Agreement, including through formal legal advice under Article 27.2 of the DSU, as well as any involvement with the dispute as an official of a WTO Member government or otherwise professionally, before having joined the Secretariat.

The Director-General shall consider any such disclosures in deciding on the assignment of members of the Secretariat to assist in a dispute.

When the Director-General, in the light of his consideration, including of available Secretariat resources, decides that a potential conflict of interest is not sufficiently material to warrant non-assignment of a particular member of the Secretariat to assist in a dispute, the Director-General shall inform the panel of his decision and of the relevant supporting information."

conflicts of interest by covered persons which may impair the integrity, impartiality or confidentiality of the dispute settlement mechanism, shall at the earliest possible time and on a confidential basis, submit such evidence to the Chair of the DSB, the Director-General or the Standing Appellate Body, as appropriate according to the respective procedures detailed in paragraphs VIII:5 to VIII:17 below, in a written statement specifying the relevant facts and circumstances. Other Members who possess or come into possession of such evidence, may provide such evidence to the parties to the dispute in the interest of maintaining the integrity and impartiality of the dispute settlement mechanism.

2.   When evidence as described in paragraph VIII:1 is based on an alleged failure of a covered person to disclose a relevant interest, relationship or matter, that fail-ure to disclose, as such, shall not be a sufficient ground for disqualification unless there is also evidence of a material violation of the obligations of independence, impartiality, confidentiality or the avoidance of direct or indirect conflicts of inter-ests and that the integrity, impartiality or confidentiality of the dispute settlement mechanism would be impaired thereby.

3.   When such evidence is not provided at the earliest practicable time, the party submitting the evidence shall explain why it did not do so earlier and this explanation shall be taken into account in the procedures initiated in paragraph VIII:1.

4.   Following the submission of such evidence to the Chair of the DSB, the Director-General of the WTO or the Standing Appellate Body, as specified below, the procedures outlined in paragraphs VIII:5 to VIII:17 below shall be completed within fifteen working days.

Panelists, Arbitrators, Experts

5.   If the covered person who is the subject of the evidence is a panelist, an arbitrator or an expert, the party shall provide such evidence to the Chair of the DSB.

6.   Upon receipt of the evidence referred to in paragraphs VIII:1 and VIII:2, the Chair of the DSB shall forthwith provide the evidence to the person who is the subject of such evidence, for consideration by the latter.

7.   If, after having consulted with the person concerned, the matter is not resolved, the Chair of the DSB shall forthwith provide all the evidence, and any additional information from the person concerned, to the parties to the dispute. If the person concerned resigns, the Chair of the DSB shall inform the parties to the dispute and, as the case may be, the panelists, the arbitrator(s) or experts.

8.   In all cases, the Chair of the DSB, in consultation with the Director-General and a sufficient number of Chairs of the relevant Council or Councils to provide an odd number, and after having provided a reasonable opportunity for the views of the person concerned and the parties to the dispute to be heard, would decide whether a material violation of these Rules as referred to in paragraphs VIII:1 and VIII:2

above has occurred. Where the parties agree that a material violation of these Rules has occurred, it would be expected that, consistent with maintaining the integrity of the dispute settlement mechanism, the disqualification of the person concerned would be confirmed.

9.   The person who is the subject of the evidence shall continue to participate in the consideration of the dispute unless it is decided that a material violation of these Rules has occurred.

10.   The Chair of the DSB shall thereafter take the necessary steps for the appointment of the person who is the subject of the evidence to be formally revoked, or excused from the dispute as the case may be, as of that time.

Secretariat

11.   If the covered person who is the subject of the evidence is a member of the Secretariat, the party shall only provide the evidence to the Director-General of the WTO, who shall forthwith provide the evidence to the person who is the subject of such evidence and shall further inform the other party or parties to the dispute and the panel.

12.   It shall be for the Director-General to take any appropriate action in accordance with the Staff Regulations.***

13.   The Director-General shall inform the parties to the dispute, the panel and the Chair of the DSB of his decision, together with relevant supporting information.

Standing Appellate Body

14.   If the covered person who is the subject of the evidence is a member of the Standing Appellate Body or of the Standing Appellate Body support staff, the party shall provide the evidence to the other party to the dispute and the evidence shall thereafter be provided to the Standing Appellate Body.

15.   Upon receipt of the evidence referred to in paragraphs VIII:1 and VIII:2 above, the Standing Appellate Body shall forthwith provide it to the person who is the subject of such evidence, for consideration by the latter.

16.   It shall be for the Standing Appellate Body to take any appropriate action after having provided a reasonable opportunity for the views of the person concerned and the parties to the dispute to be heard.

*** (footnote original) Pending adoption of the Staff Regulations, the Director-General would act in accordance with the following draft provision for the Staff Regulations: "If paragraph VIII:11 of the Rules of Conduct for the DSU governing the settlement of disputes is invoked, the Director-General shall consult with the person who is the subject of the evidence and the panel and shall, if necessary, take appropriate disciplinary action."

17.   The Standing Appellate Body shall inform the parties to the dispute and the Chair of the DSB of its decision, together with relevant supporting information.

18.   Following completion of the procedures in paragraphs VIII:5 to VIII:17, if the appointment of a covered person, other than a member of the Standing Appellate Body, is revoked or that person is excused or resigns, the procedures specified in the DSU for initial appointment shall be followed for appointment of a replacement, but the time periods shall be half those specified in the DSU.**** The member of the Standing Appellate Body who, under that Body's rules, would next be selected through rotation to consider the dispute, would automatically be assigned to the appeal. The panel, members of the Standing Appellate Body hearing the appeal, or the arbitrator, as the case may be, may then decide after consulting with the parties to the dispute, on any necessary modifications to their working procedures or proposed timetable.

19.   All covered persons and Members concerned shall resolve matters involving possible material violations of these Rules as expeditiously as possible so as not to delay the completion of proceedings, as provided in the DSU.

20.   Except to the extent strictly necessary to carry out this decision, all information concerning possible or actual material violations of these Rules shall be kept confidential.

IX. Review

1.   These Rules of Conduct shall be reviewed within two years of their adoption and a decision shall be taken by the DSB as to whether to continue, modify or terminate these Rules.

ANNEX 1a

Arbitrators acting pursuant to the following provisions:

   – Articles 21.3(c); 22.6 and 22.7; 26.1(c) and 25 of the DSU;
   – Article 8.5 of the Agreement on Subsidies and Countervailing Measures;
   – Articles XXI.3 and XXII.3 of the General Agreement on Trade in Services.

ANNEX 1b

Experts advising or providing information pursuant to the following provisions:

   – Article 13.1; 13.2 of the DSU;
   – Article 4.5 of the Agreement on Subsidies and Countervailing Measures;

**** (footnote original) Appropriate adjustments would be made in the case of appointments pursuant to the Agreement on Subsidies and Countervailing Measures.

- Article 11.2 of the Agreement on the Application of Sanitary and Phytosanitary Measures;
- Article 14.2; 14.3 of the Agreement on Technical Barriers to Trade.

ANNEX 2

ILLUSTRATIVE LIST OF INFORMATION TO BE DISCLOSED

This list contains examples of information of the type that a person called upon to serve in a dispute should disclose pursuant to the Rules of Conduct for the Understanding on Rules and Procedures Governing the Settlement of Disputes.

Each covered person, as defined in Section IV:1 of these Rules of Conduct has a continuing duty to disclose the information described in Section VI:2 of these Rules which may include the following:

(a) financial interests (e.g. investments, loans, shares, interests, other debts); business interests (e.g. directorship or other contractual interests); and property interests relevant to the dispute in question;

(b) professional interests (e.g. a past or present relationship with private clients, or any interests the person may have in domestic or international proceedings, and their implications, where these involve issues similar to those addressed in the dispute in question);

(c) other active interests (e.g. active participation in public interest groups or other organizations which may have a declared agenda relevant to the dispute in question);

(d) considered statements of personal opinion on issues relevant to the dispute in question (e.g. publications, public statements);

(e) employment or family interests (e.g. the possibility of any indirect advantage or any likelihood of pressure which could arise from their employer, business associates or immediate family members).

ANNEX 3

Dispute Number: _____

WORLD TRADE ORGANIZATION DISCLOSURE FORM

I have read the Understanding on Rules and Procedures Governing the Settlement of Disputes (DSU) and the Rules of Conduct for the DSU. I understand my continuing duty, while participating in the dispute settlement mechanism, and until such time as the Dispute Settlement Body (DSB) makes a decision on adoption of a report relating to the proceeding or notes its settlement, to disclose herewith and in future any information likely to affect my independence or impartiality, or which could give rise to justifiable doubts as to the integrity and impartiality of the dispute settlement mechanism; and to respect my obligations regarding the confidentiality of dispute settlement proceedings.

Signed: Dated:

Communication from the Director-General on Article 5 of the DSU WT/DSB/25 17 July 2001

ARTICLE 5 OF THE DISPUTE SETTLEMENT UNDERSTANDING

Communication from the Director-General

The following communication from the Director-General, dated 13 July 2001 has been addressed to the Chairman of the DSB with the request that it be circulated for the information of Members.

———

The Dispute Settlement Understanding is rightly considered a critical aspect of the international trading system. It provides an avenue for the Members to settle their disputes in a multilateral forum. Fortunately, many disputes brought to the WTO have been settled through negotiated mutually acceptable solutions. However, many have also required panel and Appellate Body proceedings.

I am of the view that Members should be afforded every opportunity to settle their disputes through negotiations whenever possible. Article 5 of the DSU provides for the use of good offices, conciliation and mediation, but this Article has not been used since the inception of the WTO. In light of that, I would like to call Members attention to the fact that I am ready and willing to assist them as is contemplated in Article 5.6. It is time to make this provision operational.

There are two attachments to this letter which will assist Members in this regard. Attachment A is a short background note and Attachment B provides some simple procedures for Members to use to request assistance.

I would like to emphasize that these procedures are purely to help Members resolve their differences and do not limit their treaty rights in any manner. I would also like to assure Members that these procedures do not in any way limit my availability to assist delegations more generally whenever they request my help.

I look forward to working with delegations and hope the note will prove useful to Members that might wish to avail themselves of the provisions of Article 5.

ATTACHMENT A

Background Note Regarding Requests for Good Offices, Conciliation and Mediation Pursuant to Article 5 of the DSU

Article 5 of the DSU, *Good Offices, Conciliation and Mediation*, has never been utilized. The predecessor procedures under the GATT were only rarely used.[1] Specifically, Article 5.6 provides that the Director-General may, acting in his *ex officio*

———

[1] (footnote original) We do not include actions taken pursuant to the provisions of the Decision of 5 April 1966 (BISD 14S/18). These are now covered by Article 3.12 of the DSU and are taken in lieu of action under Articles 4, 5, 6, and 12 of the DSU. The 1966 Decision provides some specific procedural rules.

capacity, offer good offices, conciliation or mediation to the parties to a dispute. This authority is considered inherent in the post even though not further detailed in law.[2] Thus, no new powers are being provided to the Director-General by this provision; rather, he may exercise his normal powers to assist Members in negotiating and resolving disagreements.[3]

Historical Background

The 1979 Understanding on dispute settlement provided for the use of good offices to settle disputes. Paragraph 8 of the Understanding stated as follows:

> If a dispute is not resolved through consultations the Contracting Parties concerned may request an appropriate body or individual to use their good offices with a view to the conciliation of the outstanding differences between the parties. If the dispute is one in which a less-developed contracting party has brought a complaint against a developed contracting party, the less developed contracting party may request the good offices of the Director-General who, in carrying out his tasks, may consult with the Chairman of the CONTRACTING PARTIES and the Chairman of the Council.[4]

This provision was resorted to unsuccessfully by the United States and the European Communities in 1982 regarding their dispute over EC tariff treatment of citrus products. Also in 1982, the Ministerial Declaration stated as follows:

> With reference to paragraph 8 of the Understanding, if a dispute is not resolved through consultations, any party to a dispute may, with the agreement of the other party, seek the good offices of the Director-General or of an individual or group of persons nominated by the Director-General. This conciliatory process would be carried out expeditiously, and the Director-General would inform the Council of the outcome of the conciliatory process. . . .[5]

---

[2] (footnote original) *Black's Law Dictionary* provides the following definition of *ex officio*: "From office; by virtue of the office; without any other warrant or appointment than that resulting from the holding of a particular office. Powers may be exercised by an officer which are not specifically conferred upon him, but are necessarily implied in his office; these are *ex officio*. Thus, a judge has *ex officio* the powers of a conservator of the peace."

[3] (footnote original) This should be distinguished from the provision for formal arbitration provided for in Article 25 as an alternative to dispute settlement procedures.

[4] (footnote original) Understanding on Notification, Consultation, Dispute Settlement and Surveillance of 28 November 1979 (26S/210).

[5] (footnote original) Ministerial Declaration of 29 November 1982, Decision on Dispute Settlement (29S/13).

In 1987–1988 this procedure was used by Japan and the European Communities to assist in the resolution of their dispute concerning pricing and trading practices for copper in Japan. The Director-General nominated a personal representative to submit a report on the dispute. In addition, another outside expert was retained to assist in developing the factual basis for the report. The Director-General communicated to the Contracting Parties a report which included a short factual finding as well an "advisory opinion" to the effect that the European Communities and Japan should enter into mutually advantageous and reciprocal negotiations regarding certain Japanese tariffs as part of the Uruguay Round.[6]

In 1988 The Director-General reported that he had been requested to provide good offices by Canada and the European Communities. As requested by the parties, he provided an advisory opinion on a question that arose during Article XXIV negotiations regarding whether a tariff concession granted by Portugal to Canada included wet salted cod.[7]

Paragraph D of the Decision of 12 April 1989 on Improvements to the GATT Dispute Settlement Rules and Procedures (36S/61), provided further rules for requesting good offices. These new rules are quite similar to the current Article V of the DSU. Also, the reference to appointing a personal representative of the Director-General contained in the 1982 Decision was dropped. There is no record that this provision was utilized.

Current Proposal

The Director-General is of the view that Members should attempt to settle disputes as often as possible without resort to panel and Appellate Body procedures. In this regard, he wishes Members to be aware of his willingness to actively support attempts to settle their disputes through use of good offices, conciliation and mediation. Unlike the situation under the 1982 Decision, there is no explicit authorization for appointment of another person to conduct the proceeding. Instead the DSU provides that this is to be considered part of the Director-General's *ex officio* powers.[8] Thus, it is appropriate that there be closer involvement of the Director-General as these are the powers specifically derived from his office. Therefore, it is contemplated that the proceedings will be handled directly by the Director-General or, with the concurrence of the parties, a designated Deputy Director-General. There will, necessarily, need to be provision for assistance from the Secretariat or, following consultation with the parties, other consultants retained for these purposes.

---

[6] (footnote original) Measures Affecting the World Market for Copper Ores and Concentrates, Note by the Director General (36S/199).

[7] (footnote original) C/M/225, p. 2.

[8] (footnote original) Obviously, as these are *ex officio* powers to be used in this specific setting, it follows that the Director-General could offer his services to assist in settling disagreements between Members in other settings. The language of Article 5 should not be seen as limiting his role elsewhere.

Another distinction arises in light of the considerably different situations existing with respect to dispute settlement under the GATT and the WTO. The negative consensus rule which provides certainty in access to the dispute settlement system as well as the introduction of an appellate process to ensure greater consistency have significantly changed the nature of the dispute settlement system. In light of these changes, the Director-General does not expect to provide "advisory opinions", strictly speaking, although informal non-legal advice regarding the best path to finding a solution may be appropriate. Legal conclusions regarding a particular dispute are best left to the formal dispute settlement process. Rather, Article 5 proceedings should be seen more as efforts to assist in reaching a mutually agreed solution. It should also be recalled that Article 25 provides for Arbitration and the Director-General does not wish to encroach upon this provision of the DSU.

In light of the above, the Director-General proposes to provide some procedural steps for parties to take when requesting Article 5 proceedings and such steps would be based on the following considerations:

1. Requests under Article 5 may only be made after commencement of a formal dispute pursuant to a request for consultations in accordance with Article 4 of the DSU. The nature of the Article 5 request should be specified.[9]

2. The Director-General should meet with the parties as soon as possible after a request to: (a) listen to their views of the dispute; (b) assess the resources that he should devote to the process to help reach a settlement;[10] and (c) provide any preliminary assessments as might seem appropriate.

3. The Director-General may designate a Deputy Director-General to assist and/or act in his stead. Except for the limited case of good offices, the Director-General or designated Deputy Director-General shall be present at meetings held pursuant to the process. As this is an exercise of *ex officio* powers, further delegation beyond the Deputy Director-General level should be avoided.

4. The Director-General may provide Secretariat staff to support the process as he deems appropriate. Care will be taken to insulate such staff from involvement in formal dispute settlement procedures in order to ensure the objectivity of the Secretariat.[11] To the extent necessary, outside consultants could be retained to assist in the process.

5. The Director-General and the Deputy Directors-General are not directly involved in on-going panel and Appellate Bodies cases so no further

---

[9] (footnote original) Good offices, conciliation and mediation are seen as three different levels of involvement of the Director-General with good offices being overseeing of logistical and Secretariat support, conciliation involving direct participation in negotiations and mediation including the possibility of actually proposing solutions, if appropriate. Flexibility is to be maintained with regard to changing the role.

[10] (footnote original) This will, in any event, vary depending on the type of assistance requested.

[11] (footnote original) As a general matter, staff from Divisions primarily responsible for dispute settlement will not be involved in Article 5 proceedings.

"firewalls" should be necessary in this regard.[12] With respect to other staff and consultants it would be necessary to require that they have no direct involvement in the dispute in question either before or after the Article 5 procedures. This should already be covered by the Rules of Conduct and no further action would be required.

ATTACHMENT B

Procedures for Requesting Action Pursuant to Article 5 of the DSU

1. Any time after a request for consultations is made pursuant to Article 4 of the DSU, any party to the dispute[13] may submit a request to the Director-General[14] for provision of good offices, conciliation or mediation.[15]

2. Such request shall identify whether the request is for good offices, conciliation and/or mediation. It is recognized that the Director-General's role may change during the process if the parties agree. Such a request shall include any proposed issues for such proceedings, which may include any or all of the issues included in the request for consultations.

3. The Director-General shall meet with the parties within 5 days to discuss the issues raised. If all parties to the dispute agree, the Director-General shall proceed forward with an offer of good offices, conciliation and/or mediation. The Director-General shall arrange further meetings with the parties as appropriate.

4. As soon as possible, the Director-General shall identify to the parties any Secretariat staff or, after consultation with the parties, consultants that will assist him in carrying out the procedures.

5. The process shall be terminated upon the request of any party to the dispute, except in a circumstance where there are two or more complainants and at least one complainant and the respondent wish to continue in the process. In such situations, the Director-General shall continue his efforts with respect to the remaining parties.

6. A process which has been terminated may be re-started at any time by the request of the parties. The considerations of the previous paragraph regarding multiple party situations shall apply *mutatis mutandis*.

---

[12] (footnote original) Article 8.7 of the DSU provides that the Director-General shall determine the composition of the panel if requested by one of the parties. As a general matter, this role would not seem to involve a substantive conflict of interest and, in any event, is specifically contemplated by Articles 5.6 and 8.7 taken together.

[13] (footnote original) Article 1.1 of the DSU indicates that a "dispute" in this context arises upon initiation of consultations pursuant to Article 4.

[14] (footnote original) References to the Director-General may, upon concurrence of the parties, include a designated Deputy Director-General.

[15] (footnote original) Good offices shall consist primarily of providing physical support and Secretariat assistance to the parties. Conciliation shall consist of good offices plus the further involvement of the Director-General in promoting discussions and negotiations between the parties. Mediation shall consist of conciliation plus the possibility of the Director-General to propose solutions to the parties.

7.   *Ex parte* communications are permitted. All communications made during the process shall remain confidential and shall not be revealed at any time, including during any other procedures undertaken pursuant to the DSU.

8.   There shall be no third party participation in the process unless the parties to the dispute mutually agree.

9.   If a mutually agreed solution to a dispute is reached pursuant to an Article 5 process, the notification to the DSB and relevant Councils and Committees pursuant to Article 3.6 shall so indicate.

Decision of 1966

DECISION OF 5 APRIL 1966 ON PROCEDURES UNDER ARTICLE XXIII
(BISD 14S/18)

The CONTRACTING PARTIES,

Recognizing that the prompt settlement of situations in which a contracting party considers that any benefits accruing to it directly or indirectly from the General Agreement are being impaired by measures taken by another contracting party, is essential to the effective functioning of the General Agreement and the maintenance of a proper balance between the rights and obligations of all Contracting Parties;

Recognizing further that the existence of such a situation can cause severe damage to the trade and economic development of the less-developed Contracting Parties; and

Affirming their resolve to facilitate the solution of such situations while taking fully into account the need for safeguarding both the present and potential trade of less-developed Contracting Parties affected by such measures;

Decide that:

1. If consultations between a less-developed contracting party and a developed contracting party in regard to any matter falling under paragraph 1 of Article XXIII do not lead to a satisfactory settlement, the less-developed contracting party complaining of the measures may refer the matter which is the subject of consultations to the Director-General so that, acting in an *ex officio* capacity, he may use his good offices with a view to facilitating a solution.

2. To this effect the Contracting Parties concerned shall, at the request of the Director-General, promptly furnish all relevant information.

3. On receipt of this information, the Director-General shall consult with the Contracting Parties concerned and with such other Contracting Parties or inter-governmental organizations as he considers appropriate with a view to promoting a mutually acceptable solution.

4. After a period of two months from the commencement of the consultations referred to in paragraph 3 above, if no mutually satisfactory solution has been reached, the Director-General shall, at the request of one of the Contracting Parties concerned, bring the matter to the attention of the CONTRACTING PARTIES or the Council, to whom he shall submit a report on the action taken by him, together with all background information.

5. Upon receipt of the report, the CONTRACTING PARTIES or the Council shall forthwith appoint a panel of experts to examine the matter with a view to recommending an appropriate solution. The members of the panel shall act on a personal capacity and shall be appointed in consultation with, and with the approval of, the Contracting Parties concerned.

6. In conducting its examination and having before it all the background information, the panel shall take due account of all the circumstances and considerations relating to the application of the measures complained of, and their impact on the trade and economic development of affected Contracting Parties.

7. The panel shall, within a period of sixty days from the date the matter was referred to it, submit its findings and recommendations to the CONTRACTING PARTIES or to the Council, for consideration and decision. Where the matter is referred to the Council, it may, in accordance with Rule 8 of the Intersessional Procedures adopted by the CONTRACTING PARTIES at their thirteenth session,[1] address its recommendations directly to the interested Contracting Parties and concurrently report to the CONTRACTING PARTIES.

8. Within a period of ninety days from the date of the decision of the CONTRACTING PARTIES, or the Council, the contracting party to which a recommendation is directed shall report to the CONTRACTING PARTIES or the Council on the action taken by it in pursuance of the decision.

9. If on examination of this report it is found that a contracting party to which a recommendation has been directed has not complied in full with the relevant recommendation of the CONTRACTING PARTIES or the Council, and that any benefit accruing directly or indirectly under the General Agreement continues in consequence to be nullified or impaired, and that the circumstances are serious enough to justify such action, the CONTRACTING PARTIES may authorize the affected contracting party or parties to suspend, in regard to the contracting party causing the damage, application of any concession or any other obligation under the General Agreement whose suspension is considered warranted, taking account of the circumstances.

10. In the event that a recommendation to a developed country by the CONTRACTING PARTIES is not applied within the time-limit prescribed in paragraph 8, the CONTRACTING PARTIES shall consider what measures, further to those undertaken under paragraph 9, should be taken to resolve the matter.

11. If consultations, held under paragraph 2 of Article XXXVII, relate to restrictions for which there is no authority under any provisions to the General Agreement, any of the parties to the consultations may, in the absence of a satisfactory solution, request that consultations be carried out by the CONTRACTING PARTIES pursuant to paragraph 2 of Article XXIII and in accordance with the procedures set out in the present decision, it being understood that a consultation held under

---

[1] (footnote original) 7S/7.

paragraph 2 of Article XXXVII in respect of such restrictions will be considered by the CONTRACTING PARTIES as fulfilling the conditions of paragraph 1 of Article XXIII if the parties to the consultations so agree.

Decision of 1989

DECISION OF 12 APRIL 1989 ON IMPROVEMENTS TO THE GATT
DISPUTE SETTLEMENT RULES AND PROCEDURES
(BISD 36S/61)

Following the meetings of the Trade Negotiations Committee at Ministerial level in December 1988 and at the level of high officials in April 1989, the CONTRACTING PARTIES to the General Agreement on Tariffs and Trade

Approve the improvements of the GATT dispute settlement rules and procedures set out below and their application on the basis set out in this Decision:

. . .

G. Adoption of Panel Reports

1.   In order to provide sufficient time for the members of the Council to consider panel reports, the reports shall not be considered for adoption by the Council until thirty days after they have been issued to the Contracting Parties.

2.   Contracting parties having objections to panel reports shall give written reasons to explain their objections for circulation at least ten days prior to the Council meeting at which the panel report will be considered.

3.   The parties to a dispute shall have the right to participate fully in the consideration of the panel report by the Council, and their views shall be fully recorded. The practice of adopting panel reports by consensus shall be continued, without prejudice to the GATT provisions on decision-making which remain applicable. However, the delaying of the process of dispute settlement shall be avoided.

4.   The period from the request under Article XXII:1 or Article XXIII:1 until the Council takes a decision on the panel report shall not, unless agreed to by the parties, exceed fifteen months. The provisions of this paragraph shall not affect the provisions of paragraph 6 of Section F(f).

H. Technical Assistance

1.   While the Secretariat assists Contracting Parties in respect of dispute settlement at their request, there may also be a need to provide additional legal advice and assistance in respect of dispute settlement to developing Contracting Parties. To this end, the Secretariat shall make available a qualified legal expert within the Technical Co-operation Division to any developing contracting party which so requests. This expert shall assist the developing contracting party in a manner ensuring the continued impartiality of the Secretariat.

2.   The Secretariat shall conduct special training courses for interested Contracting Parties concerning GATT dispute settlement procedures and practices so as to enable Contracting Parties' experts to be better informed in this regard.

I. Surveillance of Implementation of Recommendations and Rulings

1.   Prompt compliance with recommendations or rulings of the CONTRACTING PARTIES under Article XXIII is essential in order to ensure effective resolution of disputes to the benefit of all Contracting Parties.

2.   The contracting party concerned shall inform the Council of its intentions in respect of implementation of the recommendations or rulings. If it is impracticable to comply immediately with the recommendations or rulings, the contracting party concerned shall have a reasonable period of time in which to do so.

3.   The Council shall monitor the implementation of recommendations or rulings adopted under Article XXIII:2. The issue of implementation of the recommendations or rulings may be raised at the Council by any contracting party at any time following their adoption. Unless the Council decides otherwise, the issue of implementation of the recommendations or rulings shall be on the agenda of the Council meeting after six months following their adoption and shall remain on the Council's agenda until the issue is resolved. At least ten days prior to each such Council meeting, the contracting party concerned shall provide the Council with a status report in writing of its progress in the implementation of the panel recommendations or rulings.

4.   In cases brought by developing Contracting Parties, the Council shall consider what further action it might take which would be appropriate to the circumstances, in conformity with paragraphs 21 and 23 of the 1979 Understanding regarding Notification, Consultation, Dispute Settlement and Surveillance (BISD 26S/214).

The footnote to paragraph F(a) provides: References to the Council, made in this paragraph as well as in the following paragraphs, are without prejudice to the competence of the CONTRACTING PARTIES, for which the Council is empowered to act in accordance with normal GATT practice (BISD 26S/215).

INDEX

accelerated procedures (Decision of 5 April 1966) 60, 112–113
  Director-General, role 112–113
  precedence over DSU 4, 5, 6 and 12 (DSU 3.12) 112
Advisory Centre on WTO Law 114–115
Agreement on Safeguards
  countermeasures (Arts. 8.2 and 8.3) 81 n. 97
  implementation of recommendations and rulings (DSU 21.3), applicability
    76 n. 80
  positive implementation action, failure to take as basis for complaint 39
  standard of review 104
Agreement on Textiles and Clothing, consultations, request for 46
alternative dispute settlement 92: *see also* arbitration, competence and
    functions; consultations (DSU 4); good offices, conciliation and mediation
    (DSU 5); mutually acceptable solution consistent with covered agreements
    (DSU 3.7)
***amicus curiae* briefs**
  see also experts, panel's right to consult (DSU 13)
  admissibility 9, 98–100
    AB 65, 99–100: filing as exhibits 99; justification for (DSU 17.9) 99;
      non-participating Member 100; received direct 99; special procedures
      (WP(AB) 16(1)) 99–100
    General Council discussion 99–100
    panel proceedings 98–99
  definition 98 n. 11
  originators 98
  proceedings, justification for (DSU 12.2/13) 98
Anti-Dumping Agreement
  interpretation
    customary rules of international law and 104
    multiple permissible interpretations 104
  standard of review (AD 17.6) 104
    legal review 104
Appellate Body (AB)
  administrative and legal support (DSU 17.7) 24
  chairman
    competence and functions, direction of AB business (WP 3) 24

panel, object and purpose

mutually acceptable solution consistent with covered agreements (DSU 3.7) 6, 43, 47–48

opportunity to complainant to protect rights 47–48

opportunity to respondent to correct facts/ interpretation of WTO Agreement 47–48

panel procedures (DSU 12/Appendix 3)

administrative, technical and legal support, Secretariat (DSU 27.1) 20–21, 22

amicus curiae briefs 98–99: *see also amicus curiae* briefs

  justification for (DSU 12.2/13) 98

collegiate nature of panel 53–54

deliberations following conclusion of oral hearings 56–57: *see also* panel, reports, preparation

dispute settlement registry 54 n. 25

evidence: *see* burden of proof; standard of review (DSU 11)

flexibility 53–54

oral hearings

  AB hearings distinguished 70

  behind closed doors 55

  clarificatory questions (Appendix 3, para 8) 55: time-limits 55

  expert hearing 55–56

  first 55

  participation 55: multiple complainants, right to be present (DSU 9.2) 56

  place 55

  record: prepared written statement 55; tape 55

  second/third 55–56

  third parties, special session (DSU 10.2) 55

organizational meeting 53

preliminary issues 54

suspension at request of complaining party (DSU 12.12) 59–60

  time-limits (DSU 12.12) 59–60

time-limits, developing countries 111–112

timetable (Appendix 3) 60

  accelerated procedures: developing countries and (Decision of 5 April 1966) 60, 112–113; SCM Agreement 60–61

  agreement of parties (DSU 12.3) 53–54, 60

  multiple complaints, harmonization (DSU 9.3) 60

written rebuttals 55–56

  third parties and 55–56

  time-limits 55–56

written submissions

  confidentiality (DSU 18.2) 54–55, 97: parties' right to disclose/publish (DSU 18.2) 54–55, 97; summary in panel report 54–55, 97